THE GOLDEN THREAD

and other plays

The Texas Pan American Series

The Golden Thread

and other plays

by Emilio Carballido

translated by Margaret Sayers Peden

university of texas press

austin and london

International Standard Book Number 0–292–70039–3
Library of Congress Catalog Card Number 79–131958
Copyright © 1970 by Emilio Carballido
Printed by the University of Texas Printing Division, Austin
Bound by Universal Bookbindery, Inc., San Antonio

CONTENTS

INTRODUCTION

Emilio Carballido is Mexico's most talented and successful contemporary playwright. His presence and influence in contemporary Mexican theater are enormous. Coincidentally, it is during the span of Carballido's career—1948 to the present—that Latin American theater in general explodes into the vital form it is today. One cannot claim, of course, that Carballido is responsible for the phenomenon of a new theater in Mexico, since one can note the same process of growth and development throughout Latin America during the last two decades. On the other hand, contemporary Mexican theater *without* the presence of Carballido would be perceptibly less original and exciting.

Generally, the evolution of theater has been the same in all of Latin America: what is true of Mexico is on the whole what is true of the rest of Latin America. Theater has existed in South and Central America as long as there has been civilization there: strong physical evidence exists of a type of ritual theater that pre-dates the Conquest. In the case of the geographical area that was Maya-Quiché, the *Rabinal Achi* is an authentic survival of that area's pre-Columbian theater. With the Conquest, the Spanish soldier priests very quickly resorted to the use of theater—in this case dramatized examples of church teachings—to instruct the indigenous populations and expedite their conversion to the salvation of the One True Faith. Soon, too, Western secular theater was introduced to the continent through plays presented usually on the occasion of state visits or in celebration of viceregal birthdays or of holidays. There has been, then, since the discovery of the continent by Western civilization, and even before, some kind of theater in Mexico. There has even been an occasional flash of genius. Sor Juana Inés de la Cruz, the brilliant seventeenth-century baroque poet and dramatist, is undoubtedly the most outstanding example.

Generally, however, for three centuries theater in Mexico and throughout Latin America was a purely derivative and imitative form feeding upon the examples of its Spanish heritage. It is not until the present century that one may observe the stirrings of truly renovative and original Mexican theater. One of the first evidences of these stirrings was the Union of the Seven Authors, a group bent upon the creation of a truly Mexican (as opposed to Spanish New World) theater. One of its more important accomplishments was its insistence upon natural Mexican pronunciation. The influence of Spanish theater, Spanish plays, and Spanish actors had been so strong that it was not until 1923 that the first play was performed on a Mexican stage in which the actors spoke with a Mexican rather than a Castilian pronunciation.

The year 1928 is another important landmark in the evolution of an independent theater in Mexico. In that year the Teatro Ulises was founded by Xavier Villaurrutia and Salvador Novo. The members of this amateur group, reacting against the extreme nationalism of all art forms in the years following the Mexican Revolution, turned toward Europe and the United States for inspiration, translating and emulating authors writing in a more sophisticated theatrical tradition. But in spite of these important moments, it was only following the Second World War that Mexican (and Latin American) theater became a truly independent and vital movement. It is this generation to which Emilio Carballido belongs.

Carballido's most important single contribution has probably been the introduction of a vein of fantasy that lifts his plays from the extremely traditional-realistic strain that has been the predominant characteristic of Mexican theater. It is not that the realistic tradition has failed to produce examples of good theater. Rodolfo Usigli's *El gesticulador*, for example, is one of the better and more important Mexican plays, and it is specifically Mexican and absolutely realistic. This is, unfortunately, an isolated example. In general, Mexican theater before Carballido was bogged down in a morass of overwhelmingly traditional-realistic plays: comedies of manners or investigations of bourgeois domestic and marital situations, strong social indictments that verged on the propagandistic, or popular reviews of the music hall variety.

On the other hand, an occasional Mexican author had used the liberating element of fantasy before the publication in 1948 of Carballido's "The Intermediate Zone." Francisco Monterde (one of the Union of Seven Authors) in *Proteo* and Alfonso Reyes in *Ifigenia cruel*, both reworkings of Greek myth, are notable examples. Neither author, however, wrote any other plays in this genre. It is Emilio Carballido who is the first Mexican author to employ consistently a kind of theater that may be called fantastic, poetic, surrealistic—or simply nonrealistic. He is the first Mexican playwright who *consistently* creates plays that transcend the specifically realistic and restrictively Mexican to achieve a theater that can be called modern, contemporary, and universal.

It is this element of fantasy, or poetry if you will, that is the reason-for-being of this particular collection of Carballido plays. All, in some way, touch upon the nonreal. Each in some way is enriched by the element of fantasy. Each illustrates in its particular way the amazing variety of Carballido's imaginative creation. This collection is not a representation of *all* the Carballido fantasy-touched plays, but each of these eight illustrates an important moment in the overall trajectory of Carballido's writing, and a specific creative point of view.

For about nine years, Carballido seemed to swerve back and forth between a desire to do something new—introduce the fantasy element—and to do something good in the old strain (which produced a number of realistic provincial comedies). There is a noticeable dichotomy in his writing of those years that has been mentioned by such major commentators on Carballido's writing as Rosario Castellanos, Juan García Ponce, Frank Dauster, and Celestino Gorostiza. In Carballido's vision during those years the world is apparently divided into the real and the nonreal, and his plays during this period reflect this polarized perception of reality: they are either purely fantasy or they are purely realistic. Four of the plays in this collection are representative of the purely fantastic: "The Intermediate Zone" and the trilogy "The Time and the Place," which is made up of "Dead Love," "The Glacier," and "The Wine Cellar."

"The Intermediate Zone" (1948) is the first published Carballido play and one of the first to be produced. As the title implies, its characters and setting lie in the area of pure fantasy, the proving ground for a group of once-humans of indeterminate destinies. The Nahual "hero" of the piece is drawn directly from Aztec mythology. The word that comes most easily to mind to describe this unusual character is "charming," a word equally applicable to the play itself. This would be a damning description if it were the only quality of "The Intermediate Zone," since charm alone is scarcely enough to justify a play's existence. But beneath the superficially entertaining qualities of the play lies the author's very serious concern about the question of man's role in the world, the extent of his responsibility, and the justification for his existence, a concern that may also be seen in the "Theseus" of this collection, for example.

"The Time and the Place," dedicated to Carballido's American artist friend, Henry Hagan, is a different matter. These three plays represent a different frame of mind, and fulfill a different creative purpose. They are unlike anything that had ever appeared in Mexican theater. In Carballido's own words (from a letter to me concerning the translation of the plays), "They are my only horror pieces." And he adds that they seem more natural to him in English than in Spanish, "perhaps because one's accustomed to reading the genre in your native language."

In addition to their historical interest as the most extreme examples of Carballido's interest in the fantastic, each of the plays is fascinating in its presentation of a distinct mythical-magical reality. They are amazing examples of what Antonin Artaud wanted theater to be, a theater "whose only value is in its excruciating, magical relation to reality and danger." They are cruel, chilling, and hypnotically compelling.

"Dead Love," the first of the trilogy, exists in its own kind of intermediate zone, in another stage between life and death. Unlike "Intermediate Zone," however, there is no charm here, no humor, no hope. Claudia and the character called He are doomed, and damned, victims of their distintegrating bodies and the inevitable loss of their dissolving love.

The tone of "The Glacier" is principally mythic. In spite of its contemporary setting it would never be mistaken for a little slice-of-life piece about Mexico today. Its distortion of time, the spanning of fifty years of chronological time, its culminating magical rejuvenation, give it a flavor of "twice-told tales" or "once upon a time." It is significant that if these plays had been written in narrative prose they would invariably have been classified as tales rather than as short stories.

The last of the trilogy, "The Wine Cellar," is literally of the stuff that dreams are made of. Based on an actual dream of a friend of Carballido's, Jorge Wilmot, "The Wine Cellar" has the extra- or supra-real reality that we accept so unhesitatingly in our dreams. The disintegration of "the beautiful Zoé" recalls the disintegrating love of "Dead Love," and the unnatural attraction of the infected and noxious body of the once-beautiful Zoé is in a way similar to the necrophilism of "The Glacier." The plays constitute a whole, a unity, and they reflect a moment in Carballido's creativity, a state of mind, that he has never returned to.

"The Golden Thread" is the title play of the volume published in 1957 that included "The Time and the Place," but this three-act play reflects a different creative point of view, a consciously new one. As the author explains (again in a letter referring to the translation of the play), " 'The Thread' is quite important to me, it was the first time I attempted to join a realistic treatment with an imaginative one . . . Before, I wrote works of one genre or the other, but never mixed together."

The mingling of reality and fantasy that Carballido first attempted in "The Golden Thread" has produced a large proportion of his most successful plays, and the reinforcement of reality through the use of the non-real has become one of his most characteristic hallmarks. In addition to the interest of the play per se, it is also important historically because it marks the creation of what is virtually a new dramatic form in Mexico.

In "The Golden Thread" the examination of the many facets of reality is more important than straight plot. Again the techniques used to achieve the desired emotional and theatrical effects remind one of Artaud and of his definition of an ideal theatrical language, a physical language that is "everything that occupies the stage, everything that can be manifested and expressed materially on a stage and that is addressed first of all to the senses instead of being addressed primarily to the mind as is the language of words."

The frame situation of "The Golden Thread," the arrival of two elderly ladies at their run-down provincial estate, is conventional and realistic. It is with the appearance of Man-Silvestre, who can only enter the arena of action upon the invisible beam of a radio, that the play "takes off" from the realistic plane to enter the much more important world of truth. Man-Silvestre and Mayala have the power to recall time and to reveal the real truth about that time. It is through their revelations in the interior play that we come to know and understand Leonor and Adela and all the events of the past that lead to the present. For a brief while two worlds— truth and reality—come together, but the super-reality fades as Silvestre is identified and the action inevitably moves toward the re-enactment of his death.

Silvestre and Mayala are in concept and action the materialization of the spirit of theater, of Dionysius. Mayala, the purest representation of the nonreal world, never speaks a line of dialogue. She is the spirit of pre-oral, pre-intellectualized theater. Her counterpart in the "real world" is Leonor, obviously the medium through which the participants in the dream world are summoned to reality. Her surname, Luna (moon), reinforces this role.

"The Golden Thread," through dance, drums, pantomime, special effects, poetry, and magic, explores the depths of perceivable reality, and initiates a new direction in Carballido's dramatic writing.

Two of the plays in this collection follow the technique of "The

Golden Thread": they exist on a realistic plane, but in some way transcend or subvert that realism to create a new reality. "The Mirror," which Carballido calls a "curtain raiser," is an example-in-miniature of this concept. Here, as opposed to "The Golden Thread," the questioning of what is real is more narrowly focused, involving one character's perception of another. The confusion lies within Rubén, who perceives a fictitious reality, a creation of his imagination. It is he who imposes an ideal Alda upon the "real" Alda. The emergence of truth, through the process of disillusion- ment, reveals the Alda that the rest of the world sees, as she is literally stripped of the qualities with which Rubén's imagination had endowed her. Truth in this play is an interior process re- sulting from the dissolution of illusion in the mind of one of the characters.

The achievement of truth in "The Clockmaker from Córdoba" is more external, resulting from the active direction of don Le- andro, the comic-sophisticate judge. The setting is seventeenth- century Mexico, shortly following the founding of Córdoba, in that country. "The Clockmaker" was inspired by a Chinese short story. Its author, Pu Sung-ling, from the Shantung province of China, is introduced into the fiction of the play when don Leandro tells Elvira (incidentally giving us a hint about her) that he has a friend in China who would be interested in her story. In trans- ferring the story to Mexico, Carballido adds a few Mexican mythic touches with his use of dreams about the locality and his allusion to the legendary mulatto girl who traced the outline of a ship upon the walls of her cell, then boarded the ship and sailed away. There is, too, as in "The Golden Thread," an almost Gothic implication that *place* may have a mystery and influence of its own, as illus- trated by don Leandro's questioning the wisdom of having founded Córdoba in its present location.

Perhaps the most intriguing aspect of "The Clockmaker" is Martín's involvement in the fiction of his own creation. In the framework of "what actually happens" from the beginning to the end of the play, "The Clockmaker" also includes two plays-within- a-play. Don Leandro quite consciously sets one play in motion in the second act. The wily judge does not know the exact ending of his play, but he is convinced that it will work out to its logical conclusion, the apprehension of the guilty party.

Martín's play is much more complex and one realizes that he (unlike don Leandro) does not foresee to what extent he will be involved. Martín invents a play—the fictitious story of an assault and a robbery—and then is enmeshed as a real participant in the very real series of events that parallel his invention. It is only by the resolution of don Leandro's "play" that Martín is freed from the web of circumstances created by his own "play." The resolution of the two overlapping interior plays is also the resolution of the frame play; so that the apprehension of the real criminal serves three levels of reality, the two fictitional plays and the "what really happens" of "The Clockmaker from Córdoba."

At the same time that its Greek heritage makes it the "oldest" play in the collection, "Theseus" is also the most "modern." Although the framework of Theseus' actions is precisely the same as that of his Greek prototype—necessarily so, since his acts are limited by the prefigurations of the myth—Carballido's Theseus is a distinctly modern man, one who could belong only to the twentieth century. He is determined to direct his own actions. He wants to be the consequence of his own acts, not the result of a fate oriented and directed by the gods. This Theseus does not become king because the gods have so ordained; he does not *forget* to raise the sails of triumph. He purposely and consciously raises the black sails of defeat, knowing that his father will throw himself from his cliff vantage-point and that thereby he, Theseus, will become king. By making himself responsible for his actions, Theseus loses the possible redemption and forgiveness available to those who perform acts that fulfill a prophecy. He is truly free, perhaps, but immeasurably more cruel, and completely devoid of love. Is this the inevitable punishment of destroying the gods?

Throughout the varied and various plays of this collection, Carballido manifests two principal concerns: the questioning and exploration of "what is reality," and the problem of the extent of man's responsibility in his world. Many of the protagonists in these plays question where their responsibilities lie. Theseus, as just discussed, believes that his responsibility is to direct his *own* fate, to be free in the twentieth-century concept of freedom. Martín, in "The Clockmaker from Córdoba," finds that his first responsibility is to himself, to rid himself of self-delusion, to be true to himself so that he may then fulfill his responsibility to Casilda. The Nahual in "The Intermediate Zone" finds that his *engagement,* his commitment on behalf of another person, endows him with the responsibility that forces him to become a participant in the world of reality—a responsibility that is also man's unique privilege. Man-Silvestre's responsibility in "The Golden Thread" is that of revealing truth, and it is at this point that Carballido's two concerns become fused, since the question of truth is also the question of what constitutes reality.

In one way or another, each of the plays in this collection explores the latter question, each exists on some level of reality that is not generally conceded to be "real." Alda is two people, one to Rubén and another to the rest of the world. Martín, the clockmaker, is disconcerted to find that invention and reality have become one in his life. The Nonhumans of "The Intermediate Zone" face the ultimate limits of reality—eternity or evaporation—and each of the plays of the grotesque trilogy "The Time and the Place" probes the limits of the reality of love and time.

These two concerns—reality and responsibility—may be the two most important concerns of man throughout the history of his civilized existence. Emilio Carballido, through his creative ability and the variety of his invention, has provided what we know to be the greatest gift of the arts—new views and insights into the eternally important questions.

Margaret Sayers Peden

The Mirror

A Farce

For Ignacio Longares

Characters

ALDA
HÉCTOR
RUBÉN
ALDA'S REFLECTION
ALDA'S ECHO
ALDA'S MUSIC

A luxurious bedroom. Except for the bed, none of the furniture is practical.

Alda is getting dressed in front of the mirror, evidently dissatisfied. Someone knocks. She leaves the room to open the door. She backs into the room, impetuously embraced and kissed on the mouth by Héctor. He releases her. She takes a deep breath.

ALDA: How's everything with you, Héctor?
  (*He embraces her and kisses her again.*)
  Do you want to sit down while I finish getting ready? I don't know what's missing, but I just don't look right. There's something strange about the way I look, don't you think?
HÉCTOR: Mmmmmm. (*He takes out some Chiclets, tosses them in the air, and snaps them up in his mouth. He chews.*)
ALDA (*in front of the mirror*): Look, I put these flowers on and took them off. It's not the necklace, either. It's like something's missing. (*Looks at him.*) Hector, don't chew gum, 'cause then you get real rough and *I* swallow it. How do I look?
HÉCTOR: Okay.
ALDA: Don't flatter me so. Rubén knows how to say things prettier. Lots prettier. Just kidding—don't get mad. (*He is the same.*) You say things a lot prettier than he does, don't you? But today you can't stay because Rubén's going to take me to the opera. (*She sprays perfume, and primps while she hums.*) Al-ways fe-ree . . . Do something, read the newspaper or something. Put that down. That's one of Rubén's books.

4

HÉCTOR (*reads, very badly*): "And to hear you urinating in the darkness in the depths of the house, like spilling honey—slim, tremulous, silvery, obstinate . . ." (*He looks at her, astonished.*)

ALDA: I told you to read the paper. Here. The police reports are in the second section. (*She continues trying things on: necklaces, bracelets, earrings, flowers, feathers, anything available. She looks at herself in the mirror.*) I still say something's missing. What time is it, Héctor? (*He laughs to himself about something he is reading.*) Héctor!

HÉCTOR (*reads, very well this time*): Samuel Budiño slashed his love's belly to ribbons. He's going to prison.*

ALDA: Sure, very funny. I asked you what time it is.

HÉCTOR: Eight. (*He continues reading.*)

ALDA: Oh, it's time for Rubén to be here! He comes a half hour early, then doesn't dare come up until time for our date. I told you to be here at six. Why did you get here so late? Well, you'll have to leave, eh? Better come back tomorrow.

HÉCTOR: Is he going to sleep here?

ALDA: Go on, what a thing to say. He'll come up and have a whiskey after the performance, and—I don't know—maybe . . .

(*Héctor pulls her onto his knees and kisses her.*)

Now, don't you think I prefer him. *You* know how to accept things like they are, but *he* . . . Mmmmmmh . . . Héctor . . .

(*A knock at the door interrupts a second kiss.*)

(*Startled*) You see? Rubén's here. What'll we do now?

(*He kisses her and runs his hands over her passionately.*)

No, think about something else. What'll we do?

(*He kisses her again, still more passionately.*)

No, I tell you we can't right now. (*She yells*) I'm coming, darling! Now you've got to hide and keep still until we go. Let's see, where . . . Let's see . . . (*She puts him behind a curtain.*) No, no. I know. Get under the bed. (*He does.*) Good.

---

* For many years an evening newspaper maintained the surrealistic practice of reviewing crimes and arrests in verses of sinister humor that appeared under the picture of the accused.

(*Alda exits to open the door. A pause. Music. She returns, and after her, Rubén enters.*)

Come in, sweetheart. How've you been? (*He looks at her, entranced.*) What's the matter?

THE ECHO (*singing*): What's the matter with you?

(*The music ceases.*)

RUBÉN: I'm looking at you.

(*The music returns. Alda goes to the mirror, which no longer reflects her. In the place of the reflection is the figure of a kind of goddess, dressed in the most classic simplicity. Rubén looks, always, at the reflection.*)

How beautiful you are tonight.

ALDA: That's right. Yeah, that's right. I can see now, I don't need to put on anything. I look fine, don't I? Let's go.

THE ECHO (*singing, as always when it intervenes*): I think that's all I need. You may take me with you.

(*Alda rejects another feather she was going to put on. She looks at herself, satisfied. She steps back and forth in front of the mirror. The Reflection repeats all her movements in a kind of dance.*)

RUBÉN: I brought you something I saw. I liked the design and I couldn't picture it on any arm but yours.

(*He takes out a gift box and from it a bracelet which he places on her wrist. The Reflection puts on an identical bracelet.*)

ALDA (*looking at herself in the mirror*): Oh, how pretty, it's really swell! And it must have cost lots. Sweetie, hug me. Give me a kiss. You're so good, I love you so.

THE ECHO (*while the Reflection dances around Rubén and Alda, who embraces and kisses Rubén*): It's beautiful, it's beautiful. Such a lovely design. Hold me like a shield over your heart, for my love is as strong as death.

(*Rubén embraces the Reflection and Alda and kisses them both. The music fades. Silence.*)

RUBÉN (*sighs*): I'm mad about the way you speak.

ALDA AND THE ECHO: Yes?

RUBÉN: What you just said sounded like the Song of Songs.

6

ALDA: Go on. I didn't say a thing and there you are going on about
it.

ECHO: I express myself best in silence.

RUBÉN: And in every way. (*Sighs.*) Shall we go?

ALDA: Sure, but wait. Where'd I put my coat? Where the hell?

ECHO: Where are the white furs that caress me—where?

    (*Music. Alda searches, tripping and cursing to herself. Her
Reflection follows her, lightly dancing. Alda stops, thinking. The
Reflection continues dancing. Rubén admires it, fascinated.*)

ALDA (*shouts*): Don't you see it anywhere?

ECHO: Perhaps you see it?

    (*Music and dance cease.*)

RUBÉN: I hadn't noticed. I was watching you walk. It seemed as if
you were dancing. Your every movement seems part of a great
cosmic dance.

ALDA: Well, I don't see anything funny. Help me look for it.

ECHO (*sings, without words, and adds*): Assist me in the search.

    (*Rubén looks everywhere. He looks underneath the bed. He
straightens up, looks in other places.*)

RUBÉN: I don't see it.

ALDA: That's funny. Well, it must be hanging in the closet.

ECHO: I will find it hidden behind the doors of the armoire.

    (*Alda opens the closet and takes out the fur coat. She puts it
on. The Reflection, following her like a shadow, puts on a beautiful stole it takes from the same place. The music ceases.*)

RUBÉN: Listen.

ALDA: What?

ECHO: Yes?

RUBÉN: There was a man under the bed.

ALDA (*looking at herself in her reflection*): Yes?

ECHO: That's not possible.

RUBÉN (*takes another look*): He's still here.

ALDA: Sure. He's the plumber.

ECHO: Of course. He's the . . . (*She can't hit the note.*) He's the . . .

ALDA: Plumber.

RUBÉN: Oh, sure. (*He takes the Reflection's arm. The three walk toward the exit. Rubén stops. He looks at the Reflection. He looks at Alda.*) And is he going to stay there?

ALDA: Yeah. There was a broken pipe and the plumber's going to fix it.

ECHO: Water was escaping from its prison, and the . . . (*The music cuts her off.*) And the . . . (*She stops abruptly.*)

RUBÉN: Water under your bed?

ECHO: The plumb . . . The plumb . . .

RUBÉN: Is he working at night?

ECHO: The plumb . . . The plumb . . .

RUBÉN (*he looks under the bed*): He's too well dressed.

ECHO: The plumb . . . The plumb . . . (*She can't sing it.*)

RUBÉN: Where are his tools?

ECHO (*sings, finally*): The plumber. (*But her voice breaks and she crows.*)

ALDA: Darling, don't be ridiculous. Let's go or we won't make the first intermission.

(*Rubén looks intently at the Reflection, which returns, dancing, to its place behind the mirror. It stays there.*)

RUBÉN (*calling to the Reflection*): Alda!

(*He runs to look for her, but in the mirror he sees only his own reflection. He feels the glass. He looks at Alda again.*)

VOICE OF ALDA (*amplified*): Darling, don't be ridiculous. Let's go or we won't make the first intermission.

(*Rubén can't believe what he hears. Once again he looks under the bed, searches in the mirror. He sits down on the edge of the chair and begins to cry. The music and the Echo cry with him. The crying fades.*)

ALDA: Gee, look at the man! Rubén, what's the matter with you? Don't be silly. Why are you crying? (*She caresses his hair.*)

VOICE OF ALDA (*amplified*): Don't be an idiot.

(*Music and Echo and lament cease abruptly.*)

RUBÉN: You're right. Here are the tickets. You can still catch the first intermission. If you don't want to go alone, you can invite the plumber.

ALDA (*takes the tickets*): Aren't you going?

RUBÉN: No. (*He gives her a hard slap. There is a sound of breaking glass.*)

(*Rubén exits, and after him, walking or dragging themselves according to their nature, all the furniture and other objects exit from the room. The music, also. It ends with the exit of the curtains. The only thing remaining is the bed, its striped mattress exposed by the departure of the sheets and the bedspread.*)

ALDA: Oh, he left!

HÉCTOR (*crawls out from under the bed*): What happened?

ALDA: I think he got mad, because he hit me and left.

HÉCTOR: Ah!

ALDA: Let's go to the opera, want to? He left me the tickets.

HÉCTOR (*with horror*): The opera?

ALDA (*looks around*): The room looks a little funny, doesn't it? Like something was missing. What could have happened to it? I guess it's the light. (*She looks at herself in the place where the mirror had been.*) Oh, and something's the matter with the mirror. I don't look so good. Shall we go to the opera?

HÉCTOR (*laughs*): Opera!* (*He drags her to the bed.*)

ALDA: Héctor. Listen, Héctor . . .

(*Neruda's book is still on the bed. Héctor picks it up and looks at it. Music. He looks at it from all angles and then throws it through the balcony window as he pulls her down on the bed. The last shred of music vanishes like the book.*)

CURTAIN

* The opera had its greatest success during the six years of the presidency of M. Alemán Valdés. The legendary fortunes that each official accumulated, with transparent and open turpitude, were symbolically exhibited in the scandalous splendor of the intermission in the Bellas Artes. The effect was that of an enormous sandwich composed of great opulence—spiced with the red-hot seasoning of private lives—stuffed between slices (somewhat stale) of Puccini and Verdi. (Always "La Traviata"! Always "La Bohème," and "Rigoletto," and "Tosca" . . .) During the following presidential term the opera once again became a spectacle that took place on the stage, for thrifty, recalcitrant, and nostalgic bureaucrats.

The Time and the Place

A Trilogy

To Henry Hagan

DEAD LOVE

Characters:

CLAUDIA
HE
MARGARITA
THE YOUNG MAN

In the outskirts of Xalapa in the state of Veracruz, 1950.

Living room of a large home. The walls, dirty, with false neo-classic columns, are in blue and white and suggest those of a church or a crypt. The ceiling is vaulted and a wrought iron lamp hangs from its center. Mosses and parasitical plants are growing on the cornices and the capitals of the columns. Above the frame of the main door there are some flowering orchids. This door is at the rear of the stage, and leading down to it, from the outside, there is a stone stairway. A rusty iron gate can be seen at the top of the stairway. The furniture, Empire style, is covered in red and is very worn. There is another door, small and deepset, at the right of the stage. No paintings. No adornment.

The light, glowing with late afternoon brilliance in the beginning, gradually decreases.

A man and a woman are seated on the sofa, immobile, arms about one another. There is the constant clamor of many crickets. Then the barking of a dog, moving away.

SHE: The crickets have begun.

(*A pause. Neither of the two has moved. She is dressed in a gray, loose-sleeved dress.*)

Day before yesterday I went out to see the fountain. Someone had been cutting flowers. The water was filled with flowers. I would like to know if they are still there.

HE: It's better that you not go out.

SHE: The sun has already gone down.

HE: Someone might see you.

SHE: There are so few people who come up. It's very lonely here.

HE: But it's hot outside. Remember the sun, and the flies.

SHE: There are clouds. (*Pause.*) I enjoyed going outside so much. I wish you had come with me. That fresh air!

HE (*ironic, sweet*): The fresh air.

SHE: It smelled so good. (*He laughs quietly.*) Yes, I know. You don't have to remind me. But I would like to get some flowers.

HE: No. No flowers.

SHE: Just those from the fountain. (*Pleads.*) Just those.

HE: You're a child. I don't understand how you can still find flowers pleasing.

SHE: And I want us to be apart for a moment. It is such anguish. What relief to embrace you again.

HE: As you wish. Wait until it gets a little darker.

SHE: There's only a thin line of sunlight left. Look.

HE: All right. Go get your flowers.

> (*She moves for the first time. She gets up and goes toward the rear of the stage. She looks up the stairs toward the outdoors.*)

SHE: Truly, there's hardly any sun.

> (*She smiles, gives him a long kiss, and goes up the stairway. We hear the screech of the gate as she goes out. He does not move. From the outside come indistinct voices—a man's and a woman's. Although they cannot be heard clearly, it sounds as if they are saying*:

> > The gate is open, look.
> > It ought to be closed.
> > It just isn't possible.

> *He has heard them. He rises and exits right. The gate squeaks and a man and woman enter. He is young, blond, handsome, full of life. She is tiny and wears strict mourning. She has a small, tearful voice.*)

MOURNER: Nobody takes care of this place any more. It's so sad to see it.

YOUNG MAN: I don't know how anyone could *live* here.

MOURNER: The road we came up isn't the one they used to use. The main road has washed out. You've seen how it rains here, and the neglect . . .

YOUNG MAN: It's absurd, don't you think?

MOURNER: What is?

YOUNG MAN: To look for her here.

MOURNER: It's also absurd that she's lost. This is the only place we haven't looked.

YOUNG MAN: Lost. Like an object. Claudia lost like an object.

MOURNER: Shall we look through the house?

YOUNG MAN: Why, Margarita? It's abandoned. It smells of abandonment.

MARGARITA: Yes. Oh, I don't know. That *is* a strange odor, isn't it?

YOUNG MAN: Yes?

MARGARITA: Like bad meat.

YOUNG MAN: Some animal. There are plants growing on the walls.

MARGARITA: We used to spend weeks at a time here. When the fog got heavy it came down the stairway like a person and filtered into everything. (*She sits down.*) I feel so bad, so bad.

YOUNG MAN: You shouldn't have made Claudia postpone the date of our wedding.

MARGARITA: Why do you blame me? He was like a father, even though Claudia never loved him. It wouldn't have been right with him so sick . . . (*She interrupts herself. She has seen something on the sofa.*)

YOUNG MAN: Claudia and I weren't to blame.

MARGARITA (*speaking absently, thinking about something she wants to say, and walking back and forth*): Yes. The two of you . . . When Mama married, Claudia wanted to run away. She never called him Papa, as I did. She called him "George," and refused to speak to him at first. Claudia has always been strange . . . But he was very good. Poor Papa. I was his favorite.

YOUNG MAN: Yes, I know. (*He looks through the little door.*) It's dark in there.

MARGARITA: He always worried about us.

YOUNG MAN: Yes, I remember. He was a pleasant man. (*He looks around, discouraged.*) All right, we can go now.

MARGARITA: Everything was death and illness after the wedding. Mama lived for such a short time . . .

YOUNG MAN: That odor is offensive. It seems to come from in there. (*He gestures toward the small door.*)

MARGARITA: Claudia was always sickly. So weak, poor thing. Perhaps it was more than her weak heart . . .

YOUNG MAN: Come on. We ought to get down the hill before night comes.

MARGARITA: Yes, but . . . we must look for Claudia.

YOUNG MAN: But don't you see this place? She couldn't be here. She would have to be crazy to lock herself up in these ruins.

MARGARITA: That's just . . . Look. Oh, for God's sake. Don't you know how Mama died?

YOUNG MAN (*looking at her uneasily*): No. I don't know.

MARGARITA: She . . . died like that. It only lasted a short time, you know, but she died mad. Papa suffered so. And that's when Claudia developed her heart trouble.

YOUNG MAN: Why haven't you told me all this before?

MARGARITA: Because . . . This is Claudia's handkerchief.
(*She bursts out crying. In her hand is a small handkerchief that had beeen lying on the sofa. The Young Man sits down slowly and takes the handkerchief in his hands.*) Grandmother died that way, too. She used to say she saw things. When we were little she used to tell us how the devil lurked in corners. Claudia saw him once. She said it wasn't a devil, it was a yellow, grinning woman. I cried all that night . . . This is Claudia's handkerchief.

YOUNG MAN: There's a fly on it! (*He shakes it off with repulsion.*) An enormous green fly. (*He buries his face in his hands. He looks at the handkerchief again. He asks childishly*) Are you sure you didn't bring it yourself? (*Faced with her silence, he rises and yells into the shadows, through the small door.*) Claudia! Claudia! (*He turns.*) Is she . . . in there?

MARGARITA: Yes.

YOUNG MAN: Then it wasn't because she was upset, but because of

. . . What we were talking about, that she ran away from the farm? And you suspected . . . and said nothing to me!

MARGARITA (*lowering her head*): I hoped it wouldn't be this way. But finding this here . . . (*She points to the handkerchief.*)

YOUNG MAN: But why? Without any symptom, without any reason?

MARGARITA: I don't know. Perhaps Papa's illness.

YOUNG MAN: But why that? She didn't love him. There must be another reason. A . . . mental illness shows itself in many ways.

MARGARITA: I just don't know. It all began earlier, during the last days of Mama's illness. Claudia. Claudia got so sick. And something from that other time seemed to appear again when Papa became ill. She treated him almost affectionately, with that strange affection of hers—so strange. During his last days her heart became bad. The work, perhaps. Death is not so difficult for the one dying. But for those who attend . . . When Claudia had her attack, we sent her to the farm. She got a lot better there. My aunt wrote that she recovered her color and her animation. I intended to hide Papa's death from her for a while, because I was afraid of the damage it might do her heart. But it wasn't necessary, she disappeared from the farm the same day. They said she had been acting very strange for quite some time. She talked to herself, and wandered all over the house, as if listening.

YOUNG MAN: Why didn't you say anything to me? It wasn't fair for you to have hidden it from me. (*He sees the handkerchief.*) Till now.

(*There is a pause. A bird sings outside. The light from the sun is more oblique every minute. There are long shadows everywhere.*)

(*Rising*) Let's go look for her.

(*The gate screeches, then steps sound on the stairway.*)

MARGARITA: Claudia!

(*Claudia is on the threshold, carrying a great armload of flowers. When she sees the two waiting, she gives a soft cry. She leans against the door frame and lets the flowers fall, slowly. The Young Man advances toward her, entreating.*)

YOUNG MAN: Claudia . . .

CLAUDIA: No. Don't touch me! (*She moves away from them.*)

YOUNG MAN: What are you doing here? How long have you been here?

CLAUDIA: How awful!

MARGARITA: Claudia.

CLAUDIA: Leave me in peace.

MARGARITA: Claudia, Papa died . . . several days ago. Many days ago, now.

CLAUDIA: That's true. He died. (*She laughs softly.*)

MARGARITA: You already knew?

CLAUDIA (*walking toward the small door*): I expected it. But of course. It was natural.

MARGARITA: What are you doing here, little sister?

CLAUDIA (*pleading childishly*): Go away, please. I'm fine, just fine.

YOUNG MAN: How long have you been here?

CLAUDIA: How long? (*She looks at her hands, feels them carefully.*) I hadn't thought about it.

MARGARITA: We've been looking for you. I feel so lonely in the house. For a long time now . . .

CLAUDIA: A long time . . . Yes, of course, *time.* Have you been looking long?

MARGARITA: Yes. We must go. There's a car waiting for us down below.

CLAUDIA (*excited, her attention focused on the small door*): No! I can't. Come back for me later. That's it! You can come tomorrow. I'll have everything ready. I'll go with you then.

MARGARITA: But we can't leave you here. You look horribly pale. Auntie is ill, she feels she is to blame for your running away. We must go see her. She loves you very much.

CLAUDIA: Loves me. Loves me. I have to get my things together. (*With great weariness*) Why did this have to happen? If you had come tomorrow. You can come for me tomorrow.

YOUNG MAN: I've already bought your wedding dress.

CLAUDIA: Yes? (*Thinks*) That's right. The white dress.

YOUNG MAN: Let's go see it. It's at your house. It's covered with antique lace, the way you wanted it.

MARGARITA: Let's go, Claudia. You haven't tried on your wedding dress yet.

YOUNG MAN: It has a long veil and an orange-blossom crown. The bouquet is wax, and the sash is the one your mother and grand-mother used.

CLAUDIA: I would like to see it.

MARGARITA (*going toward her to take her arm*): Well, come on with us. It's getting dark.

CLAUDIA (*screaming*): Don't touch me! (*Panting, she shrinks into the doorway of the small door.*) At least, wait a minute . . . I'm going to . . . gather my things. I can't go like this.

MARGARITA: Claudia, what things? Listen to me. Be good. Don't shout. You're ill. We can't leave you here. We're prepared to take you with us however we have to do it. Don't fight us, please. Claudia. Little sister.

(*Claudia, frightened to a state of frenzy, looks first at one and then the other. Suddenly she yields.*)

CLAUDIA: All right. I will go with you. But don't touch me. And don't oppose me now. I would like to spend just one more night here.

YOUNG MAN: Let's go, Claudia.

CLAUDIA: Yes. Yes. But there are some things I don't want to leave, some necklaces, some old rings. I found them here, in our old room there, the dark one. Remember?

MARGARITA: Vaguely.

CLAUDIA: Yes, that's right. You were younger. But don't come any closer. Leave me alone a minute and . . . All right. We will leave together. (*Exits.*)

(*Margarita and the Young Man look at each other in silence. She begins to cry, quietly.*)

YOUNG MAN: Don't cry. Please. She won't resist. (*His voice breaks.*) She looked so beautiful with the flowers.

MARGARITA: She acts like a sleepwalker.

YOUNG MAN: It's getting dark fast. It's going to be difficult to get down to the car if she resists.

MARGARITA: She won't.

YOUNG MAN: The business of her heart frightens me. Won't we be upsetting her too much?

MARGARITA: What else can we do?

YOUNG MAN: That smell! It's stronger now.

MARGARITA: Yes, it is. How could she have stayed here so long?

(*The Young Man picks up some flowers without answering. Horrified, he throws them down and wipes his fingers.*)

YOUNG MAN (*barely audibly*): The flowers.

MARGARITA: What about them?

YOUNG MAN: They're rotten. (*A pause.*) She's taking a long time. I wonder what she's waiting for.

MARGARITA: I don't know. I vaguely remember that dark little room. It has a dirt floor. We used to hide things there, trinkets. It's next to the big gate. There's a tiny road that comes up there, but the gate was always kept closed because it's at the steepest part of the ravine.

YOUNG MAN: Is there another exit?

MARGARITA (*realizing*): Yes.

(*They both get up.*)

YOUNG MAN (*at the little door*): Claudia! Claudia! (*There is an echo, as in a vault.*) . . . audiaaaaaaaa. (*The Young Man exits.*)

MARGARITA (*wanting to follow him, but stopping*): Wait for me. I can't see a thing. It's changed. I don't recognize anything. There didn't use to be steps here. We need a light. (*Now to herself, coming back to center stage*) We need a light. (*She looks at the light outside, fading by the moment.*) We're not going to be able to find the road. Mary, help us. Mary, help us. It's getting dark. I'm afraid. Mary, help us. Mary, help us.

(*The Young Man enters.*)

YOUNG MAN: You can't see a thing. If she takes any longer, we'll wait for her outside. There's only one way to go down.

MARGARITA: We can leave at the other exit.

YOUNG MAN: Yes, you're right.

(*They walk to the back of the stage. They are on the stairway.*)

MARGARITA (*in a low voice*): Perhaps it would be better for you to stay here.

YOUNG MAN: Why?

(*Claudia enters, cautiously. The Young Man motions Margarita to be silent. He listens. He leaps into the room. Claudia screams, then breaks out crying.*)

CLAUDIA: Why don't you leave me? Why don't you? We've tried to open the gate but we're no longer strong enough. On the other side of the bars we saw the precipice, blue as evening, and below us, a black bird passed by, menacing us with his wings spread wide. We struggled with that gate, but it was so rusted we couldn't open it.

YOUNG MAN: Don't cry, Claudia. (*To the sister*) What shall we do?

MARGARITA: Dear sister, listen . . .

CLAUDIA: No! No! I can't leave. I'm not alone. I am with someone I love. He came to the farm to seek me. Perhaps I should not have, but I had resisted so long. We had tried so hard not to love each other. He came to seek me, loving, stained with earth. My heart was weak. I'm sorry. This pains me for your sake. No, don't come close to me. Don't touch me. The wedding dress . . . I don't know . . . You can keep it. Our wedding will never be now. My body, that which my body is, that which I am, I keep for someone I truly love. It already belongs to him. I am so sorry. For your sake. I don't want to say any more. Go, please. Don't make us run away. We wouldn't know where to go. Forgive me. Forgive me. Leave me now. Leave me here. You know everything now.

MARGARITA: But if there's someone here, get him, Claudia. You can go with him, and with me.

CLAUDIA: No. Not he. He is there, there in the shadow. We stood there with our arms about each other after the door wouldn't open.

YOUNG MAN: He will come to look for you at home. You can wait for him there. You and your sister. (*He is getting closer to Claudia.*)

MARGARITA (*closing the other way to Claudia*): We shall wait for him together, knitting at the window. You remember? As we used to do.

CLAUDIA (*seeing herself cornered*): No. Don't come any closer. Don't touch me. You're not to touch me. (*Almost in a howl*) Don't come near me!

HE (*appearing in the little door, standing straight, with his arms crossed over his chest*): Let her go.

(*The sister and the Young Man pause.*)

MARGARITA (*looking at him with terrified attention for one, two, three seconds*): Papa! (*She falls to the ground like a lump of dough.*)

(*The Young Man backs away and bumps into the wall, eyes starting out of his head.*)

CLAUDIA: Now you know.

YOUNG MAN: Claudia!

(*The Young Man tries to drag her outside. He takes her by the waist. She manages to get free. The Young Man takes her by an arm, intending to pull her again. She screams and draws back. The Young man is left with Claudia's arm, pulled from its socket, in his hands. He lets go and the arm falls to the floor, where it continues to move for a moment, as if it were soft rubber. The Young Man falls on his knees, emitting a hoarse, repulsive sound, like that of a slaughtered beast. Claudia cries with loud sobs. She takes hold of her empty sleeve.*)

CLAUDIA (*to Him*): Look what they've done to me. (*To the Young Man*) What right do you have? Why? Every piece I lose of my body is a little love that escapes us. Leave us alone. You've come to destroy our unhappy love that is turning to dust between our fingertips. (*He embraces her. She closes her eyes and leans against his chest. She continues speaking.*) You two don't matter any more. This is a dream *we* dreamed together, but it is becoming hazier every minute. Nobody else has a place in our dream ... (*Her voice has been getting weaker, trailing off to a thread.*)

(*The Young Man gives a hoarse cry. He takes Margarita in*

his arms and goes out with her toward the first evening shadows. Claudia sobs weakly.)

HE: Don't cry any more. Your eyes might fall out.

(*He leads her to the sofa.*)

CLAUDIA: Why is our love like this?

HE: It doesn't matter why. It is, that's all. Love should be an eternal pair of bodies. Don't cry. Don't move. We have so little time left.

CLAUDIA: So little time.

(*In the shadow, luminous pinpoints begin to dance above the torn-off arm, as if a myriad of insects were voraciously infesting it. The sound of the crickets grows louder and louder. A bird calls outside. The shadows deepen.*)

CURTAIN

THE GLACIER

"... Nor in the fiesta of love that we did not have ..."

PABLO NERUDA

Characters:

HUMBERTO SOSA (74)

AMELIA, HIS WIFE (71)

A NEWSPAPERMAN

THE CORPSE OF RUBÉN

TOWNSPEOPLE, DANCERS, UNBORN CHILDREN, GHOSTS OF 1900

In a little village high up on Ixtaccíhuatl during the first snows. Winter of 1950.

Inside an adobe house. Thick wooden poles support the roof. One window, through which one can see the falling snow. Braziers burning in the corners. A door at the rear center with six wooden steps leading up to it. Everything—walls, furniture—in bad repair, almost in ruins.

The distant music of the dancers can be heard. Humberto and Amelia are seated. A long silence.

HUMBERTO (*begins to cough, then says*): Yes, sir. Yes, sir. I'll die here coughing, or die of pneumonia. I said I'll die of this cough, or of pneumonia. And you, too. Look how you're trembling. At this height, at our age ... Oh, good God. Women will be women, even when they're a hundred years old. (*He coughs, spits into a brazier, wipes his mouth.*) No, this business'll kill me. (*He looks out the window, almost crying.*) It's snowing! We'll freeze when we leave here tomorrow. That's great! Instead of one dead, three! And why, I ask you. Why?

AMELIA: Nobody asked you to come.

HUMBERTO: As if I were going to let you come by yourself. No, sir. The lady gets a notion, well, indulge her, come with her, and die of the cold!

(*Amelia begins to cough, a cough that sounds as if it will never end.*)

God, now your cough's begun. Spit, woman, spit.

AMELIA: I don't need you to teach me how to spit. (*Spits.*) And if you say anything about that, I'll walk out of here, and you'll be talking to yourself. Even if I freeze. (*Her cough subsides.*)

(*Pause. An Indian enters.*)

INDIAN: They found him, mister.

AMELIA (*rising, electrified, and speaking hoarsely*): What? What did you say? (*She begins to tremble, especially her head and hands.*)

INDIAN: They found him, ma'am. One of the boys just ran back to say they'd found him. He looks just like he's asleep, there in that hunk of ice. They're going to chip away the ice and bring him in, in a bit. They said for you to wait here just a while, they won't be long.

HUMBERTO: That's good, that's good. Tell them to get at it, go on. And here's a little something so the boys can have a round.

INDIAN: Thanks, mister. (*Exits.*)

HUMBERTO: Look, it's silly to cry now. Just what I expected. As if he had died yesterday. But woman, look at yourself in the mirror. (*He pushes her to the piece of mirror.*) See? That's you, that pretty little old lady. What does *she* have to do with that girl from fifty years back. *I* don't know how it was. Who knows if it ever was? You're my old lady, my pretty little old lady, racing with me to see who's going to last the longest, huh? Come on, don't cry. (*He blows her nose.*) Don't cry. (*He coughs, spits, blows his nose, too. He puts his arms around her. She rests her head on his shoulder.*)

(*An Indian girl enters, the Newspaperman behind her.*)

INDIAN GIRL: I made you a cup of coffee. (*She puts the steaming pottery jar on the table.*) This man was asking for you.

(*The two old people look at him, still embraced. The Indian girl exits.*)

NEWSPAPERMAN: That's it. Just like that. (*A flash. He has taken their picture.*) You're Humberto Sosa, right?

HUMBERTO: Yes, sir.

(*Intimidated, they step back. The Newspaperman moves in on them.*)

NEWSPAPERMAN: And you're his wife, right?

AMELIA: Yes, sir.

NEWSPAPERMAN: I am here representing our nation on this solemn occasion. I wish to offer you, first of all, my admiration. The glorification of the dead is a sentiment which is fading out today, although it should be nourished because it is native to our Mexican sensibility. (*As the preceding was said in one breath, he draws a deep breath.*) Who was the deceased, sir? Your brother?

AMELIA: What's that?

NEWSPAPERMAN: I was saying, ma'am, was the deceased your brother, the one they're looking for?

HUMBERTO: He was her husband.

NEWSPAPERMAN (*writing*): Her . . . ah. Her husband? What? Her . . . Before you . . . Of course. Yes, of course. Her husband?

AMELIA: What do you want? What are you looking for?

NEWSPAPERMAN: I am the special envoy of the EXCELSIOR, ma'am, sent here to inform the nation . . .

AMELIA: The newspaper? That's what you came to do? You're from the newspaper?

NEWSPAPERMAN: Yes, ma'am.

AMELIA (*looking at her husband*): What are you waiting for? Throw him out!

HUMBERTO (*conciliatory*): Amelia . . .

AMELIA: What are you waiting for? Get out.

NEWSPAPERMAN: Madam, I'm very sorry.

AMELIA: Get out of here.

NEWSPAPERMAN: Madam, I have scaled the heights of this volcano to be with you, not . . .

AMELIA: Out!

HUMBERTO: Please. (*Takes the Newspaperman aside.*) I'll see you later, if you want. (*Gives him his card.*) This is the address of my little grocery. You can find me there tomorrow morning, or the day after. But the wife isn't at all well now, eh? Excuse us, please. Go on, go on.

NEWSPAPERMAN: All right .(*Starts to exit.*)

HUMBERTO: And . . . listen. (*Looks toward Amelia. Very low*) See if you can mention my store, eh?

NEWSPAPERMAN: Yes, sir. Of course. Sure. (*Closes the door after him.*)

AMELIA: Just like vultures . . . (*Sits down, exhausted.*)

   (*Pause. Outside, a crowd of people carrying torches.*)

   Find out what's going on, old man.

HUMBERTO (*looking out*): Hey, listen, you! Child!

LITTLE GIRL (*wearing a mask and a crown of paper flowers*): We're going to get him now. (*She leaves.*)

   (*Distant music, fading away.*)

AMELIA: I'm going out there.

HUMBERTO: What? Where?

AMELIA: I'm going out there.

HUMBERTO: Oh, no, missy. I'm keeping you here with me. That's all I need.

   (*Amelia is putting on a heavy sarape.*)

   You're not moving from here. You hear? I'm not going to have you catching cold or pneumonia! We're waiting right here until . . .

AMELIA: I don't *want* you to come with me. He was my husband before you were, so I don't want you to come.

   (*She exits, closing the door after her.*)

HUMBERTO: But . . .But at your age . . . No, you're not going out there. I positively forbid it. Listen. (*Coughs.*) Oh, my God. Now, because of your damned corpse . . . A widower at my age. Oh, Lord. It's my fault, mine alone. (*He puts charcoal on the braziers.*) Women. If only I'd never married. God.

   (*The Newspaperman enters.*)

NEWSPAPERMAN: They're bringing the body, sir. Will you allow me to take a few pictures?

HUMBERTO: You can take all you want as far as I'm concerned. Something like this always happens. What a life. What a life!

NEWSPAPERMAN: And your wife?

HUMBERTO: Dying of pneumonia, out there in the snow. Seeing as how she's so young, only seventy-one years old, she decides this is the moment to climb Ixtaccíhuatl, and here she is. Now she's gone out in the snow and the cold air, which is obviously going to do her a lot of good. She's outside there! (*Walks back and forth, furious.*)

NEWSPAPERMAN (*tentatively*): Would *you* allow me to take a picture?

HUMBERTO: Of me?

NEWSPAPERMAN: Yes. Sure.

HUMBERTO: But man, a picture of me? Pshaw! A picture of me? (*Strikes a pose.*) What for? (*Laughs softly, a conventional "he, he."*) Go take some pretty girls, or . . .
     (*Flash.*)

NEWSPAPERMAN: Thanks. (*With book and pencil ready*) So the dead man is no relation to you.

HUMBERTO: No, man. He's my wife's first husband.

NEWSPAPERMAN: But, your wife and you have been married for . . .

HUMBERTO: Twenty years, yes, sir. Twenty years.

NEWSPAPERMAN: Twenty years. And he? The dead man?

HUMBERTO: He's been very dead for fifty years.

NEWSPAPERMAN: Fifty years! Fifty years! (*He whistles happily as he writes.*) So that . . .? I don't understand.

HUMBERTO: Look. My wife was married here, in the little church in this village. In a different one that was destroyed. The church they have now has only been here thirty-five years. She was married here to her *sweetheart,* but he never got to be her husband, see? You understand. You know, I got married, but the "little widow" is not for me. No, sir. I'm not modern. With me, it's a virgin or nothing.

NEWSPAPERMAN: So you say she got married here?

HUMBERTO: Yes, right here. Her husband was a mountaineer, still a kid, you know. Going up the mountain, boyish exuberance, things of that sort, you know. He was twenty, I think. No, let's see. She told me once that he was the same age as my cousin Paco . . . No. Let's see . . .

NEWSPAPERMAN: How old was she?

HUMBERTO: She was twenty-one. And he fell, clear down into the mountain. They heard him screaming, in the air, and she was screaming up above. The business of climbing was a difficult thing then, I imagine. 1900, think of it. And he fell, up there, into a crevasse where nobody could reach him. But down at the bottom of the place where he fell, there was a glacier, you know. One of those things that moves two inches a year, or something like that. So he's been moving down, all this time. And they told Amelia about it, and there she is, waiting for her sweetheart, all this time it has taken the glacier to bring him down from the mountain.

NEWSPAPERMAN: Fifty year's waiting . . .

HUMBERTO: Yes, sir. Measured by the clock. She searched, investigated, saw geog . . . geologists, people who know about things like that. And someone told her where, and after how long she could get to him. Think of it, fifty years. I asked her what for. But one is a Christian, one is a Catholic, you know. And there's this feeling about burying the dead. Although the truth is, you know, I think she . . . Well, it doesn't matter. Doesn't matter.

NEWSPAPERMAN: Gosh. (*He shakes his head.*) Some story. And you?

HUMBERTO: Me? What about me?

NEWSPAPERMAN: Since you married her. Didn't it, didn't it make you jealous.?

HUMBERTO: No. No. I don't fool myself any. No, sir. Look. Jealous? No, sir. We were along in years when we got married, none of that nonsense about being madly in love, or anything like that. I wanted her, and she wanted me. She was a girl from a good family. Down on her luck, but from a good family. She withdrew from any social life and got used to my ham and cheese. And I got used to her cold meat, up there. (*He laughs, pleased with his joke, then thinks better of it.*) No, don't print that, eh? It's just that . . . Well, I give her pleasure, but . . . I don't understand these things. Hell, I had lots of girls, fifty years ago. One of them even died or something, I think. And so what? I'm a man seventy-four years old. Think what it would be like if *I* remembered everything as if it were only yesterday. Three quarters of a century, a century, it's all the same thing. That Amelia. Oh, that Amelia.

NEWSPAPERMAN: She wanted to come, right?

HUMBERTO: Yes, sir. Think of it. I told her: So they're going to bury him, well and good. But what can we do there? But oh, no. It was we ought to come, and we should come, and he had been her husband, and God knows what. So here we are, carried up in hand chairs. For what? For nothing, because it could be . . .

(*Distant music is heard, coming closer.*)

NEWSPAPERMAN (*about to exit*): Here they come.

HUMBERTO: Here they come. Don't take any pictures in front of her. Or not that she knows about, anyway.

NEWSPAPERMAN: Yes, sir. You bet. (*At the door*) Thanks a lot.

HUMBERTO: And listen, "The Sun of Seville," that's the name of my store, "The Sun . . ."

NEWSPAPERMAN: Yeah. Sure, sure. (*He closes the door after him.*)

HUMBERTO: ". . . of Seville." Let's see if Amelia won't . . . I hope she doesn't . . . Oh, that Amelia!

(*The music is closer. Through the windows can be seen, like lightning, the flashing of bulbs. The door opens wide and the cortege enters. At its front, dancing, masked women and small girls, dressed in bright colors, crowned with paper flowers, and carrying small, brightly colored guitars, which they play. Men carrying torches bear the cadaver, covered by a black and white sarape, on their shoulders. Amelia, looking smaller and older than ever, her voice more broken than before, bundled in her sarape, trembles between two torchbearers.*)

AMELIA: Put him down here.

(*They place the body at her feet and exit, still dancing.*) (*Be-*

fore Humberto can speak) Leave me alone with him, will you? Wait for me in the church, or in some other hut. Please. Please!

(*He exits. Amelia walks around the corpse. She drops her sarape.*)

I am trembling, imagine, but it isn't because of the cold. I still haven't seen your face. I can imagine you clearly, how you laughed, how you spoke, but something happens to me now, something. I can remember your portrait better than I remember you. What was your voice like?

(*His voice sounds in the air, distant, veiled.*)

VOICE OF RUBÉN: Girls ought to know what Bordeaux wine is.

AMELIA (*crying out*): Yes, it was like that!

VOICE OF RUBÉN (*nearer and clearer*): Girls ought to know what Bordeaux wine is.

AMELIA (*laughing, and her laughter crackles like dry kindling*): You put some in my mouth. From your mouth to mine. Ah, it embarrassed me so. How did you say it?

VOICE OF HUMBERTO (*forceful, younger*): Bordeaux wine. Authentic. Thirty-five *pesos* a bottle.

AMELIA (*screaming*): No! No! (*She squirms in disgust.*) Not now. Oh! I was fifty-one years old then and so lonely. I told him I was forty, but I was a fifty-one-year-old virgin. I got married in black, like a widow, because I was your widow. It had been so long. It was hard for me to imagine you slipping down in the glacier, second by second, fractions of fractions of millimeters. And now . . .

(*Suddenly she throws back his sarape. A burst of music. It is the body of a golden young man, blue from the cold, with a little streak of dried blood on his forehead. Amelia looks at him for a long while. The light is centered especially around his head, like a halo.*)

And so this was you. I didn't remember this blond down . . . (*She touches him.*) How cold you are. (*She uncovers him completely.*) So cold. What do you have in your hands? I don't remember. Our picnic lunch? You fell with it and left me with nothing. Egotist. You took my life's nourishment with you. Your hands were trembling in the church. They're so rigid now. (*She laces her fingers in his.*) Look at my hand. It shames me next to yours. It looks like a monkey's paw, an *old* monkey's paw.

(*The "Dolores" waltz, by Waldteufel, begins far away, the melody distorted as if squeezed out note by note.*)

That's it, that's it . . . Nothing has changed.

(*She hums it a little, very shrilly and out of tune. She sways to its beat, tremulously. Couples from the year 1900 come out of the corners, dancing. Amelia sees them, smiles to some, greets others. Suddenly she begins to wail.*)

They're all dead now. All of them, all of them. (*She wipes her nose, coughs, spits, while she continues repeating "all of them."*)

(*The couples and the music fade away.*)

(*Blowing her nose and drawing a deep breath*) Foolishness. From fifty years ago. What do you have in that package? (*She touches it but doesn't dare to take it.*) We have to bury you now. Right here, I suppose. They'll say your mass in the church. Child. So beautiful. You could be my grandson. (*She looks at herself in the piece of mirror.*) The son of my sons . . .

ECHO: Son of my sons . . .

AMELIA: Sons? What sons?

RUBÉN (*smiling, his eyes still closed*): Hadn't it occurred to you? Yours and mine.

AMELIA: Rubén! (*Her voice is young, it is a cry of scandalized delight. There is a chorus of laughter.*) No, Rubén. You embarrass me in front of everyone.

RUBÉN (*his eyes open, smiling*): Silly, why hadn't it occurred to you. That's why one marries.

AMELIA (*blushing and agile, she places her fingers to his mouth*): Rubén. Even though I'm your wife, there are things one doesn't discuss in front of people. (*Laughter from Rubén and a chorus of laughter. Her voice is suddenly old.*) That was so long ago. We have to carry you to the church now. (*Very tired*) I don't want to remember any more. That was the day we married, and I want you to give me back your sweetheart ring. It will be all I have left that is yours. A ring. Humberto made me put his on,

but I have the one you gave me hanging here. (*She pulls it from her breast, on a chain.*) Now I will have both of them together. I'm so miserable. Rubén! (*She kneels down and takes his hand. The packet rolls out and opens. From it, pale human skins spill out, like little skin balloons, deflated.*)
What's this?

(*She takes the little balloon and holds it out. It is an empty child.*)

RUBÉN: Our children.

AMELIA (*taking another, larger, empty skin, and another, and another—women's skins*): And this?

RUBÉN: They are your skins. If this one I still have hadn't frozen it would have finally worn out and another would have appeared. And another underneath it. Down to one like the one you're wearing, stretched right over the bones.

AMELIA: So many!

RUBÉN: All the ones you didn't use. That day you changed very suddenly because when I fell I carried several of your skins with me.

AMELIA: I aged years that day.

RUBÉN: Yes, years. You, the you of that time, I have here. (*He takes out one more skin, from his breast.*) Do you want it?

AMELIA: It wouldn't do me any good now. (*She takes it.*) Poor thing, empty, dry, just like I am now. These empty hands. (*She is putting on the skin like gloves, like a dress, like a mask*): This face, this empty belly . . .

(*Suddenly he is sitting up, looking at her, smiling.*)
Rubén! (*And runs laughing to his side.*)

(*Amelia and Rubén cling to each other. Then she lies down by his side. He kisses her lingeringly. They embrace, with more and more strength and vigor. The dancers come out from the corners and gradually form a living screen which shields the couple on the pallet during the whole dance. The children-skins get up and begin to move about. They are live children now, but languid and sad; like sleepwalkers, drugged, they join the dance. The women crown them with flowers and they play—almost;*

they smile, but they always stumble or fall, limp, immobile, then go on dancing. Later the music fades away. The dancers leave, one by one. The children fall, as if they had suddenly dried up. They are empty skins again. Amelia is still next to the corpse of Rubén; she lazily raises an arm and it is the nude arm of a young woman, but the skin falls away and reveals the arm of the seventy-one-year-old woman. She gets up. She is Amelia again, the seventy-one-year-old one, but the resplendent Rubén is no longer lying on the floor; there is, instead, a man as old as Humberto, wrinkled and desiccated.)

(*She sees him, and starts.*) Dear God! (*Like someone who has committed great mischief*) Dear God! And now what? (*She sees the sarape.*) Ah, that's it. (*She covers him with it, then walks wearily, lazily, stretching herself once or twice, like a virgin the morning after her wedding. She looks at the corpse. She lifts a corner of the sarape and, smiling, says reproachfully*) Why did you do all that to me? (*She covers him.*) I'm thirsty. (*But her voice is old again. She looks in the mirror, sighs. She goes to the door and opens it. The wind blows in, and the light from the mountain enters. The skins—the empty children—tumble like pieces of paper on the ground. She closes the door.*) It is morning already. (*Hastily, she picks up the skins. She looks at them, not knowing what to do. Finally, she throws them in a brazier. A great flame surges up, a last arpeggio; they are carried very high, then die down. She uncovers the body one more time. She contemplates the figure of the little old man. She kisses his forehead with cool tenderness.*) What we do to you. Some sooner, some later. (*She covers him. She goes to the door and throws it open. In her shrill, broken voice*) Humberto! Humberto!

(*Humberto enters.*)

HUMBERTO: What happened? Did you sleep, or did you keep watch all night? I was afraid you might have felt ill, but I didn't want to interrupt. I had my little nap, just for a while. And I made arrangements for the burial a little later this morning. Did you know it isn't going to cost as much as we thought?

(*Slowly the cortege is entering to carry away the body. They pick it up.*)

To the church with him, to the church. (*Music. The dancers are on the steps, forming an honor guard.*)

What did you do all that time alone with him? I was afraid you might get scared. You prayed for him, I guess.

AMELIA: I prayed for him . . . prayed. (*She begins to laugh, quietly, like a hen.*)

HUMBERTO: What are you laughing about? What's going on?

AMELIA: I prayed for him. (*She laughs like a fool, interminably.*)

HUMBERTO (*alarmed*): Amelia! What's the matter with you? Do you feel bad? Are you losing your mind? Amelia! What's the matter?

AMELIA (*suddenly she feels weak, and takes two or three deep breaths. She is still on the edge of laughter. She makes a strange noise, like the cackle of an old hen or the cry of a child. She gets control of herself, runs her hand across her forehead*): What's the matter with me? I don't know if I'm going to have a child . . . or die.

(*She gives her arm to Humberto, and they go out behind the cadaver.*)

CURTAIN

THE WINE CELLAR

Based on a dream of Jorge Wilmot's

Characters:

THE SALES MANAGER (A WOMAN)

THE EMPLOYEE

THE APPLICANT

A YOUNG WOMAN

FIGURES IN THE STORIES OF:

"*Narcissus*" *(two)*
"*The Monk and the Beautiful Zoë*" *(three)*
"*The Virgin Material*" *(three)*

A SECOND APPLICANT

THE CORTEGE

Mexico City, 1949

A dark circular wine cellar. The structure of the walls, submerged in shadows, cannot be made out. One guesses it is brick, perhaps, damp brick. The lighted area is center stage. Large packing cases are strewn about, some on end, others flat. The floor has several levels. From the entrance, right, descend three wide steps. At the rear, a black curtain visible only against the bright light seen when it is pulled.

The stage is empty. Distant music of a flute. After a moment the Sales Manager appears. Tall, with a virile, businesslike voice, she wears a long dress and a leather apron. Her face is old and lined. She has her hair combed high. Behind her, the Employee. He is old and dirty, wearing black. He wears a wig that slips when he moves. They enter rear and look at the cases one by one.

SALES MANAGER: This one.

(*She is near one of the cases, which is standing on end. The Employee exits rear. He returns leading a blond, curly-headed adolescent, dressed in Greek costume, who moves like a sleepwalker.*)

Be careful. The wood is a little rotten.

(*The Employee opens the cover of the box with meticulous care. It swings open like a wardrobe. The box is empty.*)

Good. (*She looks at the boy.*) Beautiful, eh? (*Laughing*) Put him in.

(*The Employee pushes the boy into the box.*)

His flute!

(*The Employee takes a flute from his pocket and places it in the boy's hands. The boy raises it to his lips and plays a few sweet measures. The Employee closes the box.*)

Don't close it yet. You must put the mothballs in so that he doesn't get worm-eaten.

(*The Employee nods. A discordant bell rings.*)

Hurry up. There's someone at the door.

(*The Employee nods. He picks up a label that reads* THE TRUE HISTORY OF OTHELLO AND DESDEMONA *and is about to nail it on the lid of the packing case.*)

No, you imbecile.

(*The Employee, bewildered, puts it down and picks up another, which he shows to the Sales Manager:* THE STORY OF THE MONK AND THE BEAUTIFUL ZOÉ.)

No, you imbecile. The advance scouts have just now advised us that the material for those two will arrive today.

(*The Employee, perplexed, runs from one side to another.*)

There!

(*The Employee finds the sign that reads* THE FABLE OF NARCISSUS (REVISED). *Since the Sales Manager nods her assent, he nails it on the cover of the box. The bell rings again. The Employee exits, running. He runs with little hops, as if his feet hurt. The Sales Manager waits. The Employee re-enters, preceding the Applicant.*)

36

(*Pleasantly*) Good morning.

APPLICANT: It's so dark. I, uh . . . you know. I wished to speak to the Sales Manager.

SALES MANAGER: At your service.

APPLICANT: Ah, you're the one. Well, I read in the newspaper (*showing her*) that there was an opening for new salesmen.

SALES MANAGER: What experience do you have?

APPLICANT: I've been a traveling salesman. That is, I am a traveling salesman for an Argentine publishing firm. Besides, since it says here that no . . .

SALES MANAGER: No, no training whatsoever is necessary, and there will be absolutely no conflict with any other employment you may have. This is something very new and easy to sell. There is an intensive advertising campaign prepared to be launched at any moment, and really, our agents will be in a most enviable situation. You, naturally, will begin as a trainee in the event that you meet the specifications. What is your capacity for work?

APPLICANT: Well, rather large. I mean I work well.

SALES MANAGER: Do you have recommendations?

APPLICANT: Yes, of course. (*He takes them from his pocket.*) You may look at them.

SALES MANAGER (*takes them, looks at them on both sides without unfolding them, and returns them to him*): They look very good.

APPLICANT: Aren't you going to read them?

SALES MANAGER: I said they look very good.

APPLICANT: I read that you offer a salary plus commission.

SALES MANAGER: Yes, a modest salary, which will be increased when you become an agent. But the commission is splendid, truly splendid, and sales are completely assured. You place the merchandise on view and you are completely assured of your buyer. It isn't possible to resist the fascination and novelty of the product.

APPLICANT: I understand it has to do with books, right? (*He looks around.*)

SALES MANAGER: Not exactly. It's more unusual. Books in a way, but with an added attraction.

APPLICANT: Something new, eh?

SALES MANAGER: One of these packing cases accompanies each copy. The operating technique is simple. You will need to learn it, nevertheless, so that you can explain it to every client.

APPLICANT: Yes, I read that you have to take a course.

SALES MANAGER: Just a brief course. Two lessons, three, perhaps, are enough. All this is based on a physical principle as obvious and irrefutable as the fact that you carry your own skeleton in your body.

APPLICANT (*laughing a little and feeling himself*): Yeah, sure, I never leave it at home.

SALES MANAGER (*serious*): Of course not. In the same way, you carry within you *many* men, old, mature, which one by one, in their turn, take the place of the *you* of right now, down to the one which is stuck right to your skeleton.

APPLICANT: I don't exactly understand.

SALES MANAGER: Well, that is the principle of our merchandise. Pay close attention, because this is important. (*She opens a case that is lying on the floor.*) This is the virgin material. (*She lifts out a young child, of wax, which moves a little.*) Well, inside this child there is another, larger one, in this same case. (*She puts the first away and takes out a larger child.*) This child, in the work which we will illustrate with him, will be replaced by a larger one, then by a boy, and then by a young man. O.K. You see, then, they are all inside the initial child. (*She puts away the second child and pulls out half the body of a young boy in a beret.*) You see?

APPLICANT: Ah yes. I understand. But this . . . You *sell* it?

SALES MANAGER: This is the virgin material, I said. (*She closes the case.*) But you'll see. I'll demonstrate a complete example for you. (*She takes up a pottery bell and rings it. Then she throws it down, breaking it. She makes an excuse.*) It's only good for one time.

(*The Employee enters rear.*)

Bring a light.

(*The Employee exits.*)

You must also know how to choose your clients. That's the theme of the second lesson: "Selection of Clients." Not all clients want the same story. Sometimes the title alone is enough to decide them. At other times more details are required to interest them. But it is fundamental to know what book to show each one. You'll learn that later. Help me. (*She goes behind some cases.*) Pull this out to the middle of the room.

APPLICANT: This one? (*He picks up a wooden lectern, but it falls apart in his hands.*) Oh, pardon me! I picked it up carefully, but ...

SALES MANAGER: No. It wasn't your fault. It's the carelessness of the employees. We have to fight the moss and the decay. Take another.

(*The Applicant takes another lectern, covered with stains from some long-trailing moss, and places it in the center of the stage. He brushes off his clothes. The Employee enters carrying a small lamp.*)

Give us some light.

(*In the shadows there is a shelf with seven or eight large volumes, covered with dust, that appear to be very old.*)

These are the books. There are many more, in the other cellars.

APPLICANT: Are these the ones? I thought . . . Since it's a new undertaking ...

SALES MANAGER (*severely*): What did you think?

APPLICANT: That they would be ... new books.

SALES MANAGER: What's your understanding of new? Are you capable of telling me something new? Of showing me something new?

APPLICANT: I didn't mean that.

SALES MANAGER: What did you mean?

APPLICANT: Oh, nothing.

SALES MANAGER (*pleasantly*): You can see our complete catalogue later. But, for the moment, let's study an example to explain it thoroughly. Which one would you prefer?

APPLICANT: Oh, I don't know. It's all the same, isn't it?

SALES MANAGER: It is not at all the same thing! This one is the fable of Narcissus, revised, of course.

APPLICANT: Revised?

SALES MANAGER: Yes. The absurd incident in which Narcissus dies contemplating himself has been suppressed. It includes instead the wedding of Narcissus with his own image. That is very beautiful. And it goes on a long way from there.

APPLICANT: I'm not familiar with that version. I knew that he fell in love with himself and . . .

SALES MANAGER: Yes, yes. But I just told you that this is the revised version. This is the authentic one, in reality. Here there is also the life of Saint Sebastian, the story of Othello stripped of superfluous embellishment . . .

APPLICANT: Another Othello story?

SALES MANAGER: Why do you say "another"?

APPLICANT: Because I already know one. Is it the same one?

SALES MANAGER: I don't think so. A story is different for each person who hears it and is authentic only for each person who lives it. This is what is unusual about our product. The difficulty is that no agent ever succeeds in knowing all the books.

APPLICANT: Why?

SALES MANAGER (*laughing*): For very normal reasons, really. Lack of facilities or lack of interest.

APPLICANT: What . . . what book is this?

SALES MANAGER: It's THE STORY OF THE MONK AND THE BEAUTIFUL ZOÉ. This one is THE KIDNAPPING OF HELEN. This one, BIOGRAPHY OF AN EXEMPLARY LOVER. Which would you like us to read? The one about Narcissus is still a little fresh, and the Othello is incomplete, but the others . . .

APPLICANT: Can we look at THE STORY OF THE MONK?

SALES MANAGER (*looking at him for an instant*): Yes, of course. Take it.

(*He takes the book, impeded by its great size. A cloud of dust rises from it.*)

Carry it to the lectern. (*To the Employee*) You go on now.

(*The Employee exits.*)

APPLICANT (*adjusting the book*): It weighs a lot.

SALES MANAGER: Of course. (*She opens it.*) Since this is a medieval story it makes no difference that the book is worm-eaten. You can see the beginnings: the monk lives in his grotto and knows the beautiful Zoé. She is a sort of nymph, something like that; it has something to do with water. Now, this is the corresponding illustration. (*She opens one of the horizontal boxes and directs the young girl inside, dressed in a white cloak, to sit up.*) The beautiful Zoé, don't you see? (*She puts her away and closes the case.*) Read out loud.

APPLICANT (*reads*): "That was the way they lived in the grotto, and the beautiful Zoé no longer visited the pond. Prayers were at six in the evening. Dinner was at eight."

SALES MANAGER: You read very badly. You have to declaim a little. And you skipped a bit. Before that comes the marriage of the monk and the beautiful Zoé.

APPLICANT: Shall I read it over?

SALES MANAGER: No, that would be beginning again and that isn't possible now. But let me demonstrate how you should read. (*She reads with great feeling, mannering her voice a little absurdly, but with grandiloquence.*) "Zoé was pleased with the diversions that accompanied her new situation. Many small animals and birds came to eat from her hands every day, and went away satiated, belly full and heart content." Like that. Did you pay attention? Go on.

APPLICANT (*reads*): "The monk, for his part, liked all the new pleasures accorded him by the beautiful Zoé. One pleasure was conversation. Another pleasure was that of the bed. Another pleasure—and the most important one—was that of constant companionship."

SALES MANAGER: That's a little better, but now comes the description of the pleasures and I think you mightn't read that well. Skip a page. Another. Here.

APPLICANT (*reads*): "The illness of Zoé was very vexatious. She ceased speaking, little by little, and hair began to grow within her. The monk's heart was sore, and so great was his suffering that he devoured pieces of his own flesh, leaving cruel marks from his teeth. With blood from his wounds he painted a bag red and kept Zoé inside." This is . . . ugly.

SALES MANAGER: Yes, naturally. But the story goes on. Here we have Zoé at the beginning of her illness. (*She opens the case and has the girl sit up. The girl has changed color, and hair is coming out of her eyes and mouth.*) The worm-eaten state of the arms is not part of the story, it's carelessness on the part of the attendants, but you can take it as part of the story. I suppose you've understood well.

APPLICANT: The story?

SALES MANAGER: The technique. This Zoé was inside the other. It's a question of time. The first rots and is absorbed by the second as it matures.

APPLICANT: Yes, I understand. Put her away.

SALES MANAGER: Do you see the stain of blood on the robe? It's the monk's blood.

APPLICANT: Yes, yes. Put her away.

SALES MANAGER (*putting her away*): Go on reading.

APPLICANT (*reads*): "Zoé stayed inside the bag painted with the blood of the monk, and he fastened the opening of the bag, but three times a day he loosened it and thus he fed Zoé, offering spoonfuls of food that he had first chewed. But Zoé did not get well."

SALES MANAGER: Look at Zoé in her bag. (*She opens the case and pulls out a bag the color of old blood, covered with shreds of moss.*) But if you want it to open, go on ahead. I can't open it yet. Skip a couple of pages.

APPLICANT (*doing so*): Shall I read?

SALES MANAGER: Naturally.

APPLICANT (*reads*): "The odor of the bag became more unbearable every day. All the animals that lived in the grotto fled, and all the animals that were in the forest fled, because no one wished to smell the odor of Zoé. And the monk knew that Zoé was not dead because she still moved inside the bag. And only the monk suffered the stench of the bag, which was the stench of Zoé."

SALES MANAGER: Go on reading.

APPLICANT: "And the monk wished to see now what the beautiful Zoé had become, and with a knife he ripped open the bag. And a figure appeared which was what the beautiful Zoé was now."

(*The Sales Manager opens the bag, long as it is, with a single tug, and the Applicant cries out. Inside it is a decayed figure, the size of the girl, but of a different shape. It looks like a plucked, decapitated turkey. In place of a head it has only a large tuft of long, bristly hair. It emits a harsh, hollow sound and flaps its featherless wings weakly. Many luminous insects infest it.*)

SALES MANAGER: Look, it has a zipper in it for the sake of convenience. It gives the effect of being a knife slash. The scabs are authentic. So are the insects. (*The figure begins to shriek again.*) I know the following part by heart. (*Declaims*) "That is what the beautiful Zoé had become! And her voice also had changed. But she could feed herself perfectly through the place where she once had had a mouth, and if she howled it was from strong desire for the monk." (*Explaining*) Sexual desire, you understand. Farther on it explains in detail. It would be good if you memorized a few sections. (*The figure stirs and shrieks.*) I know a few lines more. (*Declaims*) "The monk divested himself of his tunic in order to be nude, but some pieces stuck to his sores, and these sores were the places where the monk bit himself every day, and in some the whiteness of his bones showed through." (*Normal*) And it goes on like that. (*She closes the bag and thus hides the figure, then closes the box.*) Aren't you reading any more.

APPLICANT: No. No.

SALES MANAGER: All right. (*She closes the book.*) Of course the story doesn't end there. There's more, a lot more.

APPLICANT: And the monk?

SALES MANAGER: Oh, yes, the monk. But it would be better to look at another story.

APPLICANT: What is it that smells so?

SALES MANAGER: It's the odor of the case. It hasn't been very well aired. Do you understand everything all right?

(*The Employee enters, running.*)

What do you want? Don't you see that I'm giving a class?

(*The Employee presents a large card on a tray. The Sales Manager takes it and gives it to the Applicant.*) You read it.

APPLICANT: "The Assistant Sales Manager has completed his demonstration and the young lady wishes to know the salary."

SALES MANAGER: Oh, yes. She has already finished her classes and is ready to begin working. Excuse me a moment.

(*She takes the card and she and the Employee exit. The Applicant, alone, looks around him. He dries the perspiration from his hands with a handkerchief. He opens the book, but the lid of the case begins to rise. He notices it; he closes the book and the lid closes sonorously. He takes a few steps. He sees the large box with Narcissus in it.*)

APPLICANT (*reading aloud*): THE FABLE OF NARCISSUS (REVISED).

(*He opens the case. Standing inside is the figure of a very fat man, dark skinned, bald, half nude, wearing a Greek tunic that reveals folds of flesh through its rents. A very long flute is twisted about his body, beginning at his lips. The Applicant stands looking at him. The flute sounds, discordantly. The Applicant closes the case. The Young Woman enters.*)

YOUNG WOMAN: Good afternoon.

APPLICANT (*starts*): Hello.

YOUNG WOMAN: Did I frighten you?

APPLICANT: Yes, I was looking at . . . (*Forcing a laugh*) Did you say "Good afternoon"?

YOUNG WOMAN: Yes. It's almost night.

APPLICANT: Night? Do you work here?

YOUNG WOMAN: They have just given me a job, but . . . I don't know. I thought I didn't like it very much, and now, well, I don't know. They told me they'd be waiting for me in the wine cellar.

APPLICANT: I came to look for a job. I got here early. Where did you come in?

YOUNG WOMAN: There's another entrance, through the offices. (*She laughs a little.*) Those are *some* offices. Haven't you seen them?

APPLICANT: No.

YOUNG WOMAN: They pay well, but...

APPLICANT: Yes, they pay well. Do you have another job?

YOUNG WOMAN: Yes, I'm a swimming teacher. What book did you read?

APPLICANT: THE STORY OF THE MONK AND THE BEAUTIFUL ZOÉ.

YOUNG WOMAN: Oh, yes. I read that one yesterday, during the first lesson.

APPLICANT: I just finished reading it. There's . . . there's Zoé.

YOUNG WOMAN: Where?

APPLICANT: In that box.

YOUNG WOMAN: And the monk is there.

APPLICANT: There? No. (*He opens the box. It is empty.*) Well . . . (*With a forced laugh*) There's nobody now. It's empty.

YOUNG WOMAN: It is? (*She looks.*) Yes, it's empty. (*They leave the box open.*) What do you do? Do you have a job?

APPLICANT: Yes, I have a job.

YOUNG WOMAN (*jovially*): Wouldn't you like to learn to swim?

APPLICANT: I already know how to swim. I learned at the seminary.

YOUNG WOMAN: Catholic?

APPLICANT: Yes.

YOUNG WOMAN: How strange . . .

APPLICANT: What?

YOUNG WOMAN: I thought . . .

APPLICANT: What?

YOUNG WOMAN: Oh, nothing. (*Pause. They look at each other.*) I've never worked at this kind of thing. Have you?

APPLICANT: Yes, I have. For some time now.

YOUNG WOMAN: It must be difficult to learn how to sell.

APPLICANT: A little. A friend taught me.

YOUNG WOMAN: I'll have to learn by myself.

APPLICANT: I can go with you, if you want.

YOUNG WOMAN: Really?

(*The Sales Manager enters.*)

SALES MANAGER: Here are the contracts, ready for you to sign them. (*To the Applicant*) And I think we've finished with you today.

YOUNG WOMAN: When will I begin to work?

SALES MANAGER: Whenever you want. The contract is already prepared.

APPLICANT: What about me?

SALES MANAGER: You need to receive the rest of the lessons. (*Looking at them with a smile*) But you can accompany her for practice.

YOUNG WOMAN: Yes. I would like him to work with me. At least at the beginning.

APPLICANT: I'd like it, too.

(*They look at each other and smile.*)

SALES MANAGER: Can you give her your time?

APPLICANT: I can.

SALES MANAGER: And do you want to?

APPLICANT: Yes, of course I want to.

SALES MANAGER: Then there is still one small formality. Sign here, at this clause.

APPLICANT (*signs*): But... this was her contract.

SALES MANAGER: Naturally. Now, there are still a few formalities to arrange. A question of routine. Wait just a moment, please. (*She exits.*)

YOUNG WOMAN: I'm very happy you're going to work with me. I'm timid when it comes to dealing with people.

APPLICANT: I'm not. (*Looking around*) About these cases. Do they have to be carried to the clients?

YOUNG WOMAN: They haven't explained that to me. The books weigh a lot.

APPLICANT: Yes. I don't think we're going to take them either.

YOUNG WOMAN: They haven't told me. No, I don't think so. You haven't seen any other stories?

APPLICANT: No, I haven't.

YOUNG WOMAN: Me either. I'd like to know if the others are love stories too.

APPLICANT: Love stories?

YOUNG WOMAN: Yes. Like the story of the monk and Zoé.

APPLICANT: That's true. It hadn't occurred to me that it was a love story. (*They look at each other. She lowers her gaze.*) Does your family let you work?

YOUNG WOMAN: I don't have any family.

APPLICANT: Neither do I.

YOUNG WOMAN: So you're alone.

APPLICANT: Yes. I don't like being alone.

YOUNG WOMAN: Me either.

(*The book opens by itself and from inside the case comes a voice that sounds like a recording.*)

VOICE: "One pleasure was conversation. Another pleasure was that of the bed. Another pleasure—and the most important one—was that of constant companionship . . . (*As if the record were stuck in the groove*) . . . of constant companionship . . . that of cons . . ."

(*The Applicant closes the book. He and the Young Woman clasp each other's hand tightly and remain that way.*)

APPLICANT: I don't like this place.

YOUNG WOMAN: Me either. I'd rather go.

APPLICANT: But I'm going to like working with you.

YOUNG WOMAN: So am I.

APPLICANT: It seems now as if we had known each other for a long time.

YOUNG WOMAN: I would like to have known you a long time.

APPLICANT: It doesn't matter. We have all the time before us.

YOUNG WOMAN (*starts*): You and I don't have the same time in common.

APPLICANT: I don't understand.

YOUNG WOMAN: It's true. You haven't seen the second lesson, "Selection of Clients."

APPLICANT: No. I haven't seen it. I would prefer that you teach it to me. Can you?

YOUNG WOMAN: Yes. Yes, I can.

(*The Sales Manager enters. She rings a clay bell.*)

SALES MANAGER: Everything is ready now. Are you going to share your time?

APPLICANT: Yes.

YOUNG WOMAN: Yes.

SALES MANAGER: That's fine.

(*She rings the bell and the rear curtain opens. Music. A high staircase is seen. A procession with torches descends and comes toward them*).

This is only a small formality.

(*The first figure in the procession carries a white mantle. The Sales Manager puts it on the Young Woman.*)

That's just fine.

YOUNG WOMAN: What is this?

SALES MANAGER: A formality. Now you.

(*The second figure in the procession gives her a monk's habit. She puts it on the Applicant.*)

It's necessarily this way, but this way it's all right.

(*The Applicant and the Young Woman look at each other. She lowers her eyes, and he gazes at her with anguish.*)

APPLICANT (*taking her hands*): Do you think it's all right this way?

YOUNG WOMAN: Yes. I think it's all right this way.

(*They embrace, weeping. They kiss.*)

SALES MANAGER (*ringing the bell furiously*): Naturally, naturally.

(*The bell shatters on the floor.*)

(*Music, bells. The couple still embraces. The procession puts out its torches one by one, covering them with silver hoods. They retire silently. The rear curtain closes. The bells and the music cease. The Employee enters, running.*)

Although actually the monk takes up the habit the very moment he starts wearing it. (*She laughs, harshly.*) Don't you have a sense of humor any more? (*She looks at the couple.*) Well. To your world! Let's go! (*Zoé and the Monk remain embraced. The Sales Manager goes to one of the vertical cases.*) This one.

(*The Employee, questioning, points to the one that is still open on the floor.*)

48

No, you imbecile. That one was just for illustration.

(*The Employee goes to the designated one. He pries up the lid and opens it like a wardrobe.*)

Common wood, but good. (*She knocks on it.*) It will take this a while to rot. It's too bad that everyone is seduced by just one story. (*Looking at the couple*) Beautiful, eh? Put them in.

(*The Employee leads the Monk and Zoé. Music returns. They enter. A strong light comes on inside the case.*)

(*Mockingly.*) It's sad. Won't we ever be able to get any agents?

(*The Employee laboriously closes the box. The last note of music dies out with the last ray of light that touches the lid. The Employee nails it shut. The discordant bell sounds.*)

Go answer the door. I'll finish this.

(*The Employee exits right. The Sales Manager takes a sign from an open box. She nails it on the one which the Monk and Zoé are in. It says:* THE STORY OF THE MONK AND THE BEAUTIFUL ZOÉ. *She looks at it with satisfaction. The Employee enters, preceding another Applicant, a Negro, well dressed, with curly hair and a burning glance. He carries a folded newspaper in his hands. The Employee exits, running.*)

THE OTHER APPLICANT (*looking around*): Hello.

SALES MANAGER (*laying down the hammer and answering very amiably*): Hello.

CURTAIN

The Golden Thread

A Dance of Death in Three Acts

This play was written in memory of Doña Gabriela
Ferat de Fentanes, and is dedicated to
Alicia and Alfonso Trueba.

Characters:

LEONOR LUNA
ADELA SIDEL
SALUSTIO
SIBILA
THE MAN IN THE CAFTAN
MAYALA

The hacienda of Ixtla in the state of Mexico, in the year 1953. The shell of an hacienda on top of a mountain.

The room in which the play takes place was once the living room. At right, a door to the bedrooms, which one reaches by six steps that rise in two parallel stairways, one from downstage and the other facing rear; they meet on a wide landing that has a wooden bannister.

At left, a door to the outside.

At left rear, set at an angle where the walls meet, a sealed door crossed by the X of two boards.

At center rear a very high double window, bell-shaped, with two parallel single-paned windows. The balcony is made larger by a stone seat on which there are flowerpots: climbing nasturtiums and geraniums.

The walls are white.

An oil lamp with a globe, on a pulley. A large colonial painting, of a saint or a bishop. Geometrical blue stains on the walls mark the places where there were once pictures. A sack of corn in the right rear corner.

Only three pieces of furniture: a crude table in two pieces, the base made from a tree trunk and the top from a slab cut from a large tree; a colonial chair, rustic and very heavy; an ordinary straw chair, polychrome, the colors faded, perhaps a century or more old.

Halfway through the first act, a small suspended cradle made from branches and burlap will hang from the ceiling.

The surrounding countryside is harsh and cold, typical of the state of Mexico: thickets, thorny trees, some fruit trees typical of a cold climate, and pines. In the distance, a large lake. Farther still, green-gray, purplish hills. Some of this may be seen through the windows.

Sides: those of the actor.

ACT ONE

Late afternoon. The very long antenna of a portable radio poses an anachronistic touch in the empty room. It is of the sort obtained in auctions of North American army goods. Bits of music and jumbled voices can be heard between loud bursts of static.

Flashes of lightning in the distance.

Like an automaton, Leonor descends from the bedroom. She carries a large blue antique bottle in her hands. Lightning flash close by. Leonor waters the plants, then turns off the radio and stands quietly for a moment.

Adela and Salustio enter. Adela motions Salustio to be quiet and observes Leonor. Salustio is a little alarmed, but he remains still. Slowly Leonor returns to the bedrooms.

ADELA: Did you see her? Sound asleep. She was walking in her sleep. It makes my hair stand on end the nights she walks through the house like that, asleep, with those horrible eyes, like a dead woman.

SALUSTIO: Missy has always been strange.

ADELA: Missy! She's going on ninety and you still call her Missy!

SALUSTIO (*smiles*): *I'm* ninety. Missy is seventy.

ADELA: That's not possible.

SALUSTIO: Yes, Miss Adelita. Our Missy is two years older than you.

ADELA: That isn't what's impossible, you blockhead, it's that you could be ninety.

SALUSTIO: Going on ninety-one, Miss Adelita. I was twenty when

Miss Leonor was born, forty when she got married, forty-two when young little Leonor was born, sixty-four when *she* married your son, sixty-five when the boy Silvestre was born, sixty-seven when your son died, seventy-two when young Leonor died . . .

ADELA: Don't go on, or you'll have me buried too! What a memory! For heaven's sake, I can't believe it. Ninety-one! You look younger than . . . well, than Leonor. She looks worn out. (*Adela dyes her hair such an intense black that it is greenish in the light.*) Where did you leave my suitcase?

SALUSTIO: In the girls' room.

ADELA: The girls' room? Oh, our room.

SALUSTIO: Why did young Rafael leave so soon? Sibila had fixed a cot for him.

ADELA: He had things to do in Mexico City. (*Looks at him.*) Ninety-one. How old is your son?

SALUSTIO: The one you know is twenty-three, but he's the youngest. Some have gone away and some are dead now. The only one left here is the youngest, Salustio Pedro, at your service.

ADELA: Look at the lightning.

SALUSTIO: The Revolution finished Salustio Juan, Salustio José got married and went south, some Indians got Salustio Pablo early one morning in the cantina, Salustio Francisco died of the fever . . .

ADELA: But are they all named Salustio?

SALUSTIO: At God's service, and yours.

ADELA: More lightning. The storm is going to catch the car on the highway.

SALUSTIO: I hope to God it does, Miss Adela.

ADELA: Why do you hope that?

SALUSTIO: Just so it rains . . . (*Smiles.*) Everyone has his problem, right, Miss Adelita? Yours is the car, mine is my field.

ADELA: Well, your precious fields aren't worth worrying about.

SALUSTIO: I'm real pleased that Missy has come. This hacienda needs someone right here to take care of it. This building is in bad shape, almost falling down. Look at those cracks, for instance. If it rained, the corn would get all wet.

ADELA: Well, take it out of here.

SALUSTIO: Why? It's not raining. But Miss Leonor ought to stay here.

ADELA: Really? Should she really? You tell her that, tell her as soon as she comes down. She doesn't like to pay any attention to me.

SALUSTIO: They obey and respect me here because of the authority Missy gave me, but I'm old and it's not the same thing. They love Missy. She has more authority.

ADELA: That's right. That's what I say. Leonor ought to stay here.

SALUSTIO: You see the chapel, how it's fallen down. We were going around holding our masses just anywhere. The saints are scattered all over the place. We had our last masses here in this living room, but it's a long time now since the Padre's come at all. No matter how much I beg him, he doesn't want to come.

ADELA: You can still see the car, it's going down very slowly. Look how it's bumping along.

SALUSTIO: Right here in the living room is where the good Padre said mass. That's another favor I want to ask you girls, Miss Leonor and you, Miss Adela, that you get a Padre to come at least once a month, because this place is going to be so overrun with devils that no one will be able to get them out.

ADELA: What are you saying?

SALUSTIO: This place is going to be overrun with evil spirits. You can already see signs that they're around. Like Sibila's kids. Seems like the witches eat them up.

ADELA: Witches would have to be awfully hungry to eat such skinny children. And there aren't any witches, man. How could there be? (*She shrugs her shoulders and turns on the radio.*)

SALUSTIO: There used to be a good witch here, Miss Adelita. A real good witch. Imagine, once she pulled out four nails I had in my liver. And once when Sibila was dying of the fever, she gave her a cleansing by fire that left her as good as new. But she doesn't want to come any more either.

(*Buzzing of static.*)

ADELA: That's good. Women like that come and make people sick and stir up hornet's nests. A doctor, a good country doctor is what you should have. But you can't hear a thing! To have brought this thing just to hear noise!

SALUSTIO: There was a nice little doctor who was real polite and who knew a lot. He really could make people well. He brought us little pictures that were real nice, some of the Virgin, some of Saint Hippolytus, and our lady Saint Anne. And he put them on us and made us well with them.

ADELA: He made you well that way?

SALUSTIO: No. At the same time he stuck us with a needle, or gave us pills. He was very polite. But he doesn't want to come any more.

ADELA: Why not? It's his obligation. A doctor should . . . Not he either? No one wants to come? Why?

SALUSTIO: That's what I want you girls to see for yourselves, and for Miss Leonor with all her authority to take it on herself to call Salustio Pedro to an accounting, because it's all his fault.

ADELA: Salustio Pedro? Your son?

SALUSTIO: The same. At God's service, and yours.

ADELA: What about him? What's the matter with him?

SALUSTIO: It turned out that I wasn't able to give my children all the schooling that I got, because Padre Mateos, who gave me mine, he's rejoicing with our Lord.

ADELA: I know that, man. But what about your son?

SALUSTIO: Well, he's a brute, that's what he is. The business about the Padre was the worst. I think everything else happened because of it. When the first child was born, the Padre came to baptize it. Well, you see, it was an ugly little thing, and also crippled. Well, when they sprinkled the holy water on him, he was very still. It was because he was already dead as could be. Then Salustio Pedro got carried away and he hit the Padre, because he said it was his fault. That's how it happened.

ADELA: But how gross! How did he dare?

SALUSTIO: Well you see, Miss Adela, that's the way Salustio Pedro is, especially when he's drinking. That's the way he was later with the doctor, only worse, because he was trying to kill *him* with a brick.

ADELA: What a brute! What a beast!

(*Salustio, like some short people, doesn't use his hands much when he talks, but when he does it is very graphic. When he gets excited, he gesticulates a great deal more, with a confusing amplitude of gestures.*)

SALUSTIO: That's the way he gets when his children die on him. The little fellow the doctor killed for him was the one that had turned out best. He had one too many fingers on this hand (*holding out his left hand*) and that's all. The one the witch brought was born the worst. I think that's why he died. I told that to Salustio Pedro, that he shouldn't beat the woman, but he just wouldn't pay any attention to me. He hung her from that tree by her feet and piled up a lot of wood because he wanted to burn her alive. But finally, he just beat her like this (*pushing Adela with a swinging motion*) against the trunk. He was very drunk, and finally he fell asleep right there. Sibila went to untie her and helped her get away.

ADELA: What a brute, what a beast! He's an animal! How many children has he had die?

SALUSTIO: Up till now our Lord has taken away three. Who knows how many after that.

(*Leonor enters.*)

LEONOR: Aren't you cold? There is a horrible wind. The balcony window blew open by itself, I guess. I went to close it and the blackness of the sky frightened me. It looks like an abyss down there, and the black pines down below, they're moving like souls in purgatory. I had a very strange dream.

ADELA: You were sleepwalking. You must have opened the balcony window.

LEONOR: Perhaps. When I woke up I was kneeling, with this prayer book in my hand. I don't know where I had picked it up. It's the one I used at my first communion, but it's been years since I'd seen it. It's a precious book. It has prayers I've never found in any other. (*She leafs through it.*) Saint Lucia, Saint George, and this one, which enchants me:

If miracles you seek,
See death and wrong disowned,
Misery and demon flown,
The leprous and ailing, sound.
The ocean's wrath will still,
The prisoners be freed.
Young and old will see
All lost again be found.

SALUSTIO: Amen.

LEONOR: Salustio, it's awfully dark in here. Are there any lamps around?

SALUSTIO: Yes, Missy, whatever you want. (*Exits.*)

LEONOR: I don't like to walk in my sleep. You shouldn't have let me do it. (*She puts the book in the pocket of her dress.*)

ADELA: But they say it's bad to wake you.

(*Leonor is wearing a black, floor-length dress. She has a wool shawl over her shoulders. Adela, on the other hand, wears an efficient-looking tailored suit with a youngish scarf at the neck.*)

LEONOR: But it frightens me more here. This house has precipices everywhere you look out. Look here, the road way down there, and then . . . Of course, it is lovely.

ADELA: It's what you get for sleeping so much. In the car, fast asleep. And as soon as you got here you threw yourself on the bed and no one heard anything more from you. I've already been all around and seen everything.

LEONOR: I really used to enjoy coming here, but that was different, with the family, our children . . . Do you know something? Things are constantly changing. I had such a different recollection of it. Even the countryside is different, with that road down there. Look at the lake! The light is reflected on it now. It looks like a piece of mirror, like a Christmas scene. But look! Come here!

ADELA (*indifferently*): Yes, it's very pretty.

LEONOR: And what's that? Has Rafael left already?

ADELA: Yes, he left.

LEONOR: Well, yes, that's his car. There by the side of the lake. It looks like a little red ladybug. And it shines. When is he coming back to get us?

ADELA: Well, we'll see. I can go down into town any day, and I'll call him on the phone and see if he can come up here.

LEONOR: He has to come. How are we going to get back if he doesn't?

ADELA: It's just that I hate to do it. His pretty red car. Did you see how it got battered coming up? The road is so narrow, the branches scrape it all over.

LEONOR: How come it didn't get scratched the other times he brought you?

ADELA: The other times we came in the old one. He hasn't even finished paying for this one.

LEONOR: Well, he'll have to come up again, because I'm not going to be left here. I don't like the idea of your going to town. How am I going to stay here by myself almost a whole day? Something could happen to me. I already want to go back, as soon as possible.

ADELA: I was speaking with Salustio about precisely that.

LEONOR: About what?

ADELA: About how much you're needed here, and about how you ought to stay for a while.

LEONOR: The first thing they'd be doing would be burying me. Don't even say that, you frighten me.

(*Salustio enters with the lamps. There is silence while he sets them down.*)

SALUSTIO: You just say, Missy. Shall we start to go over the accounts?

LEONOR: No, Salustio. Tomorrow.

SALUSTIO: That Sibila has been outside there since you girls arrived, and she won't go away. I told her no, but she says she just *has* to talk with you both.

LEONOR: And why not, Salustio? Of course we will. Tell her to come in.

ADELA: What does she want?

SALUSTIO: It must be something about the baby. Any time now he'll be going to heaven and he hasn't been baptized or anything.

LEONOR: Is your grandchild ill?

SALUSTIO: According to what they say, he is.

LEONOR: Oh, and he's the second one, isn't he?

SALUSTIO: He's the fourth to be born, Missy, but he wasn't born right either. He has a foot that doesn't point right. Like this.

LEONOR: But that can be corrected, Salustio. These days it's easy. There are hospitals.

SALUSTIO: What for, Miss Leonor? The little innocent is already more angel than anything.

LEONOR: How can you talk like that! (*Looks out.*) Sibila! Come in, woman, come in.

(*Sibila enters.*)

SIBILA: Good evening, Godmother. Good evening, Mrs. Adela.

ADELA. Don't call me Mrs. Adela, it sounds revolting. Call me ma'am, or Adelita.

SIBILA: All right, ma'am.

LEONOR: Let me see you. But . . . you still look like a child. How many children have you had?

SIBILA: Four, Godmother. Has Rafaelito already left, Godmother?

LEONOR: It doesn't seem possible. The last time I saw you you were a skinny-hipped little thing. Silvestre and you used to run through the house like colts. You wanted to see me about your baby, didn't you?

SIBILA: Yes, Godmother.

LEONOR: Don't worry. Bring him here and we'll see what's the matter with him. I came prepared, I brought a full medicine chest.

ADELA: Yes, so full it seems big enough for a coffin. Poor Rafael could hardly manage it.

LEONOR: Well, "poor Rafael" also had to carry this big contraption so you could listen to your programs.

ADELA: I'm not the *only* one who listens to the programs, but you *are* the only one who takes all that junk. The doctor didn't even prescribe it for you.

LEONOR: What does the doctor know? My druggist knows more than any doctor. I wish you'd consult him once. You'd see.

ADELA: Why? Luckily, I'm good and healthy. But if the druggist is so good, why do you go to see the doctor?

LEONOR: I brought what the doctor gave me, too. I need to have everything right at hand. You know how delicate I am, Adela. God knows what could happen to me . . . Anything. At any moment. (*Just the idea upsets her. She sits down. She wipes her forehead of what might be perspiration.*) These chills I get sometimes. Adela! I feel chilled.

ADELA: You're not chilled. It's very cold.

LEONOR: Is it cold, Salustio?

SALUSTIO: Very cold, Missy.

LEONOR: I'm glad. I was afraid . . . Bring your son, Sibila, and let's see if we can find out what's the matter with him.

SIBILA: Godmother, I didn't want to see you about that.

LEONOR: What for, then, my child?

SIBILA: It's just that, well, you know my baby's going to die. I wish you'd take me to the city with you. I can serve you there, and I really wish you'd take me with you.

LEONOR: But what are you saying? Your baby isn't going to die.

SIBILA: Why not, Godmother? They all die.

LEONOR: But you can't say it like that. As if you knew. This one might get well. I'm here, and that's why I brought my medicine chest. Don't think that he's going to die.

SIBILA: But why not, Godmother? He doesn't cry any more, or anything. He may even have died since I came in here with you.

ADELA: How brutish! That really *is* cynicism! Barbarous! You have the instincts of a hyena, girl. I've never seen anything like that!

SALUSTIO: Get out of here, Sibila. Go on.

SIBILA: But, Godmother. Aren't you going to take me? Aren't you going to take me, Godmother?

ADELA: She's not going to take you anywhere, because she's going to stay here too. Go back to your child. What instincts!

SALUSTIO: This Sibila is no good, Missy, I tell you she's no good. I never carry tales, but I see things.

LEONOR: But don't you love your baby, child, or do you just not realize?

SIBILA: Yes, yes I do. You mean love him? Yes, I love him. But what for? They all die, Godmother, all of them. And Papa (*indicating Salustio*) says I'm bad, but it's really that I'm all dried up. Look (*striking herself*), I don't have anything to give them. And they're all born with something wrong, but it isn't my fault. They say it is, but I know it isn't. You can see what Salustio Pedro's become. It isn't good, Papa, to have children when you're old, you know that. Mine, poor little things, why should I love them? Sooner or later they all die, they all die. (*Sobs a little and blows her nose on her rebozo.*)

LEONOR: But don't stand there crying, woman. This one's going to get well, you'll see. Go bring him here. Go on. (*Pushes her toward the door. Sibila exits.*) Salustio, go get my medicine chest. It's that large box next to the bed. Go on. If it weighs too much for you, drag it, but be careful, because if anything got broken I don't know what I'd do.

SALUSTIO: Oh, Missy. What are you going to do? Better if I don't bring you those things.

LEONOR: Do what I tell you, Salustio.

(*Salustio exits.*)

ADELA: The instincts of a beast. Not even a serpent would talk that way.

LEONOR: Serpents don't talk in any way. And listen, why did you say I'm going to stay?

ADELA: Me? Oh, well, so that woman would shut up.

LEONOR: How strange. It sounded very spontaneous.

ADELA: It turned my stomach to listen to that Sibila. She's been that way ever since she was a child. Remember? Always getting into corners with Silvestre.

LEONOR: Childish games.

ADELA: Childish games! Why did they seal that door?

LEONOR: That's the fault of the person who built the house, and of my grandfather who permitted it. I don't know what got it in his head to leave the cellar connected to those enormous caverns. They go on forever. And Silvestre was so curious.

ADELA: And the tomboy there to lure him on.

LEONOR: Actually, they didn't get lost. They went a long way in, but they didn't get lost. It was the scare Leonor got that caused the uproar.

ADELA: Your daughter was always in an uproar.

LEONOR: It's only natural, since your son was always so dull. But they sealed that door because the cellar is so damp, and there might be animals. It seems there's a spring down there, Silvestre told me.

ADELA: Yes, there's a spring in the first cave. I saw it one day when I went down. It bubbles away all the time. It should be used to irrigate the land. My son meant to do that many times. Perhaps if he hadn't died . . . although it's better that way. Over and done with, rather than lose everything.

LEONOR: Why should it be lost?

ADELA: Leonor, don't be foolish. Do you think Silvestre is going to come back?

LEONOR: Naturally.

ADELA: When we're dead and the government has gobbled everything up, I guess?

LEONOR: I'm not going to be dead.

ADELA: But look at yourself, woman. Look how sick you are. How many years have I spent taking care of you?

LEONOR (*anguished*): I am not going to be dead. Not me.

ADELA: We are old, and sick.

LEONOR: I am not going to be dead. I want to see him again. I can't bear any more. That's what it is that's killing me. Why did he go? I read his letter over and over. It's so creased and crumpled, you can hardly read it, but I know the whole thing, and Blessed Mary, I can't understand it. "Dearest little grandmother, dearest, dearest. I have to go this way . . ." Three times, "Dearest little grandmother, dearest, dearest . . ."

(*She is crying with great racking sobs. Adela moves her head in dismay. She tries to be gentle.*)

ADELA: Don't cry any more. Why did I bring it up? I certainly think he's going to come back, or at least we'll hear something, but I'm concerned about the estate. And listen, it's really sad that we can't dispose of anything when it was all ours once.

LEONOR: It isn't sad to me.

ADELA: Well, that's the way you are, but not me. When your husband left everything to your daughter you were pleased as could be. But it made me furious that that donkey of a husband of mine left everything to my son. And then those two willed everything to Silvestre, leaving two stupid old women as executrices for a grandson who's been swallowed up by the earth. Beautiful!

LEONOR: It seems all right to me. The trouble is that you don't want him to come back. You didn't even like him to call you grandmother because it made you seem older. You never loved him.

ADELA: Yes, I loved him. It's just that I'm not as syrupy as you. All that business about "poor little orphan." You spoiled him, and you ruined him.

(*Salustio appears, pushing an enormous box that he can barely move.*)

SALUSTIO: It weighs a lot, Missy.

LEONOR: Be careful. I hope you haven't broken anything.

ADELA: Listen to me, Leonor. Please try to be sensible and listen to me. What will happen to everything if we both die and Silvestre hasn't come back?

LEONOR: I don't know. I don't know. I don't want to think about it.

ADELA: You must think about it. It would all be lost. The thieves in the government . . .

LEONOR: I know, I know. Don't say any more. What can we do? Nothing.

ADELA: Yes, we can. Look. We can simulate a sale. We can pretend that there was a sale twenty years ago, and that they sold me my part, and you yours.

LEONOR: And what good would that do?

ADELA: We could name an executor, in case Silvestre returns and we're . . . not here. If it all seems to be ours, we could name an executor.

LEONOR: A simulated sale, um?

ADELA: Yes. There's a man in the department of property records who could arrange everything, difficult as it is. We would have to pay him, of course, but it could be done.

LEONOR: And that way we could name an executor.

ADELA: That's right.

LEONOR: And make a will. Right?

ADELA: Well, of course, in order to name an executor . . .

LEONOR: Who gave you this advice?

ADELA: Well . . . A lawyer I know.

LEONOR: Rafael. Isn't that right?

ADELA: Certainly not.

LEONOR: Don't lie. I heard you in the car.

ADELA: So you weren't asleep!

LEONOR: I heard very little, but now I'm beginning to understand.

ADELA: I'm not going to let the estate go to waste. I want to protect Silvestre.

LEONOR: Don't lie. You want to leave everything to Rafael. But I'm going to tell him a few things when he comes back. Very decently, but I'm going to tell him. (*Realizing*) Adela! He's not coming back! You're not going to leave me here. It would be as good as killing me! It would be murder, that's what it would be! But answer me, look at me! Don't you understand? I need a doctor, I need constant medication. Salustio, be careful, please be careful!

SALUSTIO: I was resting, Missy.

(*He starts to move the large box, but it escapes him and tumbles down the stairs.*)

LEONOR: My medicines!

(*The box splits in half and quantities of books spill out and scatter all over. Leonor leaps toward them, then stops, disconcerted.*)

What is this! What are all these books? Adela, what did you people bring in place of my medicines?

(*Sibila enters with the child in her arms.*)

SIBILA: He wasn't dead, but he'd dirtied his pants. I had to change his clothes.

SALUSTIO: This is the box you brought, Missy.

LEONOR: You did this!

ADELA: I did what?

LEONOR: You switched my medicines for this.

ADELA: I swear I don't know anything about it! (*They stand looking at each other.*)

SIBILA: I brought the baby's cradle.

LEONOR: You did it! You switched my box of medicines for these other things!

ADELA: No, Leonor, truly, I don't know anything about it!

LEONOR: Then it was Rafael. But is it possible? Would you two want to kill me so you can have everything?

ADELA: Don't be stupid.

LEONOR: Where are my medicines? I'm cold, I feel sick. (*Weeps.*) It was a box like this one . . .

SIBILA: If it is full of little bottles and boxes, it's inside there, Godmother. This is the carton of Silvestre's books.

LEONOR: Is it in there? Really? Then . . . Silvestre's books! Of course. Look, Adela, these are his books! (*She looks them over.*) The mythology I gave him, Anderson, Ayesha, Sandokan . . .

ADELA: And now you're going to look at books! No! As if I wanted to murder you and steal Silvestre's pittance from you. Rob you and murder you! Besides, half of it is *mine*, because it belonged to my son. You listen to me. I'm never going to live with you again. I've swallowed these things for years, but this is the end. Call me a murderer! A thief! How coarse! What a foul mouth! And look at her! So calm!

LEONOR (*extremely anguished*): Please forgive me, Adela. I was frightened. And you were talking about leaving me.

ADELA: I wasn't just talking about it. It's a fact. After all this, it's a fact. I'm going back alone, and if you want, I'll send a car for you, but we'll see who's going to live with you and look after you. As for me, you can bid me good-by.

LEONOR: Adela!

ADELA: The best thing you could do is stay here. Sibila and Salustio can be responsible for you. Not me. Never again. (*Crosses her arms.*)

LEONOR: Forgive me, dear Adela, forgive me. You know how I am, forgive me. (*Starts to kiss her.*)

ADELA: Get away, get away! Don't touch me. (*Pushes her.*) Cynic! Impudent . . .

(*Leonor, crying and ashamed, moves away.*)

LEONOR: You shouldn't be spiteful. It's ugly. I asked your pardon.

ADELA: Never again. Never! (*Exits, trampling the books as she goes by.*)

LEONOR: All right. (*Looks at the floor.*) We'll have to put these books away. Although I want to look at them first. My baby's books . . . Pinocchio . . . Jules Verne . . . Poor little Silvestre.

SIBILA: Here is the child, Godmother.

LEONOR: That's true. The child. (*Places the books on the table.*) Let's see what's the matter with your little son. Sibila! This creature . . .! (*Feels him, looks at him.*) No, thanks be to God. What's the matter with him? But so thin. My God, so thin. How old is he?

SIBILA: Six months.

LEONOR: And what does he eat?

SIBILA: He nurses what he can, but I don't have anything. And I give him a little tea. I gave him cow's milk and he got like that because he kept vomiting it. And the same with jenny's milk.

LEONOR: But of course, girl! Poor little thing, he needs something else. Powdered milk, vitamins. Good, good. Because we old women turn into little children again, that's what *I* have to have instead of milk. Look, child, in that box you saw upstairs there are some blue tins, about this big. Put two teaspoonfuls of that powder in a cup of boiling water and fill the bottle with that. Give me the child while you do that.

SIBILA: What bottle, Godmother?

LEONOR: How do you give him the warm tea?

SIBILA: In a cup, or with a spoon.

LEONOR: Lord save us. Well, go on, prepare a cup. Give him to me. (*Sibila starts to obey. She hesitates.*)

SIBILA: Godmother, Salustio Pedro is wandering around out there.

LEONOR: So . . .?

SIBILA: If he finds out, he'll kill you, Godmother. He's drunk, and he already noticed that the box is yours.

LEONOR: Well, tell him that it's for me. Go on.

SIBILA (*to Salustio*): Papa, put up his little cradle. (*Exits toward bedrooms.*)

LEONOR (*cooing to the baby*): Big little man, you're so thin, poor little thing. But sou'll see, tweet lil' sing, sou'll ha' da' wich milk, and sou'll dit so fat, hum? Gurugururuguru. (*Sings*)

> For the rurru baby
> New born to the cat,
> Five tiny piglets
> And a spider fat.
> For the rurru baby,
> For the rurru rong . . .

SALUSTIO: Missy.

LEONOR: He doesn't laugh, or anything.

(*Sibila crosses through the room, returning from the bedrooms on her way to the kitchen. Exits.*)

SALUSTIO: Missy, it would be better to give him to me. I'll take him now.

LEONOR: Where?

SALUSTIO: To his house, Missy.

LEONOR: Let him have his food first.

SALUSTIO: You don't know what's the matter with him.

LEONOR: Go on. It's easy to see.

SALUSTIO: It's Sibila's fault.

LEONOR: Why?

SALUSTIO: She holds her milk back, just like a cunning cow will.

LEONOR: But do you think we women are like cows?

SALUSTIO: Well, yes, Missy. And she has a doll stuck with needles and pins. She says it's for her sewing, but that's not true. It's a very old doll, and she won't give it to me. And look, I know it's Sibila who makes Salustio Pedro act the way he does. It was her fault about the priest and Chonita the witch, because that Sibila is bad and she makes things up. She didn't want the priest to sprinkle the holy water on him because she had heard it was very cold. Do you believe that? Holy water is always good. Naturally, the little innocent would be full of devils . . . Give him to me, Missy. I'm going to take him.

LEONOR: I'm not giving you anything. Please pick up those books, I don't like to have them scattered about. (*Indicating the cradle*) And this? It's the child's, isn't it? Hang it up.

SALUSTIO: It's so the rats won't eat him. (*Obeys.*) Missy, I've thought about it real heard. Miss Leonor, you'll have to pardon me, but as much as I respect you, I'm going to take the child. Better if I take this down again, because I don't want Salustio Pedro to do something terrible. He's a real bad character, Missy, and he doesn't obey me any more because I'm old. You understand he never had any schooling. Give him to me.

LEONOR: I am not going to give him to you. Leave me alone. (*She puts the baby in the cradle.*)

SALUSTIO: Missy, I'm weak and no match for Salustio Pedro and even if I tried to defend you, it'd be the same.

(*Sibila enters.*)

SIBILA: Godmother! Salustio Pedro saw me!

LEONOR: What difference does that make?

SIBILA: He said he was coming to pay his respects. But he's drunk, Godmother. And he saw me when I was fixing the food. I'd better take my little baby away.

SALUSTIO: These are not things of this world, Missy. Sibila says not, but she knows it very well. I've already told you there is evil around here because we never have mass anymore.

LEONOR: Evil! Bring that cup here. Give me a spoon and take the baby out of his cradle. I'm going to give him some of this.

SIBILA: Don't burn yourself.

SALUSTIO: With all respect, Missy, I've never let you down, I've been obedient to you, but there are some things I know better. (*Places himself between them.*) Take the baby away, Sibila.

SIBILA: It's better, Godmother. (*She is going to obey.*)

LEONOR: But . . . you stupid lout! Bring him here.

SALUSTIO (*stepping between them, firm and respectful*): Pardon me, Missy. This has nothing to do with you, Missy. You don't know anything about it. (*He pushes Sibila.*)

LEONOR: Listen to me. What don't I know about? Just what?

SALUSTIO: There's witchcraft, Missy. This is strong business.*

LEONOR: There's no witchcraft, or anything like it!

SALUSTIO: You don't believe because you don't know.

LEONOR (*after a brief pause, during which she looks at him reflectively*): Yes, I believe . . . and yes, I know. There's the book of darkness and there's the book of light. It's as simple as saying there's day and night. Look. Do you see this? I found it in my hands when I woke up. What do you think it is?

SALUSTIO (*doubtful*): Well . . . it's a prayer book.

LEONOR: Yes and no. You don't know what's in it. You don't even know what I know. I know things. What do you think? That I can't take care of myself? Everyone prays, but everyone doesn't know how to direct his prayers like arrows, or what gestures to make as he prays. Everyone says the Lord's Prayer, but not everyone knows that it is also the prayer of the spirits. I can read something, here, that would make any wandering evil spirit howl with pain. Your son, for example. You don't know how it is to lash with St. Francis' cord. And you don't know what I have tied at my waist . . . or what I have here in my breast. Do you know? Do *you* know, Sibila? (*Her voice has been rising.*)

(*Salustio and Sibila shake their heads with respect and a little alarm.*)

Leave the child here.

(*Salustio obeys. Adela enters.*)

ADELA: Is the child still here? That savage is going to come in and beat us up.

LEONOR: Adela, go to your room.

---

* After this play was published in Spanish, the author partially rewrote the remainder of this act; his revised version has been used in this translation. *Tr.*

ADELA: I'm not going to. Why should I? It's very dark.

LEONOR: Not as dark as you are.

(*She mutters things over the cup, circles Adela, and traces the sign of the Cross in the air over her head several times.*)

ADELA: What are you doing?

(*Leonor throws the cup of water on her.*)

(*Screaming*) You've got me all wet! And burned me!

LEONOR: Be quiet. Here. (*She looks at the cup in her hands; she looks around.*) Look what happened. (*She speaks in a normal voice.*) All the water splashed out. Sibila, it would be a good idea for you to bring me a lighted brazier.

SIBILA: Yes, Godmother.

ADELA: Leonor . . . you're very strange.

LEONOR: A lighted brazier. And a glass of clean water, from the spring. And a red rose. And salt. And copal incense. And honey. And a little tobacco.

ADELA: And how long have you been smoking?

LEONOR (*almost singing*): Something they may eat, something they may smell, something they may smoke, and something they may drink. And be sure it's pure. Go on.

SIBILA: There aren't any red roses, Godmother.

LEONOR: There *have* to be. (*Interrupts herself.*) There aren't any . . . what? Bring . . . whatever there is, child, to feed the child. (*Sibila exits.*)

ADELA: Leonor, what is it you're doing? Why did you get me all wet?

LEONOR (*imposingly*): Come here.

(*She leads her to a corner, puts her hands on her shoulders, and looks into her eyes. Adela steps back. Leonor lowers her hands.*)

ADELA (*alarmed*): Why did you bring me over here?

LEONOR: I? Ah, well . . . (*Quietly*) Can't you see that they won't let me look after the child, because of their . . . foolishness and superstition? So, I have to make them think that I know a lot about those things, and . . . that there are stronger powers.

(*She raises her voice without intending to.*) There—are— stronger—powers. (*She shakes her head.*) Oh, Adela, I'm so sleepy. But why *am* I so sleepy? It's . . . I feel almost as if I'm walking in my sleep.

ADELA: You act as if you're walking in your sleep.

LEONOR: In a triangle?

ADELA: What?

LEONOR: I am. I'm doing as you say.

ADELA: What am I saying?

LEONOR: Yes, I'm going to place them that way. (*She is confused.*) Did you tell me to place the candles in a triangle?

ADELA: Candles? I didn't say anything to you!

(*Leonor starts toward the door without paying any attention to Adela.*)

LEONOR (*at the door*): Did you bring the candles?

(*Sibila enters.*)

SIBILA: Yes, Godmother. Three. You asked me to, didn't you?

LEONOR: On the table, in a triangle. And the brazier down there.

SIBILA: There *was* a red rose! That rose bush that never blooms has a red rose. So I cut it and brought it to you.

(*She places the things as she has been directed.*)

LEONOR: The honey on the table. The glass of water in the center. The salt next to the honey. Give me the incense. And put the water on the fire. When it boils, the child will be able to take his milk.

SIBILA: Shall I light them?

LEONOR: Yes, light them. And put the water in the cup. And the rose. Here. And the tobacco?

SIBILA (*who has obeyed*): I couldn't find any cigarettes. There was just this cigar.

LEONOR: Give it to me. And light it for me.

ADELA: Are you really going to smoke a cigar, Leonor?

(*They are all nervous, disconcerted, somewhat afraid, but above all fascinated in some special way. Leonor smokes and claps her hands, she sways back and forth a lot, mutters rhythmically; she hums, stamps her feet, and reads her prayer book.*)

She throws copal incense on the brazier fire. A great puff of smoke.)

SIBILA: Godmother, the water in the glass . . . it's full of bubbles. They're making pictures through the glass.

LEONOR (*as if in a dream*): Yes, that's it. Join hands, all of you. In a chain, around the table.

(*Salustio and Sibila obey.*)

ADELA: I'm going to my room. I don't like this nonsense. (*Leonor, swaying, signals to her with one finger.*) I don't see the least reason for . . . Why me? Why do you want me?

(*She walks away. Leonor's finger pursues her, signaling her. She obeys. They form the chain.*)

SIBILA: What is all this, Godmother?

(*Smoke keeps billowing up.*)

LEONOR: Aha! That's it. (*She lays down the book and closes the chain around the table.*) Powerful and glorious Mother of Shadows, Protector of newborn bats, Custodian of mushroom and mandrake, Black Mistress, we are here to rescue the prey from between your brilliant white teeth, we are here beneath the wings and wonders of your slimy mantle.

ADELA: I can't believe that that prayer is in your prayer book. You're making it up. Don't deny it.

LEONOR: Open the doors of hardest mahogany, set free your radio-graphic light and the sulphurous tremor of your shadows.

(*The radio turns on by itself and a long buzz of static begins. The lights dim without any apparent change in the flame of the lamps.*)

ADELA: Who turned on the radio? Let me go. Who turned on the radio?

(*Adela holds the hands of Sibila and Salustio, and the latter two, the hands of Leonor.*)

SIBILA: Look at the light!

SALUSTIO: Missy, Missy. Better let me loose. Missy!

ADELA: She's asleep! Those are her sleepwalker's eyes! Leonor, what is it?

(*They try to break loose. Blue lights around the radio. A*

blue blaze on the tip of the antenna. The sealed door slowly begins to open.)

SIBILA: The sealed door!

(They finally drop hands and move back. Salustio falls to his knees. A slim young man enters, wearing black trousers and a shiny black leather jacket with a fur collar.)

LEONOR *(as if awakening)*: What's happening? There's too much wind blowing in. Close the window. *(She turns.)* Oh. Good evening.

THE MAN: Good evening.

CURTAIN

ACT TWO

LEONOR *(as if awakening)*: What's happening? There's too much wind blowing in. Close the window. *(She turns.)* Oh. Good evening.

THE MAN: Good evening.

SALUSTIO: Master, Master. We beg you to give health back to this child, my grandson, and to do us no harm. *(He makes the sign of the Cross.)* Cross, Cross, Holy Cross.

MAN: This child? Is it yours? *(Sibila is frozen, unable to move.)* I would like to help, but the plane burned. I don't know whether there's anything left.

(He exits the way he entered. The door closes. The radio stills.)

SALUSTIO: No, Missy Leonor. No. May the Holy Cross shelter me. This isn't any good, Missy. We could all lose our souls. May the Lord God protect us and the Holy Virgin shelter me. *(He is trembling.)*

LEONOR: Who was that man?

SALUSTIO: The devil you called, Missy. I don't want to see him again. I don't want to. No, Missy, I don't want to. *(Exits.)*

(Sibila begins to whimper.)

SIBILA: I'm afraid, Godmother.

LEONOR: But . . . how did he get in? Who is he? Who is he, Sibila?

(*Adela runs to the door, pulls it, pushes, beats on it.*)

ADELA: It's nailed shut! And there are spider webs in the cracks. It won't open! It won't open!

LEONOR: How did he get in? (*She pushes too.*) Who is he? Who is he, Sibila?

ADELA: He's a phantom, a phantom!

SIBILA: I'm afraid, Godmother.

LEONOR: He came in here? It's nailed! Don't try to fool me. I don't understand. Who is he? How did he get in?

(*The radio buzzes loudly. The door opens. Adela screams stridently. Sibila huddles in the chair with her arms in front of her face. The Man enters again.*)

MAN: This is all I found. (*He is carrying an enormous coral branch and a branch, laden with fruit, from some strange tree. The door closes.*)

(*Adela screams again with all her might.*)

What's the matter with this lady? Is she ill?

(*Adela sobs and screams in a tremendous fit of nerves. Leonor seems not to understand anything that is going on. Sibila remains hunched up like a frightened puppy.*)

Yes, I think the lady is ill. Epilepsy?

LEONOR: Oh, but . . . I don't understand. Give her something. Alcohol, ammonia. I brought some in my chest, but . . . Oh, you, sir. What can I do? Adela! Adela!

(*Shakes her.*)

ADELA (*hiccupping*): I-uh, I-uh! He isn't . . . I-uh. Ah-h-h! (*Noises and sobs.*) He couldn't come in, he couldn't. (*More noises.*) I thought he was . . . (*To Leonor*) It's your fault. I thought he was . . . Ah, me. Dear God, what's the matter with me. What is this?

LEONOR: Well, *I* don't know. What in the world is the matter with you?

ADELA: Ah . . . Ah . . .

MAN (*moving closer to her*): Do you feel better now?

ADELA: Don't you touch me!

MAN: Why are you screaming? Because of me?

ADELA: Who are you?

MAN: Our plane fell near the grotto. There was a subterranean river. The spring, actually, is an entrance.

ADELA: What plane? Don't touch me.

MAN: Naturally I'm not planning to touch you. We were coming from Ceylon when the motor began to fail, and I haven't been able to clear up what happened to the other pilot.

ADELA: How did you get in here?

MAN: Through that door.

ADELA: It's sealed up! Don't you see the crossbars?

MAN: I'm very sorry. You can't see them from the other side.

ADELA: How did you get in? That door doesn't open.

MAN: No? (*He opens and closes it.*)

(*Adela runs to try. The door doesn't move. She looks in the crack.*)

ADELA: Spider webs!

MAN: Spider webs mend themselves. The old nails go in and out with a certain amount of effort. Of course, it takes strength to get the door to move, but look. (*He opens and closes it.*)

LEONOR: There's no one like you for doing the ridiculous, Adela. Now I understand what's the matter with you. (*To the Man*) She thinks you're a ghost.

MAN: But tell me, do you really think I'm . . . Ah, yes, I see you do. Come on, now, tell me something. Now, in the year 1953, do you believe in apparitions? Do you really believe in those things?

ADELA: No. Certainly not. (*She sits down, trembling.*)

MAN (*to Sibila*): And you. Do you believe in ghosts?

SIBILA: Yes. Yes, I believe.

MAN: So do I, but don't be frightened. (*To Leonor*) And you, who do you believe I am?

LEONOR: I don't know. The whole thing seems very strange to me. *They* seem like phantoms to me, too.

MAN: We all seem like phantoms. Will you forgive me for appearing like this. My caftan is covered with dust, and my pants are filthy.

LEONOR (*incredulous*): Caftan? Is that (*indicating his jacket*) a caftan?

MAN: I bought it in Fez. Rather, I traded it for a Siamese cat and a spider monkey. They were two delightful animals, but very bad companions in a plane.

LEONOR: That's right. You had an accident! But you told us a dozen times. You must have come looking for help, didn't you? You're not wounded? Can we help you?

MAN: I don't think you can do anything now. The co-pilot is lost. The pearls too. The plane burned up, completely.

LEONOR: And nothing happened to you?

MAN: Nothing. Mayala and I jumped out in time. I left her among the pines, resting. The coral branches are hers, the fruit is mine—our whole fortune at the moment. Is there a sick child?

SIBILA: Yes. (*They look at each other.*)

LEONOR: But I don't understand. Did someone come with you?

MAN: Mayala. It's a common name there.

LEONOR: But . . . Don't leave her out there, she might be feeling bad. Is it a young lady?

MAN: She's . . . Well, she's a young girl. Nothing will happen to her. When I want, she'll come. I can call her by concentrating. (*To Adela*) Are you feeling better?

ADELA (*shortly*): Yes, thank you. (*Looks him up and down.*) Did your plane come down very near here?

MAN: Very near.

ADELA: How strange that we didn't hear anything.

MAN: That *is* strange. We transmitted signals in every direction. Don't you have a radio? Of course, here it is. You must have heard something.

ADELA: Well, this thing was buzzing.

MAN: That was it, naturally.

LEONOR: Dear Lord, I'm so happy that I've never gone up in an airplane. Do you think the other man is dead, the one who was with you?

MAN: No, I don't think so. He must have got away with everything. He wasn't a very good person. As a matter of fact, we might find out that he engineered the accident.

LEONOR: Really? Is that possible? But you and the young lady might have died.

MAN: Imagine that.

LEONOR: What are you going to do?

MAN: Get back to work again. Beginning in theaters.

LEONOR: He's an artist!

MAN: In a way. I'm a magician. (*To Adela*) Yes, a magician. I transmit thoughts, I read them. I do elemental and advanced exercises. Do you understand?

ADELA (*with superiority*): Yes, I know. I've seen things like that at the circus.

LEONOR: But ... where do you plan to go?

MAN: I don't have the least idea.

LEONOR: Well, in the meantime you can stay here. We can fix a room for the girl, and ... It's just that ... there are only three beds, but ... Well, Adela and I can sleep in one, or ... The girl, is she your wife?

MAN: No. But it doesn't matter.

ADELA: What do you mean, it doesn't matter? It matters to me! I'm not going to give up my bed to the first pair of tramps that come along and scare the life out of me. Especially if they're not married!

LEONOR: Adela, don't be common!

ADELA: He's the one who said they weren't married.

MAN: But I didn't say we're going to sleep together.

ADELA: Well, of course. It's just that ... (*Brusquely*) It's just that there are only three beds, and I'm not going to sleep with you, Leonor, because you snore.

LEONOR: *I* snore! A lot you know about it. You've just never waked up in time to hear yourself blaring. And besides, the house is mine, and the beds are mine. Either you sleep with me or you sleep on the floor.

ADELA: Yours? Yours? So now they're yours, right? Well, they're not! They're Silvestre's, and I'm just as much in charge as you are.

LEONOR: Well, I'm in charge and I say that the beds . . .

ADELA: Leonor, don't try me!

MAN: Please. We never had a bed in Malacca. In Tibet we slept two nights on horseback. Now, if you'll excuse me, I can always do this.

(*He goes over to the flowers, leans over, and from among the plants draws out the end of something. He pulls, and an endless cord of multicolored triangular pennants emerges. After pulling out fifteen or twenty yards, he stops, embarrassed.*)

I'm sorry, I made a mistake. It's lack of practice.

(*He takes out some large scissors and cuts the rope at the roots.*)

LEONOR: How pretty.

MAN: Yes, but *this* is what I was looking for. (*He leans over; in the same way, he makes a hammock appear. He unfolds it and shows it to them.*)

MAN: You see. Personally, I prefer it, but if you want I can make a bed appear, or anything else you want.

LEONOR: A hammock!

ADELA: Things like that don't fool me. They carry it all in their sleeves.

MAN: Not everything, I assure you.

(*From the same place he pulls out a bouquet of flowers, a handful of long ribbons, and a large bunch of very ugly weeds.*)

For you. (*He gives the flowers to Leonor.*) And this is for you. (*The ribbons to Sibila.*) You're not frightened any more?

SIBILA (*who moves and takes them*): Not any more.

LEONOR: Thank you, how pretty.

MAN: Well, too bad. This is all there is left for you. (*He gives the weeds to Adela.*)

ADELA: I don't want anything.

(*She throws the weeds on the floor. They explode like dynamite. Adela screams and Sibila laughs.*)

MAN: I forgot to warn you. Be careful.

LEONOR: How did you do that? Where were all those things?

MAN: Everywhere. There's matter everywhere. Everything is created, everything is destroyed. Energy takes the most unexpected forms. It changes, grows, or disappears forever.

LEONOR: Did you do that?

MAN: I only know a few ways of creating matter. It's like spinning the threads of the spider webs we always have around us. (*He gestures.*) Matter, you see? All around. As if everything were webbed with little strands of glass. As if we saw everything through a great shattered glass. Take any end at all. Where do you want it from? From your radio, here. A thread. (*He takes it. A low hum.*) Pull it out. (*He pulls it.*) See? (*Through one hand he pulls a line of colorful silk scarves tied together.*) These, or anything else. It isn't difficult. You just have to know how—the key, the formula, the incantation, call it whatever you like. Anyone can do it.

LEONOR: Do you mean I could do it?

MAN: Naturally. You want a bouquet? You take seeds, you sow them, water them, wait for days, or weeks. The plants flower and you cut a bouquet. Well, I do the same thing at a different speed. If a camera recorded my movements, slowing them down to the maximum degree, one by one, they would look equally magical, equally simple. (*He puts the scarves around his neck.*)

SIBILA: The water still isn't boiling.

LEONOR: I still don't understand very well. The flowers, maybe, but ... the hammock?

MAN: It's for me. (*He lays it across the table.*) What's the matter with your child?

SIBILA: Look at him. I don't know. Can you do something?

MAN: That's difficult to answer.

SIBILA: I don't want him to die.

MAN: Why?

SIBILA: He's mine.

MAN: That's a good reason. What's his name?

SIBILA: I don't know.

ADELA: Why don't you know?

SIBILA: I just don't. We haven't baptized him, or anything.

ADELA: He'll be called Salustio, like all the others.

SIBILA: No. Not that. I don't know.

LEONOR: You could give him a pretty name. Something like . . . Let me think. Silvestre! You should name him Silvestre. You and he loved each other so much when you were small. I could be his godmother. Poor thin little thing. If I had my choice, I would always have a child this age.

   (*Drums begin in the distance.*)

MAN: Careful! Do you hear? (*He covers his ears.*) Do you hear them?

LEONOR: It's drums, or seems to be. And someone singing! What is it?

ADELA: It sounds like . . . savages.

MAN: I don't know, they must have followed me, and if they catch me, it's the end. (*He sits down. He is sweating.*) They're going away now. (*The radio buzzes.*) Another message. I will have to go very soon.

LEONOR: What's going on?

MAN: The drums. (*Calls*) Mayala! Mayala! I can't call her, there's some interference. Everything's vibrating, isn't it?

LEONOR: No, I don't think so.

MAN: Permit me, then. (*He turns in circles, his arms open.*)

ADELA: Ah, what's the matter with him?

MAN (*looks at his hands, held at varying heights*): I'm trying to verify positions, but the light is failing. (*The buzzing stops.*) It's like the beginning of a dream, your head's heavy and images come and go according to their own will. That's the danger.

ADELA: What danger?

MAN: Reality gets away. Haven't you seen how logical everything seems in our dreams? And one's memory believes whatever is most convenient. Now—pardon me—now memory is beginning to work again. Suddenly the clock is wound up. It was outside of time, and it takes a while for the hands to assume the position that corresponds to a determined position of the earth and the sun and the place where the clock is situated within incandescent circles and cosmic wheels and explosions and laws of gravity and infinite spirals. The spider web I was telling you about, the web of matter, do you remember? Memory is the shortest distance between consciousness and time, and now I feel it slowly coming back.

LEONOR: Sit down, won't you? (*In a low voice*) I think he's going to faint.

MAN (*after an effort of will*): Impossible. I can't. Isn't it miraculous? We all remember what we've imagined, read, desired, that which falls upon our senses from the outside, and here it all falls into place. What is one's own? What is other? A mystery. I'm terribly sorry, but I will have to employ automatism and incoherence. It's a recipe I can give you. When you feel yourself lost or sinking, touch yourself, feel yourself (*he does so*), and recite your memories in prayer, because that's what we are. It welds us together, it unites us, body and memory. That's it. I remember, I remember. But the name is missing. The name is like a trap. (*He takes the branches from the table and shakes them.*) Here it comes. Yes, now. (*The drums begin again.*) A few images, a woman's face covered with tears. Mayala. Long, loose hair. Hammocks. Jungle. The whole tribe dancing. More than 104 degrees, wind from the northeast. Static. The radio in the plane. The hum of the motors. *Sacrifice.* And the victim on the stone. The dance of death, and the stone knife. The chopped-off trees. (*The drums are slower.*) The hut of mud and straw . . . (*He is slumping over the table.*) The buzzing . . . the buzzing . . . southeast, 104 degrees . . . and the drums . . . 104 degrees . . . the sa-cri-fice . . .

(*He has fallen to the floor. Silence. The women, astonished, tiptoe close to him.*)

LEONOR: Young man, young man. Oh, Adela.

ADELA (*dogmatically*): He's lost his memory. That's what happens to aviators, I've seen it in the movies.

LEONOR: Look, young man. Do you know where you crashed? This is the hacienda of Ixtla. I am Leonor Luna, this lady is Adela

Sidel. The girl is Sibila, my goddaughter. You came in a plane, you told us, and you told us there was a young woman with you whose name was, what was it? Mayala. That's what you told us.

ADELA: Leave him alone! Don't touch him! You might give him an attack.

LEONOR: The plane. Do you remember? The plane.

MAN (*slowly*): The hacienda of Ixtla . . . Leonor Luna . . .

LEONOR: Oh, Adela, I think he's in bad shape.

ADELA: He certainly is, he looks like a corpse.

LEONOR: Where is my chest? Let me see what I can find.

MAN: Leonor Luna . . . Adela Sidel . . .

ADELA: No, not the medicine chest. You'll make him worse.

MAN: Adela Sidel . . . Sibila . . .

SIBILA: He said my name. He said my name, too.

MAN: Silvestre Sidel. Silvestre Sidel!

LEONOR: He's calling him! He's going to bring him here.

ADELA: Don't be a fool. He's repeating names he heard.

(*The Man slowly gets to his feet. Circus music, very far away. He lets himself fall again.*)

MAN: It's over now. Sorry. Now all the memories are united again.

LEONOR: Come, I'm going to put some compresses on your head. Come lie down. (*To Adela*) I suppose you won't object. This young man is very sick.

ADELA: Yes, I see that. (*Trying to sound casual*) You know, it isn't very late. I think I could go into town and stay there with Rafael. We could send you a doctor . . .

LEONOR: And what is Rafael doing in town?

ADELA: Rafael? I mean, maybe if he didn't go on to Mexico City . . . If he were at the hotel . . .

LEONOR: Aha! Maybe! Go on, if you want! Get out of here and don't invent excuses. Go on. Don't come back. Do you think I can't see what you mean to do?

ADELA (*realizing she has revealed her hand*): Excuses! (*Resolved, she decides to be offended.*) Good evening.

MAN (*without rising, in a natural tone*): There's some problem, isn't there?

ADELA: Not with me. I'm going to my room, and no problems. It's a good thing I'm going to live by myself now.

MAN (*one leap and he is on his feet*): If you will forgive me, problems are my business. I have answered the letters of many readers of the most frequently read section of a magazine, I have given private and public consultations. Is your boyfriend unfaithful? Is a loved one far away? I! (*He beats his chest.*) I resolve your case! (*With sympathy*) Do you have problems?

LEONOR: Some.

MAN: And you?

ADELA: Me? Yes, but I'm not going to tell them to anyone. I'm going to get my things. (*She goes to the staircase.*)

MAN: And you? Do you have problems? Are there difficulties in your home? Are you suffering?

SIBILA: Yes, sir.

(*The magician bounds to the top of the stairs, blocking Adela's way. He claps twice, then declaims as at the beginning of a circus.*)

MAN: Attention! Attention! We're going to begin!

ADELA: But . . . Let me by. What do you think you're doing!

MAN: Are you going?

ADELA: Yes, I am.

MAN: And you're not going to see my performance? Well, now, you're planning to go away and leave me your place here, and I thank you for it from the bottom of my heart. I have nothing to give you in exchange except tricks and fortunes, but I was planning to dedicate a very special one to you. That wouldn't be so bad, eh? (*Takes a rose from his hand, or somewhere.*) This is for you. Special. You can throw it away, if you want, it only perfumes the air.

ADELA: Thank you, but . . .

MAN: Stay, little Adela, pretty Adelita.

ADELA (*startled*): Who are you?

MAN: Why are you surprised?

ADELA: It's . . . Rafael calls me that sometimes.

MAN: That's strange. (*Smiles at her.*) It must be that he loves you very much. Will you stay?

ADELA: It's a long way to town, and it's getting late. I'll be sleepy . . .

MAN: That's better.

(*He claps twice. Circus music: trumpet flourishes, a march.*)

(*He declaims*) Attention! Attention! The most admired personage of our day, the possessor of the powers and secrets of the ancient Pharaohs, the marvel of five continents, specially arrived from Asia for the amazement of our public . . .

(*A drum roll. While shouting these words, the Man has taken the banners and draped an X from the four corners of the room. He has not interrupted his speech except as necessary in expectation of the drumroll.*)

(*Continues*) Ladies and gentlemen, here is . . . the Magician of the Caftan!

(*He points to the stairway. A spotlight on the landing. With one leap he places himself in the light, then bows. The three women applaud and he waves in all directions. The march continues.*)

(*Modestly*) Thank you very much. Thank you very much. Now, ladies and gentlemen, before you all I am going to send a telepathic summons to my assistant and she will present herself to answer, through the mouths of the listeners themselves, whatever you want to ask her. I am concentrating . . . (*He places his fingers on his temple.*) And I call her!

(*The march ceases. Drum roll. The lights lower. A great light strikes the sealed door. It opens. Sound of galloping. Malaya enters in a silver and rose dress, in the style of a ballerina or a bareback rider. She takes the chain of silk scarves as she dances through the room. She passes the scarves between her fingers and makes them change color. She finishes with a bow and stops with her arms crossed at the foot of the stairway.*)

Here before you . . . Mayala!

(*Applause. Another bow by Mayala.*)

And now, young lady, we are going to hear what this select public wishes to ask you. There is no trick, no deceit, the answers are within yourselves. Yes, ladies and gentlemen! The answer to every question lies within the person who formulates it! Who has a problem? Advance one step.

(*Leonor and Sibila step forward.*)

Very well. (*To Adela*) Ma'am, do you not wish a consultation? Don't you have any problems?

ADELA: I don't have any great . . . The only one I had I've already decided. Why can't I live by myself? Of course there is the inheritance. And Rafael. That's all. My life is not very complicated.

MAN: What is this about the inheritance? What is this about Rafael?

ADELA: Well . . . my husband, may he rest in peace, was an imbecile. He said that I was too foolish to manage money and he left it all to my son. The poor thing was an ingrate, a very bad son, to tell the truth. He married Leonorcita, *her* daughter, and left everything to her. She, of course, left a will in favor of their child. (*To Leonor*) I'm amazed that she didn't leave everything to you. One thing, he very generously named me executrix "to look after the child while he was a minor." He left me something, of course, but it's all gone. And now the earth has swallowed up the child, and we're going to die and it will all be lost. Or just supposing, he may come back to reclaim it, the Silvestre we don't even know any more. The truth is, Leonor, when Silvestre comes back—if he comes back—he's going to be a stranger. We won't matter to him, if he even recognizes us. So why can't I have my money? Silvestre or not, I want it so I can do whatever I want to with it.

(*The drums have begun while Adela was speaking.*)

MAN: Be careful. Did you hear? Again.

(*Mayala becomes terrified; she sniffs and searches for a scent like a wild animal, following the rhythm of the drums.*)

We must hurry. The drums are a constant danger. Mayala! Hurry. Run and change.

(*Mayala exits. The drums fade away.*)

They're passing now. We have to continue, as fast as possible. And Rafael? Tell me.

ADELA: He's my nephew, but that's something else. I don't know.

MAN: Naturally not. Ask.

ADELA: It's that . . . He's a distant nephew who began to visit me. He's very handsome, very affectionate. He's brought me to the hacienda several times. He's a darling boy. Sibila knows him, ask her.

SIBILA: Yes, it's true.

ADELA: He takes me to the movies and gets me whatever I want. He borrowed this radio from some friends so I wouldn't miss the story of Gilda Miramar. Then . . . I know that I'm not very . . . very likeable, or very . . . It's just . . . What if he doesn't love me for myself, but for my money?

MAN (*taking notes*): Why couldn't you live alone? Why can't you have your money? Does Rafael really love you? Now you. What about you? What do you want to know?

LEONOR (*very quietly*): I'm very lonely.

MAN: Louder, please, so we can all hear you.

LEONOR: My grandson went away. He fled from the house, leaving me a letter, and he was all I had in this world.

MAN: I'm very sorry about that. Do you want to know where he is?

LEONOR: Where he is, why he went away, why he left me all by myself, what's going to become of me, what will happen if he comes back and I . . . and I'm not here anymore?

MAN: Just a minute, please. Three questions are all I can answer during one consultation. (*Takes notes.*) Why he went away . . . What was the gentleman's name?

LEONOR: The boy's. (*Smiles.*) Gentleman!

MAN: Why he went away . . . where he is . . . why he left you all alone.

SIBILA: The water is still cold, Godmother.

MAN: Naturally. We haven't heard from you. What do you want to know.

SIBILA: Nothing.

MAN: You don't want to know anything?

SIBILA: Well, no. I want . . . things.

MAN: What things?

SIBILA: I can't say.

MAN: There must be something you want to know.

SIBILA: What for? Although . . . Yes. Will I get what I want?

MAN: That's a good question. (*Notes it.*)

(*Sibila sits down in a corner. She covers her head with her rebozo. Very distant, a waltz plays.*)

You hear? Now the answers are coming.

ADELA: That music?

MAN: It's Mayala. She's ready now. This is going to be for you. Are you listening to it?

LEONOR: It's a waltz.

(*The sealed door opens suddenly, as if pushed by the wind. Through it can be seen a brilliant light. A handful of dry leaves blows in.*)

MAN: Come. (*Takes Leonor by the hand.*) Look there. Look in there.

LEONOR: It's bright in there. What is it? (*She looks in.*) A mirror! No. It's me! But . . . so long ago. Is it my portrait? It's moving! (*She steps back.*)

(*Mayala advances, dressed in grey, in the mode of the 1900's. At her breast she wears some enormous roses. The "Dolores" waltz by Waldeteufel, at first very weakly, then stronger, finally very strong, although at times distorted. Mayala advances, dancing. Dry leaves spin around her as if they were hanging from her dress. She crosses, turns, weaves the watchers into her circles.*)

How pretty I was!

ADELA: Not terribly. I remember, too.

MAN: Youth. Look at it. Remember. What else was there?

LEONOR: I don't know. It seemed like that. They brought me that dress from Paris. I was . . . Oh, Lord, I was so young. Look at me, Adela.

(*The magician is close to the sealed door.*)

MAN: Who's missing? Who should be with her?

LEONOR: It was that night! Was it that night?

(*The magician takes off the caftan. He puts on a jacket that appears to have been hanging on the inside of the sealed door.*)

MAN: I'm going to act for him, because it would be difficult to bring him here. You speak your lines, which Mayala will act out for you.

(*Mayala, the young Leonor, places herself at the window looking toward the outside. The magician approaches her slowly. Leonor will say the lines and Mayala will enact them. The magician has transformed himself into Gabriel.*)

GABRIEL: Leonor.

(*She starts and turns.*)

Did I frighten you?

LEONOR: Yes.

GABRIEL: Didn't you know it was I?

LEONOR: Yes, that's the reason I was frightened. What did they tell you?

GABRIEL: I will go speak to them tomorrow. Do you love me?

LEONOR: I don't know. You'd better leave. They'll say you were with me the whole time. Go. (*He starts to leave.*) Gabriel! (*He stops.*) No, don't go. What did they say to you?

GABRIEL: Your father said to me, "Young man, you must understand that this is not the proper place to deal with these matters. Come to the house tomorrow and we will talk about it."

LEONOR: Are you afraid?

GABRIEL: No.

LEONOR: No?

GABRIEL: Yes. (*He takes her hand.*)

LEONOR: Don't take my hand!

(*Gabriel lets go, startled. She extends it toward him nevertheless, insisting.*)

No, don't take it. Let go. (*He takes it. She smiles at him apprehensively.*) You're so daring.

GABRIEL: Will you give me a flower?

LEONOR: No!

GABRIEL: No?

LEONOR: What do you want it for?

GABRIEL: To keep. Because you wore it, because it was next to you.

LEONOR: To keep?

GABRIEL: Yes.

LEONOR (*looks to see if anyone is watching her, then quickly unfastens the entire bunch of flowers at her breast and gives them to him*): Here, hide them.

(*Gabriel does not know what to do with the enormous roses. Finally he puts them under his shirt, where they stick out terribly.*)

GABRIEL: Thanks. (*Steps back.*) Thanks. (*He exits through the sealed door.*) (*Pause.*) (*Sticks his head out.*) End of this scene. The next one begins a year and several months later. (*Disappears once more.*)

(*Mayala—Leonor—stands for a moment with her hands where the roses had been. Then she goes to the door and takes down a full dressing gown that opens at the back like a doctor's tunic. She puts it on over her dress and loosens her hair. She changes her position. Sound of water.*)

LEONOR (*timidly*): There were lots of stars.

MAN (*looking out*): I'm sorry, there can't be as many as there were.

(*He whistles, claps twice. The window becomes sprinkled from the outside with large radiant stars, obviously false. The magician hides himself. Moonlight. Mayala—Leonor—is walking in her sleep in the garden. She cuts a nasturtium and sits on the stone bench. Gabriel enters, his hair in disarray, also wearing a robe, beneath which can be seen the shoes and pantslegs of the magician.*)

GABRIEL (*quietly*): Leonor. What's going on, Leonor? (*She does not move.*) Are you disgusted with me? Don't you love me any more? (*He takes her hand.*) Why did you go out? Leonor.

(*She cries out and awakens, looks around her in terror, and then begins to weep.*)

LEONOR: What happened? Why did you bring me here?

GABRIEL: You came by yourself. You got up and walked out. Do you walk in your sleep?

LEONOR: I don't know. I was dreaming something horrible. I wasn't married. We were walking along the seashore and there was a thread binding us together. You wanted to cut it with an enormous knife. I was crying, but I said yes, go ahead and cut it once and for all. And when you touched it, it shone, as if in protest. "What if it's gold?" I said. Then you didn't cut it, but you wounded me in the stomach with that knife. That's when I woke up. I still feel a pain. What are we doing here?

GABRIEL: You got up in your sleep. Does that happen to you often?

LEONOR: I don't know. It never happened before, walking in my sleep.

GABRIEL: Let's go inside, darling. You might get cold.

LEONOR: No. I like the air. Look. (*Holding up the nasturtium.*) Did you give it to me?

GABRIEL: No. You must have cut it. (*Laughs.*) We look like ghosts in our white robes.

LEONOR: Yes. We look like spirits. Tell me, I already knew, of course, but . . . is it always like that?

GABRIEL: You mean . . . No, darling. (*Embraces her.*) Only the first time.

LEONOR: They should teach us when we're young, don't you think? I feel so . . . stupid, so ridiculous, but don't think that . . . that I want to pretend. I didn't expect it. No matter how much one imagines . . . Nobody tells us, nobody says anything clearly. If the girls were here, they would start to ask me questions. Of course. How could I tell them! Never. Listen, couldn't we live like brother and sister, without any of . . . that?

GABRIEL: Look, that's why you get married. To live as husband and wife.

LEONOR (*with horror*): Is that right? For that? Truly?

GABRIEL: That's why. It should be why, so that life can go on happening, developing. You can't break the thread. As in your dream. You see? I believe it. That must be what it means. I love you and because of that it's good that we have pleasure together. It's good, the church blesses us for it.

LEONOR: The church blesses anything. And look, I didn't have any pleasure, you needn't think I did. My mother told me about that. There are women like that, you know which ones, the ones that feel things with men. I am . . . Oh, Gabriel. (*She cries. He embraces her.*) I'm cold.

GABRIEL: You see? Let's go to bed. (*They rise.*)

LEONOR: Gabriel, listen. Do you think we will have children?

GABRIEL: Of course, darling. Many.

LEONOR: Not many, but two, or three . . . (*They exit through the sealed door.*)

(*The magician peeks out.*)

MAN: End of this scene. Let's go on to the next one.

LEONOR (*as if sighing, quietly*): Two or three . . . How I would have liked to. Or many, as he wanted.

ADELA: What about me? Aren't I going to masquerade?

MAN (*entering*): You?

ADELA (*confused*): That is . . . I think that when my scenes come it would be better if I got dressed up, don't you think? I mean, you've seen Leonor's, how pretty they came out. Mine could be much better.

MAN: And you want to dress up?

ADELA: Yes. It was good that Leonor's part was played by the . . . young lady, but I'm the same as when I was young.

MAN: Fine. Get dressed. (*She goes to the sealed door.*) Not there. Wait. It's a little difficult, but I'm going to try.

(*He makes a great effort. He is pushing something that does not want to shut tight. Noise of doors slamming, closing one after another. The magician turns the key and rests.*)

You can go on. The whole place is locked up now and the house is ours. Have you noticed the value of a door? On the other side there can be cold, wind, night, time, nameless things. And we lock up and we are in our own kingdom. I have closed all the outside doors. Now the whole house is our kingdom. You can change in there.

(*Mayala hands some clothes through the door.*)

ADELA: Thank you. Oh, how pretty. (*Happy, she exits left, rapidly.*)

MAN: Now, away with the stars! (*They go out.*) That can indicate the passage of time. And a little later . . .

(*Mayala enters wearing a large black shawl and widow's mourning. She looks about, sighs. It is evident that she is suffering. She sits down.*)

(*He peers through the door.*) At this moment there is one person missing. Since he is so close, it will be better for him to come in person, although as a younger man. (*Disappears.*)

(*Enter Salustio, as he was at 49, dressed in a modest, dark charro suit.*)

SALUSTIO: I'm sorry, Missy. Excuse me. (*He is going to leave.*)

LEONOR: Salustio! Don't leave. (*Sighs.*) I'm so happy to see you. I mean, it pleases me. Oh, look at all this, this garden, these trees, without him.

SALUSTIO: Missy, it's more than a year now since Master Gabrielito died. What can we do? And you still such a young girl. You're as pretty as a rose.

LEONOR: Salustio. (*She smiles, and rejects the compliment with a gesture.*)

SALUSTIO: But Missy, look at yourself. There are plenty wandering around who'd like to marry you. And why not, Missy, what'll you do without someone to look after you and someone to love you? (*A little embarrassed*) Excuse me, Missy, if I've gone too far.

LEONOR (*surprised*): No, don't worry, but don't say things like that. I'll never forget Gabriel. There could never be anyone like him. Never.

SALUSTIO: Well, no. Not like him, no. But someone different, someone who loves you very much.

LEONOR: Oh, Salustio. (*With concentration*) My daughter loves me, and nobody else. I'm so lonely. But that's the way I want to be always. With my heart empty, the way Gabriel left it. (*She rubs her eyes, shakes her head, sobs.*)

SALUSTIO (*angered*): You see? You see? You're making yourself cry. You do it, look at yourself. You say things and say things, on purpose, till you cry. And that's the way it'll be your whole life, when there are people who love you. Your husband is in heaven now, or someplace. And what about those of us who're still here? You ought to get married, because it isn't good or right for widows to go around without a husband. You ought to marry someone who knows your business affairs, and who doesn't care if you're rich because he loves you for being pretty and for being good—someone who would defend you, someone strong, someone you know real well, someone who knows you, who's known you since you were a child. Look, really (*he shakes her by the shoulders*), it's what you ought to do. Marry, Missy, marry a man who . . . (*Releases her, steps back.*) A man like . . . (*Loses his breath. Falls to one knee.*) Missy! Missy Leonor! (*Kisses her hand fervently.*)

LEONOR (*steps back, frightened*): Salustio!

(*Salustio covers his face with his hands. He rises.*)

SALUSTIO: You'll have to excuse me, Missy, 'cause sometimes . . . I didn't mean to step out of line, Missy, but . . . (*Lowers his hands, pulls some papers from his pocket.*) Do you want us to go over the accounts?

LEONOR (*upset, looking at him with surprise, through new eyes*): The accounts? Let's see them. (*She continues looking at him with intense amazement.*)

SALUSTIO: Here are the wages for the year, Missy. This month was the worst, because we had to bring in some workers from outside to help with the plowing. Then, on this page, there are the household expenses. This is for food, this is for . . .

(*His voice is fading out little by little until he falls silent. They stand immobile, like a photograph. Lights down where he is standing and up on Leonor. The magician looks out.*)

MAN (*quietly*): End of this scene.

(*Leonor begins to sob, with restraint at first, then openly.*)

LEONOR: So long ago, so long ago.

MAN (*approaching her slowly, and speaking softly*): Why are you crying?

LEONOR: I don't know.

MAN: Could you have loved him? Would you have married him?

LEONOR: No. Not then, under any circumstances. (*She dries her tears.*)

MAN: And later?

LEONOR: I don't know. (*Blows her nose.*) He never said anything to me again. He was a widower then, but he got married again . . . Who knows? I can't forget him as he was that evening, but it's difficult now to see him. Afterward he began to show his age, he got careless . . . That was forty years ago! It seems that something happens, it's over and done, then suddenly you see it right before you, and it's fresh, as if it just happened. I keep on being the same as I always was, but I was still different all the time. How is it possible?

MAN: Did you love him?

LEONOR: No! I mean . . . It's really strange. I can't explain it, I don't know. I never would have planned it.

MAN: What a shame! But that was one answer.

LEONOR: An answer? How?

MAN: Think. Don't you realize? Why you remained so lonely?

(*Adela enters, dressed in the height of the style of the 1900's, plumes and all.*)

ADELA: I'm ready. It fits me very well. Didn't I tell you, I'm the same as I was then. (*Turns around.*) Aren't I just the same as I was then, Leonor?

LEONOR: Yes, poor dear. You always looked like a little old lady.

ADELA: An old lady? Go on. Listen to her. Even now men still spy on me. Your husband, Sibila, was up in a tree peeking in a window. Fortunately I had already dressed. All right, you say when we begin.

(*The magician claps twice. Mayala and Salustio leave the stage.*)

(*Goes to the window.*) I could do what she did, the night my husband asked . . . Well, no, because my husband didn't propose to me at night. He went to ask my parents first. I didn't even know his intentions. My husband was a little older than I was. He had money, quite a bit of money. (*Sits down.*) That's it. The day he asked for my hand. I was sitting like this, waiting . . .

No, I wasn't like this. I was . . . I don't remember! My papa told me about it, dying with laughter. But I can't act it out by myself! Help me. You, help me, or call that girl!

MAN: All right. Who do you want us to be?

ADELA: You could be my husband, the night that . . . No. No, not that night. That man. Weak and sickly. He had asthma, you know? And it came on him in the most . . . inopportune, the most . . . absurd moments. No, it's not necessary for anyone to play the part of my husband. His death! That's it. His death. I was very sad. (*She settles into a trance of profound sadness.*) My son . . . (*Furious*) He was mesmerized, I'm sure. His only heir! And I, subjected to whatever . . . What a night. Everybody was commenting about the will. We opened it the moment he died. No. We could do the scene about . . . (*searches and searches*) about . . . When my son got married I wasn't able to go to the church. I had a cold, and I wasn't going to get out of my bed to see him get married to this one's daughter. Or maybe . . . some scenes with my mother! No. She hit me so often. She loved my sisters more. So did my father. They gave them everything, because they were smaller, they said. And I worked and worked. We were poor, that's why they didn't want me to get married. "Miss Ambitious is marrying the old man for his money," they said, and for that reason they never accepted a penny. Of course I loved my husband, plenty. A lot. I adored him. Let's do a scene with him. One scene. Let's see, which one? Or something with . . . I don't know. I don't have any to do. Only . . . Yes! A fiesta, one of those happy, beautiful fiestas from long ago. When I wore this dress for the first time. It was really too small for me. It was much too tight, I thought I looked ridiculous. Only you, Leonor, only you were able to say it looked nice on me. Of course, since you had given it to me. Your rejects, your old clothes. How you must have laughed that time. You with your fine things, always trying to make me envious. You never liked me, you loved to humiliate me with your old dresses, like this one, your old cast-off hats, like this one. (*Throws it on the floor.*) You were glad when my husband didn't leave me anything, when my son didn't leave me anything. You don't like me, you have never been my friend. Faker, egotist, schemer. (*Sobs.*) I'm so miserable. Nobody ever loved me, nobody. I'm so miserable!

MAN: I'm very sorry. Do you want to do a scene with Rafael?

LEONOR: It's better to leave her alone. It's good that she's crying.

ADELA (*dries her eyes*): With Rafael? Yes!

MAN: The scene in which you came to an understanding.

ADELA: What? I don't understand.

MAN: Yes, you understand. Isolated allusions, complaints, suggestions . . . Shall we do it?

ADELA: No, better not.

MAN: He told you that story about his friend the lawyer. Do you remember how his eyes sparkled? And he gave you that explanation about the false sale . . .

ADELA: No! I don't want any more scenes!

MAN: Then how you planned this trip.

ADELA: I don't want any more scenes! I don't like them! I'm going to change again.

(*Begins to unbutton her dress.*)

MAN: One must dare to look!

ADELA: Don't shout at me. I told you I don't want to.

LEONOR: Listen. She doesn't want to. So, couldn't I see something with Silvestre?

MAN: Anything special?

LEONOR: Perhaps . . . Our arrival at the hacienda, after his mother died. I became a mother to him from that time on. But we'd need several . . . Salustio, and him. Sibila was a child.

MAN: Sibila can look like a child. Salustio can come back. And I'll have to play the part of Silvestre as a child.

(*He claps twice. The light focuses on the antique chair that Leonor will occupy. He curls up at her feet. Leonor places a mourning band on his arm. Guitar music.*)

LEONOR: Well, now you see, child. Now this whole hacienda is yours.

SILVESTRE: I want to go down to the grottoes and the spring.

LEONOR: No, child! It still isn't the time to have fun. It's scarcely four weeks since . . . (*A pause.*) Look at the evening, how melancholy, how lonely. Your mother and I used to sew together in this room. She played here as a child. No, son, we have to protect each other and look out for each other, I for you, and you for me. We have been left alone. Son, don't cry! My little orphan, my darling. (*She weeps too.*) Yes, child. We must cry for her, we must remember her. What are we going to do without her?

(*The magician makes an aside in his role as Silvestre the child.*)

MAN: And here Salustio enters.

(*He claps twice. Salustio, once again ninety years old, can be seen through the wall.*)

LEONOR: Salustio! How you have aged! But so much! (*Steps outside the recalled scene.*) Listen, he wasn't like that then.

SALUSTIO: Missy, Missy, this is dangerous. We can all lose our souls, Missy.

LEONOR: What is he saying? He didn't say that then.

SALUSTIO: Salustio Pedro is throwing water in my face and I won't be able to do anything, because I'm old and I've lost authority.

SIBILA: The water's beginning to boil, Godmother!

(*A reddish glow at the window. The drums begin again.*)

MAN (*rising*): Now, you hear, I won't be able to stay much longer.

(*A rock breaks the window. Cries outside.*)

ADELA: They're throwing rocks! (*Looks out.*) It's your son, Salustio. (*Gives a cry.*) No! Who is *he*? Look, Salustio is out there. *He* isn't Salustio. Salustio is down there, stretched out on the ground near his son, and there are other men, with torches

SALUSTIO: It's true, it's true. I didn't mean to tell things about you and the Devil, but I came out all trembling and I let something slip without meaning to. It's because I'm old, Missy. And suddenly I fell on the ground and began to talk about things from the past. And the doors closed by themselves, no one can come in here. Because of that they want to force the doors and burn the house. They say you're a witch, Missy. And now I have to go, because Salustio Pedro is throwing water in my face, and I'm going to wake up now. With your permission, Missy. (*Disappears.*)

(*The drums grow louder.*)

MAN: We have to do the scene, hurry, come. Sibila, here.

ADELA: But what did Salustio say? I saw two Salustios, two. One stretched out down there and the other here.

LEONOR: Wait, be quiet. This is Silvestre's scene.

MAN: Come here, I must go.

SIBILA: Why?

SILVESTRE: She is taking me to the city.

SIBILA: Why?

SILVESTRE: I heard her talking with Salustio. I don't want us to go back, because I'm going to study. Here, take this. (*He hands her a little doll.*)

SIBILA: What is it?

SILVESTRE: A doll, for your pins. If anything happens to me, the points will get blood on them, because I put some of my hair and my saliva and my nails inside it. I read that in a book. That's the way the voodoo witches do it.

SIBILA: Don't give it to me, it scares me.

SILVESTRE: Yes, take it. Now you have to take it. And give me a kiss.

(*Sibila laughs and blushes.*)

Come on, now, hurry, because they're going to call me. Remember to look at the pins from time to time.

(*They kiss each other, childishly, on the mouth.*)

Good-by. They're calling me now. Good-by. (*He exits through the sealed door. It closes after him.*)

LEONOR: What was that scene? Is that the way Silvestre said good-by? How did he know we weren't coming back?

ADELA: Do you hear that? It's stronger now.

(*Shouts outside. The noise of the drums grows louder, the beats have become more measured.*)

LEONOR: Yes, it's the drums.

ADELA (*running back and forth like a madwoman*): That's not drums at all! They're beating down the doors! Don't you hear?

It's a battering ram beating the door. And smoke! Look, it's true. They're burning the house!

LEONOR: We have to speak to the magician. Sibila, what's the matter, Sibila?

SIBILA (*dries her eyes, blows her nose*): But didn't you notice? It was him and he's never coming back.

LEONOR: Him?

SIBILA: It was Silvestre, and he went away again. And the points of the pins are covered with blood.

LEONOR: Silvestre! Son! Silvestre! (*Tries to open the door.*) Silvestre!

(*Another stone through the window. The smoke is thicker.*)

ADELA (*looking outside*): They're beating Salustio! Look at the smoke! They're burning the house!

(*The baby begins to cry.*)

LEONOR: Silvestre! Silvestre! (*Continues trying to open the door.*)

CURTAIN

ACT THREE

The smoke is growing thicker. The magic objects have disappeared.

ADELA: They're beating Salustio! Look at the smoke! They're burning the house!

(*The baby begins to cry.*)

LEONOR: Silvestre! Silvestre! (*Continues trying to open the door.*)

SIBILA: He's crying. It's the smoke, it's very bad for him. What shall we do, Godmother?

ADELA: Well, do something, for God's sake! (*From the window*) Help! (*Another rock.*) Everyone, everyone. If we go out they'll kill us. (*Shakes Leonor.*) Stop crying. Where is that man? The magician. Where is he?

LEONOR: It was Silvestre, it was him. He's gone away from me again.

SIBILA: You haven't cried for days.

ADELA: Silvestre, my foot! Don't be stupid. (*Authoritative and realistic, she knocks on the door.*) This isn't a game. Open up. We have to escape through there. (*Waits. Knocks again with her knuckles.*) Listen to me, you magician or whatever you are, open up. The imbecile thinks this is the time to play tricks.

LEONOR: But . . . it was Silvestre.

ADELA: You don't seem to understand. It was another scene, like all the others he did. If the magician were Silvestre, Mayala would be you and you wouldn't be anyone. Damn this smoke. (*Coughs.*) Help me open the door. Give me something, a hammer, anything. Help me, Sibila, don't stand there like an idiot. Put the baby down, give him to Leonor. Go on! (*Sibila obeys.*)

LEONOR: I don't understand. Blessed Lord. Don't cry, my big little fellow. There. That smoke . . . (*Coughs.*) Wasn't it he, then?

ADELA: Hard, Sibila, pull hard.

(*Sound of wood creaking.*)

SIBILA: It's moving.

ADELA: Another big tug. Again. Careful!

(*The entire door comes loose, crossbars and all, and falls on them. Stones and mortar dust fall all around them. Behind the door there is a brick wall covered with moss and spiderwebs and a few mushrooms.*)

But what is this? (*She touches the wall, then pulls her hand back nervously.*) How the devil could he do it? They're bricks, it looks like a real wall. (*Wipes her hand on her dress.*) Even the dampness seems . . . But the dress? This is my own dress! But . . . he took the other one from me! Then, he must be here! (*Shouts.*) Listen to me! Where are you? Listen!

(*The magician enters, right. He stops at the top of the stairway.*)

MAN: Quick, the door is burning, it will fall in in a minute and they'll come in. Do you hear? The pounding has stopped.

ADELA (*shouts*): Don't you think it's time to help us now?

MAN: I know it, forgive me. I couldn't use the sealed door and I

had to come the long way round. I can't find Mayala. Have you
seen her?

ADELA: How long before you plan to get us out of here, magician,
or whoever you are?

MAN: At this moment. All you have to do is turn on the radio.

LEONOR: I've been thinking and thinking whether it could really
be Silvestre.

ADELA: This isn't the time to be playing foolish tricks!

(*The light from the fire begins to be seen in the room.*)

MAN: It isn't a trick. The radio. Turn on the radio. Don't you
realize? It's very simple.

SIBILA: I hear them laughing outside.

MAN: An enormous web of long and short waves comes together
here, a great cluster of coordinates and waves to everywhere.
The sun is setting at one point and rising in another. The earth
spins and balances, it turns and tumbles, like a weight on the
end of a tense yellow thread held by the sun. And here we are,
stuck here. (*He stamps on the floor.*) In the east it is already
tomorrow, it is dawning, the day is tomorrow, and nevertheless
it is the same point in the great time which envelops us.

(*While he is speaking, the three women walk around, coughing, stupefied; the room is filled with reddish light.*)

The west is yesterday. The west is dark, and it awaits today's
dawn. Here it is night. Don't you realize? Turn on the radio.
One wave from yesterday, or tomorrow, so I can get in.

(*A pause.*)

ADELA: Are you going to leave us here?

MAN: No, no! Don't you understand me? Turn on the radio!

SIBILA: They're quiet. I don't hear anything except the noise of
the fire. The wood crackles.

ADELA: He went away. Could he have been afraid of those men?
Coward! You see, Leonor? I'm so glad I didn't give him my bed.

MAN: But . . . (*Runs down the stairs.*) Don't you hear me?

LEONOR: I think he's going to come back.

ADELA: What do you mean come back? He was afraid and he went away. Let's go to the back of the house. We can hide in the bedrooms.

SIBILA: The only doors are glass, Mrs. Adela, and they'll look for us everywhere.

MAN (*to Sibila*): You, at least. Do you see me? Hear me? Do what I tell you, because time's running out.

LEONOR: Let's go to the bedrooms anyway. Maybe we can hide in a clothes closet.

MAN: No! No! Don't leave here!

ADELA: That'll be the first thing they open to steal everything. (*They go to the stairway.*)

LEONOR: Your baby, take him, easy. I feel very weak. It's the cold, I can't walk. Help me.

MAN: Don't leave here or I won't be able to do anything. Don't go away from this table. Don't take the child away.

LEONOR: Help me, Adela.

ADELA: Hurry, I'm going to look for a place we can hide.

MAN: Don't go, don't go! Turn on the radio! (*Adela exits.*)

SIBILA: You weigh a lot, Godmother.

LEONOR: Leave me here, you go hide. I think I'm dying.

MAN: Sibila, Sibila. Do you hear me? Sibila. (*He falls on one knee and covers his face.*)

LEONOR: My strength is going.

MAN: Mine, too. I think this is the end.

SIBILA: Godmother, the child and you ... Don't lean on me so hard. (*Stumbling, they walk toward a corner.*)

MAN: I lost Mayala, too. (*Adela runs in, rigid with fright, almost unable to speak.*)

ADELA: There are men in there. They're drunk, in the farthest bedroom. I think they got in by climbing the big pines. They're talking about us.

LEONOR (*her voice is fading*): Didn't you ask them to help you? (*She drops into a chair.*)

ADELA (*weeping*): Help me! They were talking about burning us alive. They're afraid of us and that's why they're going to burn us. You, too, Sibila. Do you see? I told you not to get mixed up with the child. We're surrounded, Leonor. Leonor! (*She passes her hand in front of Leonor's eyes.*)

That's all we needed. She's asleep.

LEONOR: We have to turn on the radio.

ADELA: The radio! Wake up, woman. Wake up! (*She shakes her.*)

LEONOR: What? Adela . . . Was I asleep?

MAN: Don't wake her!

ADELA: There are men there, they want to burn us alive. They're in there, Leonor. Listen to me. Leonor!

LEONOR: We have to turn on the radio.

ADELA: Leonor! (*Shakes her.*)

(*Without their touching it, the radio turns on. Adela steps back. The buzz of static.*)

MAN (*rises*): That's it! Now, the short wave. Quickly. Yesterday or tomorrow, another place, another time, the coordinate.

LEONOR: There it is.

MAN: Look for the exact wave. Look!

ADELA: Leonor, wake up.

LEONOR: There. There, I found it.

MAN: Now, music for the flight!

(*Music. Everything sways. Adela yelps and falls to the floor on all fours. The window flies wide open. The lamp swings, as in an earthquake. The red light ceases. Darkness. Clouds pass by the windows, stars, constellations.*)

There they go now. One, two, three, the twelve Greek constellations. That one like a spherical zebra is Uranus, striped by shimmering bands and with its sputtering moons; and that one whirling along, that incandescent red bubble, is Mars. The moon! It's at the crescent, a worm-eaten rose in the east. Let's go there, toward tomorrow. Look how it whirls. Routes, clouds of gasses, masses in combustion. Listen to it! That is the music of flight.

ADELA: Who is that speaking? What happened to the light?

SIBILA: Godmother! Mrs. Adela!

ADELA: It was like an earthquake. Did the hacienda sink in the ground?

SIBILA: It's like being dead. Godmother, we're flying.

ADELA: What? Light a lamp. I think I broke my kneecap.

SIBILA: Look out there, Godmother.

LEONOR: There's a lot of wind coming in.

SIBILA: Those are stars! And there, an airplane! We're as high as it is.

(*An airplane passes slowly across the window. Its flight lights are lighted, its eyes winking red and green. The sky recedes slowly in the opposite direction and it is as Tamayo has painted it at times: almost a spiderweb.*)

MAN: More travelers going toward the west, robbing an hour every time they tear the thread from the spindle. They dangle brilliant shreds from their wings, pieces of the great web. Like a knife in the net of the sky, they hasten or slow the hands of the appointment: the time and the place.

LEONOR: Who is that speaking?

ADELA: The magician, or whatever you want him to be. But he's caused me to run one of my stockings with his jokes.

SIBILA: It's so beautiful it makes me want to cry.

LEONOR: Where is he?

MAN: Here.

LEONOR: Is it you, is it my . . .? I can't see a thing. Where are you? Tell me.

(*The magician claps twice: everything is bathed in light like strong moonlight.*)

Let me look at you. Please forgive me if I'm mistaken, but . . . Is it possible that you are my . . . (*almost touching him*) that you are . . .?

MAN: Don't ask. You must wait. I haven't completed the numbers. There are still questions to be answered, but I can't find Mayala.

ADELA (*screams*): Animal! You're going to murder us. What have you done? (*She moves away from the window.*)

LEONOR: What's the matter, Adela?

ADELA: This . . . makes me seasick. What's the matter? Look out the window and you'll see what's the matter with me. Listen, just take me down. I'd rather be burned alive than splattered to death.

LEONOR: How beautiful. Can you all see? It's Orion. I've never seen it shine so.

MAN: Now hurry, even though Mayala isn't here, because soon we'll be coming close to the sun. At the moment, it's a star like any other. If we should lose contact we'll never be able to pick it out. It's neither larger nor smaller, it shines neither more nor less. It is its proximity that gives it its dubious title of shepherd or wolf.

SIBILA: I can't stop looking at it.

ADELA: I don't want to look, I can't breathe. Something is happening. What is happening to me?

MAN: It is the missing answer. There throbs Mars. Look at it, dare. That is Mars throbbing over there. Put your hand on your breast. Feel it? There it is. Close your eyes. Go into yourself.

ADELA: No, no!

MAN: Turn into yourself.

ADELA (*wails*): Oh, oh, oh!

(*The light changes. It becomes a throbbing red.*)

LEONOR: What are you doing to her?

MAN: I am forcing her to look at her heart, cold and red, shriveled like a wornout planet. That's why she can't be alone. That's why she searches for Rafael. Sick and alone. Isn't that right? Your heart lies in a thin, poor atmosphere. It is going out. It is getting cold.

ADELA: I'm so alone, dear God.

LEONOR: Don't say those things to her!

MAN: She knows it very well.

ADELA: My doctor told me I am very ill. I may drop dead any minute and there's no cure.

LEONOR: Oh, Adela, no.

ADELA: And what difference will it make to you? You're happy, dosing yourself in good health, spoiling yourself, babying yourself. You swallow barrels of medicine while you're strong as an oak. For me, nothing. I don't want anyone to know, they'd all be pleased. No one loves me, not even Rafael. If he knew it, he'd be tickled to death.

LEONOR: No. Adela. He loves you very much.

ADELA: You should be the last one to tell me a fool thing like that. *No one* loves me.

LEONOR: I do. We're related through our children, aren't we? We have always been friends. Why didn't you tell me?

ADELA: Our children are dead, so that relationship doesn't have any bearing any more. I have nothing. Let go, let go. Don't hang all over me. I don't like to be babied.

LEONOR (*to the Man*): You see?

MAN: It doesn't matter. You all know now. (*To Adela*) You can't live alone. Rafael doesn't love you.

(*The red light is fading.*)

ADELA: I'm going to die very soon.

SIBILA: A star fell. Can I make a wish?

MAN: Make it.

SIBILA: There it goes, trailing its thread. It's gone. (*Silence.*) I made my wish.

MAN: Now, your question. You will have to answer it yourself, within the hermetic circle. (*A circle of light stage front right.*) Now, walk in.

SIBILA: What for?

MAN: Take your child and go in.

(*Sibila resists a little.*)

SIBILA: I don't like it, I feel funny. I can't get out, Godmother.

MAN: No, stay there. You're alone now. Go on, it's your number. Speak, or sing. Sing a lullaby to your baby.

(*Sibila sits on the floor and begins to sing to the child, humming something indistinguishable. In the distance, a cradle song.*)

SIBILA: Poor nameless child, why should I baptize you now? Why don't you die? I don't love you. You're always the same, you die and are born worse each time. Look at your little foot, so ugly. I guess it hurts you and that's why you cry. You were worse the last time. Oh, God, you make me sick, with that head, your eyes shut tight, always looking for my breast, dead with hunger. Why do you come back to be born again? You're never going to be good for anything, and because of you I'm just going to keep on screwing up. It's really a good thing you're going to die. There you are, so skinny and quiet, like that Christ child the priest used to bring. Just look at you, and those mosquitoes keep on stinging you. I don't know what there is left to get out. You don't know anything, and you yell, and I'm the one who suffers. Every cry of yours hurts me here, right down to my bones. You get sores, and they hurt me here. I can't even eat, hoping that you'll die and not cry anymore. But you take so long at it, I'd like to leave you on the ground for the pigs to eat, even though Salustio Pedro would kill me for it later. As if it made any difference to him. He'd probably get drunk and beat me. It would be better for you to die. Once and for all, just die.

(*The magician turns out all the lights except for the circle. Shadows.*)

MAN: Now everything is dark. Look, you can get the whole thing over with here. You'll never see him again, I promise you. He'll never be born again. It would be better that way. (*A little cry from the infant.*) He's not breathing any more. His little hands are limp. He's dead now.

SIBILA: No! Oh, Godmother, what did I do? I killed him. Baby. He's not moving or anything.

(*The Magician claps twice. Lights. Sibila wails, with the child cradled in her arms.*)

ADELA: She killed him.

SIBILA: I didn't ask for this. I didn't want it, it isn't true. I asked to be able to go with my godmother, and be far away from Salustio Pedro, and see young Mr. Rafael often. That's what I asked for, that's what I asked for.

LEONOR: Rafael, Sibila?

SIBILA: It's just that he's very good to me. Rafaelito brings me presents when he comes and he's . . . very good to me.

ADELA: Now I know, now I know what this hyena's been up to. It's all clear to me now.

SIBILA: But I didn't want him to die.

LEONOR: Did you really do something to him?

108

SIBILA: No, Godmother, not really.

MAN: No, naturally you didn't really. That's the way of wishes, they're simultaneous, like two electric poles. Nothing happened to the child, but now you know what the price is.

SIBILA: He's alive!

MAN: Of course. This was only a scene like the others.

LEONOR: Thanks be to God.

ADELA: Well, I thought this wild woman had finished him.

LEONOR: Silly thing, don't cry. I'm going to take you to Mexico City, and he'll get better there. Don't cry. I love him very much. I'm going to be his godmother. Don't cry.

SIBILA: It's very bright. (*Covers herself, goes to a corner.*)

ADELA (*to Sibila*): Be a fool. You know what Rafael wants. Don't you know? Don't you?

LEONOR: Leave her alone.

ADELA: I can see what's going to happen. That's the way Rafael is. She'll think it's wonderful to believe he isn't like that . . . She plans to give him everything, destroy herself, to please him. What a fool you are, Sibila.

MAN: Now all the questions are answered. Look. It's getting light. I think we're getting close to the sun.

LEONOR: Is it hot? I feel hot.

MAN: It's getting more like summer, the short heavy nights—nights filled with thoughts like relentlessly repeated dreams. Forgive me, it always happens to me in this weather: a sudden sadness. Life is a difficult thing. It could be, too, that the performance is over.

LEONOR: No! Over? And Silvestre?

MAN: Madam. Are you still asking questions? Search, you already have the answer.

LEONOR: No. There's still one scene to do, the one of the meeting with Silvestre, the one where he comes back.

MAN: Suddenly it's as if everything has fallen in on me, at one blow, in a dream. I am tired, tired, tired. I think there is something very sad to tell.

LEONOR: About Silvestre?

MAN: About everything. About people, everything.

LEONOR: And the scene?

MAN: All right. We'll do it.

ADELA: I'm cold.

LEONOR: Don't cry any more. Come on, the scene with Silvestre's coming now.

ADELA: And what difference does that make to me?

SIBILA: And me? I want to . . .

MAN: What?

SIBILA: In the thing about Silvestre.

MAN: Yes, you'll be in it. Let's start, we can do it any way we want. For example . . . Of course, I'm going to play the part of Silvestre.

LEONOR: Of course, of course. And you . . . Silvestre . . . will arrive suddenly, right? At any moment.

MAN: And at any absurd place. Through the window . . .

LEONOR: Or the sealed door . . .

SILVESTRE: And no one will recognize me.

SIBILA: I will. I will know.

SILVESTRE: But you won't say anything.

ADELA: And me?

SILVESTRE: It doesn't matter to you.

ADELA: That's right. I'm going to die, alone, like a dog.

LEONOR: He came to stay, didn't he, without my knowing who he is. And I become concerned because, where can he sleep?

SILVESTRE: Anywhere, in this hammock, on the floor.

LEONOR: And his plane?

SILVESTRE: It doesn't exist.

LEONOR: It burned.

SILVESTRE: It never existed. Don't think about the plane.

LEONOR: But I don't understand. You told me . . .

SILVESTRE: Yes. Look. Here it is. (*He shows her the books.*) And here is Tibet. Everything is here.

LEONOR: They were lies.

SILVESTRE: They were dreams.

LEONOR: The pearls, too?

SILVESTRE: The pearls are dead seeds, don't think about the pearls. This is a jacket, it never was a caftan.

LEONOR: Do it now, then, please. The meeting, the recognition. Don't make me wait any longer.

SILVESTRE: All right. (*He opens his arms a little, standing facing her.*) Now.

(*Leonor rushes to embrace him. She cries.*)

LEONOR: I already knew.

SILVESTRE: Grandmother, dear. No, no, dearest, don't cry.

LEONOR (*standing away, looking at him*): There's something about your face . . . I can't see it clearly now. What is it that's strange about it?

SILVESTRE: How can you see me clearly through so many tears?

LEONOR: Hug me. Don't go away. Give me a handkerchief, Sibila.

(*Adela gives one to Sibila, Sibila gives it to Leonor, who buries her face in the handkerchief.*)

I can't. I thought it would give me some pleasure. Oh, I don't know. Maybe it is pleasure. It's like something breaking inside me, here . . . Dear child, it hurts. No, yes, now I can die.

(*Sibila approaches. She and Silvestre look at each other.*)

SILVESTRE: Did you keep that little doll I gave you?

SIBILA: Yes. I have it here.

SILVESTRE: We were really funny, weren't we?

SIBILA: You gave me a kiss.

SILVESTRE: I'm going to give you another. (*Kisses her. She laughs, twists a little.*) Why did you marry Salustio Pedro?

SIBILA: Oh, well . . . (*It was an embarrassing question.*) Well . . . he wanted to.

SILVESTRE: And you?

SIBILA (*laughs, nervously*): Me, too.

LEONOR: Son, Silvestre, you're very different. No, you're the same. Although . . . I expected the child from long ago, how could I recognize you. Oh, son, why did you go away?

SILVESTRE: Because I didn't like the mourning.

LEONOR: For that? For . . . a little band like this? You went away for that?

SILVESTRE: For that.

LEONOR: But dear Lord, I don't understand. And later?

SILVESTRE: Later? Listen, there I go now.

LEONOR: Where?

SILVESTRE: It's coming close, do you hear?

(*The sound of a moving train. The whistle blows. It approaches, passes, at top speed. Its noise fades away in the distance.*)

LEONOR: Where did you go?

SILVESTRE: To another town. In spite of everything, I found out how to spend my money. My savings lasted almost three weeks. I swam in the sea. I met some boys who sold newspapers.

LEONOR: And then?

SILVESTRE: I sold papers, too.

(*A cock crows. Another. Silence. Silvestre paces back and forth.*)

There in the south, people sleep in hammocks.

LEONOR: Yes?

SILVESTRE: Did you hear the cocks?

LEONOR: Yes. What's the matter with you?

SILVESTRE: With the fever one doesn't know anything. Not what his own name is, or anything.

LEONOR: What do you have?

SILVESTRE: There was a woman.

LEONOR: Mayala?

SILVESTRE (*laughs*): No, after that, much later. The thing with Mayala was . . . You know? No. Who's going to know what a child thinks about? You know? All sorts of people lived with me.

LEONOR: When you sold newspapers?

SILVESTRE: No, when I lived with you. When I went to bed, I didn't go to sleep. I saw all those people, pirates, friends, a girl . . . The girl used to do things with me.

LEONOR: Silvestre! Is that true?

SILVESTRE: Yes. Everything a child imagines is true.

LEONOR: Did you imagine bad things? How could that be? You were so innocent.

SILVESTRE: They weren't bad things, and I wasn't innocent. They were forms of pleasure, dreams without substance that almost made me cry with desire. The dream was so real that it was worse, worse not to touch it. Mayala was more alive than you, and I wanted to find her. With the mourning and your tears, it wasn't possible, Grandmother. That's why I went away. Mayala was a circus performer, a ballerina, everything I wanted. We had lots of adventures. Since I invented her, perhaps it was in my mind to look for her. Yes, perhaps I went to look for her.

LEONOR: But you imagined all that. It wasn't true.

SILVESTRE: But I went away.

(*Leonor starts to cry again.*)

Why are you crying?

LEONOR: I'm just remembering when I found your letter. I was desperate! The police were looking for you. I was like a madwoman, running from one room to another, screaming, yes, screaming. You don't know, you can't even imagine. Silvestre. Don't you hear me? What's the matter?

SILVESTRE: A cock crowed.

LEONOR: No, son.

SILVESTRE: Then he's going to crow. Listen to him.

(*The cock crows.*)

LEONOR: And then, son?

SILVESTRE: Nothing.

LEONOR: You were selling papers. And then?

(*Sound of cell door. The shadows of bars fill the room. Leonor looks around her.*)

Was it that! Jai ... (She covers her mouth.) That?

SILVESTRE: No, no, no. I was very happy then. I lived very well. I had everything I wanted. (*He moves his hands, tries to erase the shadows.*) I traveled, I learned about a lot of places, I married ... more or less. (*Sits down.*) There are many ways to learn about life. Everyone has what he wants if he knows how to desire it with truth and strength. You didn't teach me to wish. You didn't teach me to wish, Grandmother. (*As he walks back and forth, the shadows disappear.*) Then I worked, I traveled,

I worked at whatever I could. Illness. I think about it and I feel weak. 104 degrees of temperature. Then the cock crowing, constantly, crickets, wheels. (*Sounds of these.*)

LEONOR: Aren't you going to tell me? What did you do then? How did you live?

SILVESTRE: Try to imagine the best.

LEONOR: It frightens me. How have you lived?

SILVESTRE: The worst was the illness. There's something like a drum in your ears. It's your pulse, but you begin to hear it inside, and the drums are there, ready for the dance. (*Drums far away.*) Your desires come. You're like someone in a story, floating through the air in an absurd, endless chain of keys and objects and papers. And that's the way they tie you down, and weigh you down, because now you know that your dreams will never be. There was a woman close by me there, my woman. She wasn't pretty. She earned her living washing clothes. She had a big, stupid child.

LEONOR: I don't understand, son. Did you live with this woman? You? Was it your child?

SILVESTRE: No. She already had him when I met her. We lived together. How she cried by the side of my hammock.

LEONOR: Why was she crying? For you? Were you very sick?

SILVESTRE: The drums. They always mark the end of scenes: change of dream, change of set. It's as if someone were moving a giant handle somewhere and the pale blue light begins to grow red. There in the south the dawn is the din of birds. How poor we all are. You can see the sun through the walls, because the hut is as fragile as a toy. The sun is the color of fever. A witch is rubbing the sick man, and in his ears are the drums of fever. It must be at least 104 degrees because everything is rocking, everything is whirling, everything is turning, everything is real. Out there are the fierce teeth of the buzz saw. Do you hear them?

(*Sound of the buzz saw. The drums are nearer. The spot-lighted arms of someone dancing are thrust through the window. Then the head. Then there she is, silhouetted against the sky, but now she is dressed like an African priestess, after Rider Haggard. She enters with a leap and begins the dance of death around Silvestre.)*

(*Silvestre has not interrupted his speech.*) Jungle in Oaxaca, 104 degrees of temperature, perhaps more, there's no thermometer. And the saw forming a helix, turning upon itself to chew the wood. The sick man would have liked to write, to ask for help, but there is no money for stamps. The sick man wonders if his grandmother still lives and if she remembers him. Things grow confused in his mind. The imaginary girl who accompanied him through his childhood returns.

LEONOR: Mayala?

SILVESTRE: He is no longer in command of his dream. The nightmare comes and goes. His blood is a drum beating, always more slowly. The saw is a shrill motor receding in the distance. Everything turns inward, the sobs, the drums . . . Thus begins the sacrifice. (*Shouts.*) Now comes the end, the realization of the end! A red day. "If he sees the dawn, he'll live, if he sees the dawn, he'll live," but there is no more essence, only the dream will remain. Now he comprehends everything, because the galloping beat is interrupted, the opportunities, all of the game and the delight. He can see her there dancing, screaming, greedy. Now there will be only desires, there will be no body. You ought to know. This one dream is a second, or an hour, perhaps a century, because the dream of him inside the dream is eternal. That is the simple well of delights, Paradise Regained, the infinite cave where time reaches every point but does not intrude. Nothing else, nothing else, because there is no body, only the nightmare where boundaries are broken and everything is desire, where memory is shattered to bits and the body is paralyzed and corrupt. This is She—broken strings, unfulfilled desires, the unfinished letter, interrupted work, images scattered like waves, engulfing everything, a voracious palpitating well absorbing everything. You pass by out there, isolated voices reach me from out there, distant memories, news of yesterday and tomorrow. Everything blends and touches.

LEONOR: Silvestre!

SILVESTRE: A cry like that, a summons. But I am no longer I, he, Silvestre, but the other, my frustrated possibilities, my non-being, the reflection of my broken potentials. The cry comes, I share the same instant, and then the well continues, unabated, free, its voracious suction . . .

LEONOR: Silvestre!

SILVESTRE: And there I go, tumbling, I've lost the end of the thread. Don't drop it, don't let go! Go on weaving, tend the web, seize the threads, remember, touch, so there are no more desires, no more fetters, the empty dream, memory lost, absorbed. What? Who? Which? How?

ECHOES (*from differing distances*): What, what, which, which, how . . . ?

SILVESTRE (*without interruption*): Look at your hands, touch yourself, remember, time, taste, live, give. Live! Smell, remember me, good-by, body, touch yourself. Life! Love, listen, see, space, good-by, her, him, them, Mayala, him, good-by, good-by-y, good-by-y-y.

ECHOES: Good-by, good-by-y, good-by-y-y . . .

(*The light has been slowly fading. Now Mayala's silhouette is scarcely distinguishable as she continues dancing and shouting in front of the magician. Lightning outside. Total darkness.*)

LEONOR: Silvestre!

(*Silence. Two long screams: Adela and Sibila. Loud thunder. The baby begins to cry.*)

The light. Light a lamp. Light a lamp.

ADELA: I'm dying.

(*Sibila is lighting a lamp, then another. Smoke is still drifting through the room. Red light comes from outside, but it is fading. Another clap of thunder. Wind shakes the lamp and the windows.*)

LEONOR: Silvestre! (*She screams again, through the window into the night.*) Silvestre!

SIBILA: Were we killed, Godmother?

LEONOR: No.

SIBILA: Put your arm around me, Godmother.

(*Adela is lying on the stairs, whimpering.*)

LEONOR: He's gone.

SIBILA: Was it really him, Godmother?

LEONOR: I don't know. Perhaps it was . . . No. He wasn't the same one who left. It wasn't the boy. Oh, I feel bad. (*Quietly*) Silvestre. He doesn't answer now. I don't understand. I'm drained, I can't cry, or even cry out.

SIBILA: Look at the smoke.

LEONOR: Do you hear? It's raining now.

SIBILA: I think they killed Papa. Will Silvestre come back, Godmother?

LEONOR: No. Never. Come, Adela is very ill. Adela. Adelita. I must have something in the medicine chest.

(*The baby cries.*)

SIBILA: I'm all fuzzy, like when I first wake up.

LEONOR: Take care of your child. I have to get Adela to bed. Silvestre is gone. Help me.

ADELA: I'm dying.

LEONOR: No, don't say that. Oh, Holy Mother. Let's see what's in the chest. Don't leave her alone. From now on we'll have to take care of her every minute. You'll have to come with us. I'm going to need you very much. (*Exits.*)

SIBILA: You too? Godmother! (*Prepares the baby's food.*) Don't cry. Poor little thing. And you too, baby. And her. (*Holds the baby in her arms and begins to give him spoonfuls of food.*) Don't burn yourself, it's boiling hot. Poor thing. Oh, Lord, I can't even do anything for you. (*Kisses him. Crosses herself. Continues feeding him.*) Come on. You won't vomit this, will you? You like this. Oh, son, you're so heavy!

(*She looks outside. She kisses him, puts him in the cradle, covers him with her rebozo, and runs out.*)

ADELA: Leonor. Oh, Holy Mother, like a dog! What happened? Leonor!

(*Leonor enters.*)

LEONOR: Don't be upset. Look what I found. These are magnificent. Take this pill. And Sibila?

ADELA: I don't know. I feel very sick.

LEONOR: Take this. Those drunkards are stretched out in there snoring like pigs. I stepped over them and they just grunted. Water is pouring in on them through the windows, and even that didn't stir them. (*Looks out the window.*) The others are laid out down there. They don't notice the rain. Just one got up and went home, like a drowned rat.

ADELA: Did they try to burn the house? Or was that a dream?

LEONOR: They burned the doors, but just a little. The rain put it all out.

ADELA: Where is the magician? Something happened to me, I don't remember very clearly. The magician, and that woman, dancing like a black . . . I think I'm very sick.

LEONOR (*gravely*): Don't worry. I remember.

ADELA: Put on a little music will you? Go on.

LEONOR: The radio!

(*Leonor tries to turn it on, plays with the dials.*)

It won't come on. The battery has burned out.

ADELA: But it was new.

LEONOR: It's dead.

ADELA: I'm sleepy. Look what an old pin cushion.

LEONOR: It's Sibila's.

ADELA: The pins in it are rusted. I want to go to bed. I'm cold. (*Cries.*) Leonor, Rafael isn't going to come. We had agreed to . . . to . . .

LEONOR: There, don't cry. I can go to town to look for a doctor and whatever we need.

(*Salustio enters, beaten and covered with mud.*)

Salustio, what a mess they made of you!

SALUSTIO: They didn't do anything to you, Missy?

LEONOR: No.

SALUSTIO: I cursed him, Missy. I cursed Salustio Pedro and he fell right on the ground.

ADELA: He must have fallen down drunk.

SALUSTIO: They beat me and everything, but I didn't let them burn the hacienda.

LEONOR: Did you put it out, Salustio?

SALUSTIO: Yes, Missy, I prayed to Saint Isidro to make it rain.

ADELA: Carry me to the bedroom.

SALUSTIO: And listen, Missy, that Sibila did terrible things. She stole a horse, Missy, and she ran away. I saw the devil hovering over her as she galloped away. There they go down the mountain, look.

LEONOR: She went away? (*Goes to the window.*) In this storm? I can't see a thing, it's very dark.

SALUSTIO: He was circling around her like a bat. I saw him. Her guardian angel was flying after her, too. It was white. The two of them were fighting in the air above her. And her on horseback, tearing down the mountainside.

ADELA: It was the ends of her rebozo flying behind her. Carry me to the bedroom.

LEONOR: Go on, and then come back. (*To Salustio*) Do you think the angel won?

SALUSTIO: I pray God not, Missy, so she'll get made over in hell, begging your pardon.

LEONOR: And she didn't finish feeding him.

ADELA: My God! I forgot that the bedroom is full of drunks.

SALUSTIO: They'll be sound asleep, now, Miss Adela. I'll go with you and throw them over the balcony. (*They exit.*)

LEONOR: They left you with me, little fellow. Come on. Finish your milk. There's nothing to see out there. (*One, two lightning flashes.*) There she goes! Down the mountain very fast. She must be soaked. It's raining so hard. And you, baby, you're not going to cry. You're going to live. You're going to be named Silvestre and you'll have lots of friends, and since you're a little lame, you're not going to be able to get away. We'll have to see Rafael to arrange about the estate. What a blow it will be to him that it won't be his. Little baby Silvestre. Silvestre. You're going to live. (*She sits down and sings to him.*)

For the rurru baby
Newborn to the cat,
Five tiny piglets
And a spider fat.

For the rurru baby,
For the rurru rong,
Sleep now, my baby,
While I sing this song.

(*Something has burst forth in the sack of corn. It has been rising slowly since the beginning of the scene. Now it can be seen clearly: it is stalks of corn, many of them, which stretch upward while Leonor sings and the curtain falls.*)

CURTAIN

The Intermediate Zone

An Auto Sacramental

This play was written under the continuing presence of Sor Juana Inés de la Cruz. For that reason, the author places it, humbly, at the feet of the humane spirit which created "Joseph's Staff," "The Martyr of the Sacrament," and "The Divine Narcissus."

Characters:

FIRST ASSISTANT

SECOND ASSISTANT

THE MAIDEN

THE CRITIC

THE LITTLE MAN

THE WOMAN

THE NAHUAL*

THE DEVIL

THE ANGEL

ANOTHER ANGEL, AND DEVILS

Cupola Twenty-Five of the Intermediate Zone.
Time elapses very relatively.

A circular glass cupola, its interior luminous. An enormous sky can be seen through the large glass panes, which are sustained in a metallic armature that rests upon a low wall about a half meter in height. At the left, downstage, a small door. On the same side, upstage, a large sliding door. At the right, an enormous panelboard covered with levers and electric switches. Next to it, a broad, flat-sided piece of metal furniture, a type of elaborately wired and insulated wardrobe in which a standing person can fit. Upstage, by the wall, a blue easy chair.

It is completely dark. In the silence a musical vibration is perceived. Dim vapors, illuminated by a blue light, move across stage rear behind the wall of glass.

---

* The Nahual is a figure deriving from Aztec mythology whose major characteristic is the ability to assume varying forms.

FIRST ASSISTANT: Intenser light.

(*The vapors begin to dissipate behind the panes and now, through them, we can distinguish a night sky, star studded, with drifting clouds.*)

Still more intense. Slowly, slowly.

(*The silhouettes of the two assistants are now discernible. The second one manipulates the electrical panel, which is emitting blue sparks. The sky begins to grow light.*)

Faster now, and begin to make the stars disappear.

(*The Second Assistant obeys. The sky becomes a paler blue and the stars begin to fade.*)

Faster with the light. Faster.

(*The sky is now pale blue, and only one star remains. The two assistants and the objects are vaguely distinguishable through a smooth bluish light.*)

That's far enough. Combining colors is more difficult. You'll practice it tomorrow. Give me the panel.

SECOND ASSISTANT: Did I handle it all right?

FIRST ASSISTANT: Very well. A small mistake in putting out the stars. But, in general, very well.

SECOND ASSISTANT: May I help you with the musical effects?

FIRST ASSISTANT: If you want to. But open the door in the back. I'm going to loose the fourth breeze.

SECOND ASSISTANT: That's the best!

FIRST ASSISTANT: Yes, let it in.

(*The First Assistant takes charge of the panel. He begins to light a pale rose in the sky, while the Second Assistant slides the door and a brighter light pervades the room. The assistants wear striped blue coveralls.*)

Hurry, if you want to be in charge of the music.

(*The Second Assistant returns to the panel and manages it. The music becomes more radiant. Sharper colors are staining the sky and the light is changing from blue to red.*)

SECOND ASSISTANT: May I put a little of the gold?

FIRST ASSISTANT: Yes. Correct the mauves and add a green fringe.

(*The sky undergoes the indicated changes. Then the music*

and color rise in tone and volume. The light, brilliant, rosy, illuminates the interior and makes the glass shine. There is a more intense note, then suddenly the music ceases and the Maiden stands profiled in the doorway. She is wearing white, her hair is loose, and she is carrying a lily in her hand. She is seen radiantly illuminated.)

MAIDEN: May I come in?

FIRST ASSISTANT: Yes, of course. But you've lost your way.

SECOND ASSISTANT (*in a low voice*): The Blessed Virgin!

FIRST ASSISTANT: No, not at all. She almost never comes.

MAIDEN: What is the way, then?

FIRST ASSISTANT (*steps out and points*): Take your right, that way. That brilliance radiates from the Hall of Judgement.

MAIDEN: But I've just come from there.

FIRST ASSISTANT: Didn't they open up for you?

MAIDEN: No.

FIRST ASSISTANT: Then you'll have to wait. In a little while the trumpets will sound. Didn't some angel point that out to you?

MAIDEN: Yes. I met the custodian of the doors. A golden angel. He told me I couldn't pass.

FIRST ASSISTANT: That you couldn't pass! But surely you're not a nonhuman ... or are you?

MAIDEN: He said I am. He showed me a list with my name. There will be four of us nonhumans arriving today.

FIRST ASSISTANT: Go on. I wouldn't have believed it. You a nonhuman. But, why?

MAIDEN: Down there in my home they said I was. "She's an angel," they said. But now you see that I'm not. (*Looks curiously around the room.*) Will you allow me to watch what you're doing?

FIRST ASSISTANT: If you like. We're dawning.

MAIDEN: You two? Dawning!

FIRST ASSISTANT: Yes. He's just learning.

SECOND ASSISTANT: But I don't do too badly. Look, how about that? I did those colors by myself, while you two were chatting.

MAIDEN (*entranced*): Dawning!

SECOND ASSISTANT: Would you like some musical effects?

FIRST ASSISTANT: It isn't quite time. But give a few, light ones.

MAIDEN (*very quietly*): Dawning!

(*The music begins in a murmur.*)

SECOND ASSISTANT: You see?

MAIDEN: Yes. I heard it down there, but in a different way. I heard it deep inside me.

FIRST ASSISTANT: Now everything is deep inside.

MAIDEN: It was on the hill. Down below, the bells were ringing for mass. I didn't want to go. Perhaps that's the reason they won't let me enter for the Judgement. I wanted to be part of everything. I wanted to dawn, too.

(*In the sky the blue of day is blending with the fading gold and light rose.*)

FIRST ASSISTANT: Why do you have that lily?

MAIDEN: They put it in my hands. For being a virgin, I guess. Did I do wrong to bring it?

FIRST ASSISTANT: No, but now it will never wither.

(*A strange figure appears in the door, a mixture of cubist painting, with variations on the figure of a man, and the sculpture of Picasso.*)

FIGURE: Good morning.

(*The three start.*)

MAIDEN: My God, what is that thing?

SECOND ASSISTANT: Another of the nonhumans. But on him you really notice it.

MAIDEN: I'll say you notice it!

FIRST ASSISTANT: Come in, sir ... or madam?

FIGURE (*indignant*): Sir, of course! Do I look like something else?

FIRST ASSISTANT: No, naturally. But you do look a little strange. Or haven't you seen yourself?

(*He opens the metallic wardrobe, which has a mirror on the inside of the door*).

FIGURE (*looks at himself*): It seems strange to you? It is a Carlos Mérida, with Mayan influences . . . although perhaps it is a

Tamayo . . . M-m-m, although perhaps it would be better to say that it is a . . .

FIRST ASSISTANT: The best thing is for you to step into the regenerator of figures, if you will.

(*He pushes him inside the wardrobe and closes it. Blue sparks and humming come out of the wiring and insulators. He opens the wardrobe. The Critic steps out. He has a broad forehead and is wearing thick spectacles. He is dressed in grey, with a bow tie.*)

MAIDEN: There, now you're more presentable. Perhaps they'll even allow you to enter for the Judgement.

CRITIC: For the Judgement! I got as far as the foot of the great staircase. A perfectly academic angel stopped me. One in the worst taste. He sent me here, saying that I am one of the four nonhumans for today. Would someone like to explain this to me?

FIRST ASSISTANT: It will be a little disagreeable for you all, I'm afraid. We in this cupola are in charge of dusks and things like that. Furthermore, we receive the nonhumans while they're awaiting the moment of . . .

(*As he is speaking, a fat little man appears in the door, dressed in black. He looks at all of them, hesitates, and finally, still outside, walks toward the small door at the left. He knocks. The Second Assistant opens the door. He enters.*)

SECOND ASSISTANT: Why didn't you come in the other door?

LITTLE MAN: I didn't know whether it was permitted. I thought that this was more . . . discrete. (*To everyone*) Good morning.

MAIDEN: And are you another nonhuman?

LITTLE MAN: I think so. That's what a very pretty angel I met told me.

CRITIC: Pretty! Bah! It looked like the angel on a fifteen-year-old's birthday cake. Sweet little colors, a so smooth style, what hideous taste! I have always said that angels . . .

(*They hear inhuman screams approaching and a terrible angel, tall, carrying a sword of fire in his hand, enters carrying a woman under his arm. She screams and they struggle.*)

FIRST ASSISTANT (*to the Critic*): You were saying?

CRITIC: No. Nothing.

(*The angel puts the Woman on the floor and exits. The Woman has a tangled mane of hair. Her arms terminate in feline claws. She is dressed in skins, and her face is a mixture of human and feline characteristics. She does not speak. Incessantly she emits a kind of inarticulate, sobbing roar.*)

SECOND ASSISTANT: To the regenerator, right?

FIRST ASSISTANT: Right. Help me.

(*The Woman has been on the floor like a bundle since the angel left her there. They pick her up and carry her to the regenerator of figures. They close it. The same business of the blue sparks. They open the wardrobe, and a small woman, wearing a sweater, steps out. She looks all around, stunned, and breaks into inconsolable sobs. The Maiden goes to her side.*)

MAIDEN: Come, woman, don't cry like that. It makes me feel funny.

LITTLE MAN: What's the matter with her?

MAIDEN (*after looking in her eyes*): She's in love.

CRITIC: And she's crying about that! (*Laughs lightly.*)

(*The Second Assistant and the Maiden look at him, wanting to strike him down with a glance. Then the two women sit down, upstage. Trumpets sound in the distance.*)

LITTLE MAN: Are they calling us to eat?

SECOND ASSISTANT: They are calling you for the Judgement!

LITTLE MAN: Oh, I'm sorry.

CRITIC: And what about us? Finish explaining. What will we do meanwhile? We ought to be judged. We have rights.

FIRST ASSISTANT: Why?

CRITIC: Man! Well, because . . . At least, I think I am a child of God, aren't I?

SECOND ASSISTANT: I have my doubts.

CRITIC: Your doubts! Go on, because of that foolishness about my form, right? That happened for want of critical spirit. You remain on the most superficial level without penetrating the spirit of the work. I have spent my life interpreting, judging . . .

SECOND ASSISTANT: Well, judge yourself now.

LITTLE MAN (*brightly*): If we all made a petition asking to be judged, and we all signed it, and one of us carried it to . . . (*He runs out of words as he notices the faces of the others.*)

CRITIC: After all, what prevents their treating us like everyone else? Aren't we men?

FIRST ASSISTANT: You *were* men, at least, but that's the motive. For some reason or other, you ceased to be men. You were then an empty form.

CRITIC: I? Empty! Do you know that I have been called the most profound critic of my country?

FIRST ASSISTANT: That may be. But you've already seen how you arrived here. A monstrous form, that's what you had become.

CRITIC: An artistic form.

FIRST ASSISTANT: Not even that. A mishmash of artistic forms.

CRITIC: What insensitivity! Diversity of influences does not diminish the value of a work. Look at many beginners.

FIRST ASSISTANT: A work. But for a man the result is monstrous.

CRITIC: Many great men have been influenced by others, and their spirit has been a mixture.

FIRST ASSISTANT: Of diverse human presences, yes. But what you showed us was not this mélange. A finished work of art is not human, and so it cannot step out of the painting and walk among us. Michelangelo's creations in the middle of the street would be frightening; El Greco's figures, if they came in this door, would move us to laughter. It would be something like your entrance.

CRITIC: And what does this have to do with the Judgement?

FIRST ASSISTANT: I will try to make you understand. Man is potential. If for some reason he becomes stationary, he ceases to be.

CRITIC: To be *what*?

FIRST ASSISTANT: Potential, *and* man. He must choose between one thing and another, realizing the worthwhile, rejecting what is not worthwhile. He has a powerful weapon, pain, and he polishes it with the tears of his decisions. He has pleasure, too, for purifying his errors. Almost all pleasure originates in man's errors.

CRITIC: That's not true. Beauty gives pleasure, and it is not an error.

FIRST ASSISTANT: Beauty does not give pleasure, it causes emotion. True beauty is oppressive, it is pain in one's breast. Grace makes one tender, it stirs one. It is a small pain. And so with truth, and goodness, all are pain. Emotions are never pleasure. They are just that—emotions.

CRITIC: According to that, man does not have pleasure.

FIRST ASSISTANT: Yes. Lies and error give pleasure. Ugliness vibrates with pleasure, and evil above all—evil in general. Ask the Devil. He has an enormous catalogue of pleasures to which man can give himself without ceasing to be a man. He can reject them, though, and choose the heroic path and become more than a man. Or he can oscillate between one pole and the other, although then he pays for his doubt with anguish, and until Judgement Day he does not know which weighs more in his work.

CRITIC: These are all the ways, I think. I don't see how we have ceased to be men.

FIRST ASSISTANT: The individual can remain in a spiritual intermediate zone.

LITTLE MAN: Like this?

FIRST ASSISTANT: More or less. Man can close his ears to his vocation for something worthy, or something unworthy. He can live between two worlds. He can do evil or good incidentally, unconsciously, like a weak little animal. Then he is lost. He has ceased to be a man.

LITTLE MAN: He becomes . . . something else?

FIRST ASSISTANT: He ceases to be a human being, I mean. He is perfectly nonhuman; he is an unliving thing. And he can no longer be judged. Judgement, I have already told you, is not for the shadows of the Intermediate Zone.

CRITIC: That is to say that we were not men?

FIRST ASSISTANT: Not you nor many like you. You had a vocation and you avoided it. You rejected it completely, or you accepted it only in part—in idea, perhaps, but without any live emotion. Did you ever feel anything, once?

CRITIC: As little as possible, and only at the beginning. Emotion inhibits lucidity. It is necessary to think, not feel. For a critic it is fatal to let emotion invade him at every step.

FIRST ASSISTANT: Well, now you see why you're here.

CRITIC: Then we ought to surrender ourselves to emotion, like her. (*He points to the Woman.*)

FIRST ASSISTANT: To pure and lucid emotion, not to the instincts. To several emotions, not to one. A man should be the solar spectrum, not a single color.

CRITIC: That's all very complicated, and very boring. How is that woman getting along?

MAIDEN: She's calmer now.

LITTLE MAN: Her face is frightening.

MAIDEN: What can we do for her?

FIRST ASSISTANT: Nothing right now. An angel will come at nightfall, to see if there's anything redeemable in you, a trace of humanity that will let you go to Judgement.

MAIDEN: What little humanity I had ended when I arrived here. Since then, I have been seeping into everything around me. The horizon, the sound of a tree, all serene, gentle. Even into the storm, where everything seems to be chaos. What is it? Drops of water that fall from above, fall. They touch, and the earth drinks them. Sometimes, a vivid light, and a jubilant crash. If this is all there is, why is it necessary to be human?

FIRST ASSISTANT: It isn't all. Man was put on earth to feel everything. Light, flowers, the simple things too, even though they're not human. But you filled yourself with that only, Maiden. You were converted into that, a kind of gentle flower. And only men and women can be judged. When have you ever heard of their judging a cactus, or a bull?

CRITIC: And what about the arts? Can't a man devote himself to them?

FIRST ASSISTANT: Yes. If you had created something, a puppet, or a child, it would be different.

CRITIC: But I have a child.

FIRST ASSISTANT: I said create, not engender. And the same thing is true in art. Perhaps once you felt the desire to do something?

CRITIC: Yes.

FIRST ASSISTANT: Why didn't you do it?

CRITIC: I had enough lucidity to see that I wouldn't be a genius. And art doesn't provide a living. And the family . . . and above all, since I was young I have had a lot of critical sense, and the first thing I criticized was myself.

FIRST ASSISTANT: And you killed yourself as a man. Criticism freezes the blood if the warmth of creation is lacking.

CRITIC: God criticized his work. "And He saw that it was good."

FIRST ASSISTANT: First he had done it, hadn't he?

(*Trumpets sound. In the distance a chorus is entoning a miserere.*)

SECOND ASSISTANT: They are opening the doors.

LITTLE MAN: May we go and see?

FIRST ASSISTANT: If you wish. But you must be here when the Angel comes.

MAIDEN: You said he would come at nightfall.

FIRST ASSISTANT: Yes, but time here is very different. They manage it in Cupola Three, which is far below us. They govern us with a rhythm that we vary according to our taste, although it has its rules. When we create the dark, the Devil will come. All of you must be here. He does not have the right to take anyone away, but if anyone prefers to go with him . . .

CRITIC: The Devil. How interesting. What's his style?

SECOND ASSISTANT: Diabolical, in general.

CRITIC: I mean what artistic style?

FIRST ASSISTANT: Several, the most diverse.

CRITIC: Ooh.

FIRST ASSISTANT: What? Don't you like that?

CRITIC: It's just that I thought that one might come like an Orozco. I would prefer a popular style. We would all prefer that, wouldn't we?

FIRST ASSISTANT: I'll tell him that.

CRITIC: Meanwhile, I'm going to watch the Judgement. Aren't you coming? (*He exits.*)

LITTLE MAN: Am I permitted to go?

SECOND ASSISTANT: Go on, man, go on.

LITTLE MAN: There isn't any danger, is there?

SECOND ASSISTANT: No. What would there be?

LITTLE MAN: But I won't get lost?

SECOND ASSISTANT (*resigned*): I'll go with you. (*The Second Assistant and the Little Man exit.*)

FIRST ASSISTANT: Don't you want to see the Hall of Judgement while it's open?

MAIDEN: What for? I'd like to know what's going to become of us. Could the Devil take us away?

FIRST ASSISTANT: Only if you want to go with him.

MAIDEN: Of course I don't. But if he doesn't take us, and if we aren't judged, then what?

FIRST ASSISTANT: It would be a matter of wandering for a while in empty space, and dissolving little by little into nothingness. (*The three are silent. The trumpet sounds in the distance.*)

WOMAN (*suddenly, in a harsh and thoughtful tone*): And I'll never see him again? Never?

FIRST ASSISTANT: Someone from there? No.

WOMAN: Then I'll go with the Devil.

MAIDEN: No! What are you saying?

WOMAN: I need to see him again. I need the desire to see him again! I need to see him again!

MAIDEN: You can see him from here, follow him in your mind while you are dissolving, imagine that you are caressing him.

WOMAN: I don't want to caress him. I want to tear him to pieces. How I detest him! I don't even know what he was like. I was a woman like any other. I met him and I didn't realize it, but he was in me, always deeper and deeper inside me. One day I turned my eyes inward and I saw him shining there. Then I ceased to live for myself. I lived for him. And then I lived no longer. How horrible it was, how horrible! Always burning, consuming everything human in me. It was not only physical desire; it was all the desires represented in him. I only had to see him to be calm and clean, or one of his gestures was enough to set me on fire. I couldn't stand any more. I lost everything human. I was no longer a woman, I was a walking sore, a beast, anything except a woman. I wanted to tear him to pieces. I threw myself on him, to wound him with teeth and nails. But when I touched him, I could do nothing. I kissed him and leaped from the balcony. I don't know why. Perhaps because I couldn't hurt him and had to hurt myself. And now I haven't seen him. I need to see him! I'm burning all over because I haven't seen him. I need to see him! Anything is preferable to his absence! If the Devil will allow me to see him only once, I will go with the Devil. Hell will be nothing. I need to see him, see him, see him! (*She falls on the sofa, writhing.*)

FIRST ASSISTANT (*in a low voice*): Better leave her. You can't help her in any way. Do you want to see the Hall of Judgement?

MAIDEN: Let's go. Can we leave all this?

FIRST ASSISTANT: Yes. Let me arrange for the midday music to play by itself. (*Moves some levers and comes back with her. They are ready to exit.*)

MAIDEN: Have you noticed what friends we've become?

(*They exit.*)

(*The Woman is gradually becoming calmer. The light is growing more intense and the warm music of midday is playing. It is slow, heavy, and brilliant, and it forces the woman to rise as if possessed. She sees the Maiden's lily and tears it to pieces. She looks around her and twists and turns frenetically. She falls to the floor, completely destroyed. The music soars and the lights rise in intensity. Through the panes on the right appears a face with both human and animal characteristics: the Nahual's. He crouches and turns, so that through the glass one can see him pass by, cautiously. His body is a mixture of coyote and man. He has a long tail. He is wearing only tight, red trunks. With a leap he plants himself in the doorway and laughs out loud. The Woman rises to look at him, startled. They stand face to face for a moment.*)

WOMAN: Are you . . . the Devil?

NAHUAL: No. (*When he speaks, his voice is at times satanic, at times childishly ingenuous.*)

WOMAN: You are . . . a man?

NAHUAL: No.

WOMAN: Are you a nonhuman, like me?

NAHUAL: No.

WOMAN: What the devil are you, then?

NAHUAL (*loud laughter*): I won't tell you. (*He advances toward her and makes her retreat.*)

WOMAN: What do you want? Leave me in peace. Go away.

(*The Nahual follows her covetously. It can be seen that his intentions are not the most decent. The Woman screams and begins to run. He follows her. She tries to get out the door and he places himself in the doorway. He pursues her again. The Woman screams and the Nahual laughs.*)

Maiden! Angels! Please, angels!

(*The chase continues until the two assistants run in. Then the Maiden. The assistants grab the Nahual. The Critic enters and looks at him with admiration.*)

CRITIC: What a curious mélange of pre-Columbian styles. Traces of the Teotihuacán, the Aztec . . .

NAHUAL: Mélange your grandmother.

SECOND ASSISTANT: What were you doing? You know you're not allowed to molest anyone here.

FIRST ASSISTANT (*after examining him*): But you're not a devil!

SECOND ASSISTANT: No? He's wearing devil's clothes.

NAHUAL: Yes. I took it off one I met.

FIRST ASSISTANT: What kind of thing are you?

NAHUAL: I am a nahual.

FIRST ASSISTANT: And what are you doing here?

SECOND ASSISTANT: He wasn't on the list of nonhumans. He must be human.

FIRST ASSISTANT: How could he be? How did you get here? You're the first one I've seen in all my life.

NAHUAL: It wasn't difficult to get here.

FIRST ASSISTANT: Didn't anyone tell you anything?

NAHUAL: Yes, the devil who owned these tights.

136

MAIDEN: They won't let you in looking like that. Take him to the regenerator.

NAHUAL: Don't you like my looks?

MAIDEN: Of course not. Although it's better than some. (*Looks at the Critic.*)

NAHUAL: I can change. I have some sixteen forms I can improvise, and if you'll tell me, I can take the one you want—a bat, a winged serpent, a pig with shoes, a dog with the head of a child. I have many forms.

MAIDEN: No. How horrible! You'd better stay as you are.

CRITIC: It would interest me to see those forms. If you want to show me some, I could study what influenced them and help you improve them.

NAHUAL: I'm not showing anything to *you*. Perhaps I'll turn into a vampire and bite you.

CRITIC: You savage. And please do not address me so familiarly.

NAHUAL: First a mélange, and now a savage. Do you know I've already taken a lot from you? (*He advances menacingly. The assistants hold him back.*)

FIRST ASSISTANT: Don't pay any attention to him. It would be better for you to go back to your land. You have nothing to do here.

NAHUAL: And do you think I want to stay? I've tried to find the road. And there's something here that bothers me. (*Coughs.*) Look at my throat. It hurts. (*Moans.*) It wasn't hurting before. Ah! (*Remorsefully, he opens his mouth and shows the Second Assistant, who looks inside.*)

SECOND ASSISTANT: You have something stuck there. Come over to the light. (*He looks, places his fingers in the mouth of the Nahual, and pulls out a crucifix.*) Look at that. Where did you swallow this?

NAHUAL: I don't know. Oh, it hurt me. (*He wipes his eyes and sits down, very sad.*) The boy I ate yesterday must have been carrying it.

FIRST ASSISTANT: That you ate yesterday?

NAHUAL: Yes. He was really tough. I think he wasn't really a boy. I was on my way after raping two maidens when I met him on the road. I started to play with him, and then I ate him. He must have done me some harm. That must be why I'm here.

MAIDEN: Or perhaps because of the crucifix in your throat. They're not for nahuals to swallow, are they?

SECOND ASSISTANT: Yes. A crucifix is enough to make a nahual fall into our zone.

(*The trumpets sound from the Hall of Judgement. Songs of hallelujah. The First Assistant goes to the panel and the light begins to turn crepuscular.*)

CRITIC: Why are they singing?

FIRST ASSISTANT: The Judgement is over.

CRITIC: I would have liked to see it. But that scandalous woman! And that . . . thing.

NAHUAL: I'll have you know I'm not a thing. I'm a nahual.

(*They look at each other defiantly. The Little Man enters.*)

LITTLE MAN: My crucifix. I didn't realize I had lost it. Many thanks.

MAIDEN: My goodness! So it was *you* he ate. (*She gives it to him, moving to one side, and the Little Man sees the Nahual. He gives a cry and steps back.*)

NAHUAL: So it was you. You're not much of a boy, you fat old man.

LITTLE MAN: How horrible! That monster! He chased me yesterday. I was coming from my aunt's house. He came out from among some trees. He dragged me over the stones, and bit me.

NAHUAL: I was playing with him.

LITTLE MAN: Get him out of here, don't let him come near me!

NAHUAL: I'm not going to do anything to you. Be quiet and stop shouting or I'll bite you.

(*The Little Man screams and starts to run away. The Critic stops him.*)

CRITIC: Calm down. Those gentlemen are taking care of him. Did you see the Judgement?

LITTLE MAN (*hugging the wall opposite the Nahual, on the other side of the stage*): Yes. Very pretty. Those who were singing were the blessed. The condemned were cursing in chorus, but it didn't sound so pretty. I saw the Devil at a distance. He said he was going to Cupola Twenty-Six.

138

SECOND ASSISTANT: That's the one next to ours. There they lock up the devils who do improper things.

LITTLE MAN: Yes. That's what he said. That he was going to free a devil who had been locked up for walking around naked.

(*The Nahual snorts with glee and leaps about. He shows his trunks to the Woman.*)

NAHUAL: Look, Woman, this is what the devil was wearing.

WOMAN: Let me alone.

NAHUAL: Are you angry with me? Only because I wanted to rape you? Be happy, come on. (*He takes her by the arm and tries to dance with her.*)

WOMAN: Let me alone, let me alone! (*She beats him and sobs, despairingly. She flees. The Little Man prudently has left the stage as soon as the Nahual began to leap about.*)

NAHUAL: What's the matter with her? I looked in her eyes and there was a fixed form in them—a man's. And she isn't a woman. She is something very different. You'd think that she was a female nahual, if it weren't for the fact there aren't any.

MAIDEN: She is in love.

NAHUAL: I know something about that. It's bad, isn't it?

MAIDEN: Who knows? If I had ever fallen in love I wouldn't be here. She fell in love too much and that's why she's here.

(*The Little Man enters, terrified.*)

LITTLE MAN: The Devil is coming this way! How ugly he is!

CRITIC: Yes? (*Looks out.*) Ah, good. A popular style.

MAIDEN: Thanks to God, the poor enamored creature will not go with him. Don't anyone say anything about her to him.

FIRST ASSISTANT: Maiden, I'm sorry, I must tell him about her.

MAIDEN: You wouldn't dare.

FIRST ASSISTANT: It is my duty. I can't do anything else. If you wanted to go with him and you weren't here, I would have to inform him. Naturally I detest doing it, but what can I do?

MAIDEN: You work for him then.

FIRST ASSISTANT: No. But you see how it is. I'm only an assistant in the Intermediate Zone, and I have many unavoidable duties.

(*The Second Assistant begins to turn the sky red. The solemn music of dusk is heard. The Devil enters. He silently examines each of them, one by one. The Nonhumans look at him with fear, the Nahual with cynicism. The Devil is black and white, tall, plump, with a big belly. He has a long, turned-up snout; his long mustache and his long hairy tail are blue. His horns are black and brilliant.)*

DEVIL: So it was you who took the clothes off one of my devils?

NAHUAL: Yes, it was me.

DEVIL (*to the First Assistant*): What thing is this?

FIRST ASSISTANT: A nahual.

DEVIL: How curious. I didn't think there were any of them left. And I didn't think they could end up here.

NAHUAL: Well, now you know.

DEVIL: A maiden in white. Do you know what's waiting for you?

MAIDEN: Yes.

DEVIL: Dissolving little by little, the same as any cloud. Nothing, finally.

MAIDEN: Yes.

DEVIL: You could go with me. I have practically nothing for you to do but I like you. I'll teach you a lot you don't know. You'll no longer be a page on which no one wanted to write. You'll have temptation, without having to resist it. It isn't so bad in hell. The wisdom you never possessed; the inquietude you have missed. Of course, some tortures. But you have to pay for everything. For you, heaven wouldn't be much better.

MAIDEN: No. You must have tempted me before. To struggle against you, yes, it pleases me. But to surrender myself to you, completely, for always—no. I prefer to dissolve little by little, anywhere at all.

DEVIL: It will be sad and full of anguish.

MAIDEN: I've always had a vague feeling of anguish about everything. I've come to love my anguish, it's so calm. It nourishes me. It's the only live thing there ever was in me. I'll stay.

DEVIL: As you wish. And you? A critic, aren't you?

CRITIC: Yes.

DEVIL: Do you like my style?

CRITIC: Yes, certainly.

DEVIL: I thought you would prefer something slightly more high-brow.

CRITIC: In paintings, yes. But here, in front of me, I prefer this. You know that art is one thing and reality another, that painting is not...

DEVIL: Yes, I know that. I can give you lessons, and then some. I don't know how you would be any help to me. We've never paid any attention to each other. We've never struggled and you've always been between two worlds. That can't be. You have to be for me or against me.

CRITIC: Yes, I see that now.

DEVIL: Yes, finally, you want to be with me. Let's go. You can no longer be against me.

CRITIC: I don't know. I beg you to wait till tomorrow. Perhaps I could be judged.

DEVIL: I never make deals, and I don't think the Judgement would do you any good. And you?

LITTLE MAN: Me? All right, sir. Thank you.

DEVIL: Do you also want them to judge you?

LITTLE MAN: If it were possible...

DEVIL: I don't think so. Amorphous matter, grease. If they judge you, you're probably going to end up with me anyway. Would that displease you?

LITTLE MAN (*very courteously*): No, of course not. I would be very pleased.

DEVIL: Well, once and for all, let's go.

LITTLE MAN: But I prefer... I mean... I didn't want...

DEVIL: Of course you want to. You're coming, aren't you?

LITTLE MAN: I don't know. The Judgement would be better.

DEVIL: But you already accepted. Here's one who wants to go with us! Because you do want to, don't you?

LITTLE MAN: Yes, but...

DEVIL: Good! Enter!

(*Small devils enter. They are blue and black, with little*

wings; they are wearing trunks like the Nahual's. They take the Little Man by the arms.)

Say good-by.

LITTLE MAN: Yes, sir. I'm very sorry, but, you see . . .

CRITIC: But, man, aren't you going to wait?

DEVIL (*to Little Man*): You don't have time, right?

LITTLE MAN: No, I don't think so.

MAIDEN: But don't be crazy. That's the Devil!

DEVIL: You prefer me to dissolving, don't you?

LITTLE MAN: Well, maybe so.

DEVIL: Take him away.

LITTLE MAN: Good-by . . . that is . . . I think that . . . the Devil with it.

(*The two devils exit, dragging him.*)

DEVIL (*to the Nahual*): You weren't on the list. But if you want you can come with me. You've never been human, so you can learn to be a devil. In a few centuries you can become a first class devil.

NAHUAL: A good devil.

DEVIL: No! A bad devil.

NAHUAL: Submissive to you, rigorously involved in my work.

DEVIL: Of course. Damning souls, torturing.

NAHUAL: It doesn't interest me. I'm free, do you understand?

DEVIL: Libertine.

NAHUAL: Yes. And I feel antipathy for you. You are your own slave. You can't do good even if you want to. *I* can. In other days, there were gods in my land. They were neither good nor bad. They had their principles, of course. They made it rain and they made the corn grow. They also loosed the locusts and the destructive sun. They liked sacrifices. But the angels arrived with their cross, and it was all over. Those gods fled and have never been seen again. It's so sad. Their temples exist only for types like him. (*He indicates the Critic.*) With notebook in hand they walk around taking notes without doing anything to revive the gods. "Marvelous! Great!" and that's it. But they don't give their blood for the poor dead ruins. There are some who do. They say they paint and they sculpt, but they do something more: they are men. They have immobile children, brightly colored. They give life to the dead. In a different form, but they give it life. And they fight against you, against everything. But they are not free; they are men. I don't want to be a devil *or* a man. I live well the way I am, free, running like the lightning, like the ancient gods, free from any standards but my own. So . . . leave me alone. Don't bother.

DEVIL: Liberty, libertine. Yes, if that's what you like. But you can't be like that here. The Intermediate Zone is narrow. You must go to one side or the other, or dissolve like a cloud, with no remaining trace. You can't be judged—you don't want to come with me. You go over there. Someone is missing, isn't there? A woman.

FIRST ASSISTANT: Yes.

DEVIL: Will you please call her?

MAIDEN: I will go for her.

SECOND ASSISTANT: You won't know the way. We'll go together. (*They exit.*)

CRITIC: Now there are no ladies, I must clear something up. I have committed a number of sins, and I need to be judged. Of course, I repent them.

DEVIL (*bursts out laughing*): Sins! Repentance! Have you felt that?

CRITIC: No. But I'm thinking about it now.

DEVIL: You weren't human enough even to sin. A human suffers for his sins. *You* committed them tranquilly and impassively. Without pleasure, or the pain of doing evil, there can be no man.

NAHUAL: Oh, yeah? You wouldn't say that I'm a man, but I've enjoyed myself many times doing evil.

FIRST ASSISTANT: You will suffer, Nahual, you will suffer.

NAHUAL: But I've also had pleasure from doing good.

CRITIC: How do you know that the evil was evil and the good, good? I know because I'm a critic, but it isn't a bit easy. Values are not easy to distinguish.

NAHUAL: I feel immediately the value of everything. What I like— is good.

CRITIC: No, it's something much more complex. Beauty, ugliness, good, evil can be equally enjoyed; you said so earlier. So, what is the difference?

NAHUAL: Whether I like it or not.

CRITIC: You don't know how to think.

NAHUAL: I don't miss it. And now you've bored me, you know that?

CRITIC: You are incapable of rational thought. A lively emotion wouldn't do a thing for you. Couldn't *I* prepare to be a devil instead of him?

DEVIL: No, certainly not. How amusing that would be! You, a devil!

CRITIC: I'm worth more than he is, aren't I?

NAHUAL: More than me! (*The Nahual lays his paw on him, but the First Assistant intervenes.*)

FIRST ASSISTANT: No, Nahual! No fighting here.

(*The Woman enters, running; then the Maiden and the Second Assistant.*)

WOMAN: You are the Devil. Were you looking for me?

DEVIL: Go on. A wild little beast with nothing human about her.

WOMAN: Nothing human.

DEVIL: Do you know you have only two choices?

WOMAN: I only know that I love him. I need to see him. If you can show him to me, even if only for an instant, I'll go with you.

DEVIL: I can.

WOMAN: Well, take me wherever you want.

DEVIL: All right. Come here! (*Another group of devils enters.*) I'll show him to you there. Come on, Woman. You'll see him for a moment before you enter.

MAIDEN: Wait, please, it isn't worth it, I tell you. I'm a woman like you. Surrender yourself to the Devil? What for? Your lover will come here someday. Wait for him, and don't renounce everything.

WOMAN: That's what *you* tell me, you who prefer to dissolve. What do you know! Don't you see that I'm burning? Everything is red. I need to see him, nothing else matters to me. Let's go, Devil.

NAHUAL: Wait. What's this all about? Why do you want to see him?

144

WOMAN: Because I want to.

NAHUAL: Is he that fixed image behind your eyes?

WOMAN: He *is* that fixed image.

NAHUAL: Would it be enough for you to see him?

WOMAN: To see him, at any cost.

NAHUAL: Look in my eyes. You know, I can transform myself. Being an illusion is better even than reality. Look in my eyes, Woman, so I can copy the image. Keep looking, hard. (*The Nahual steps back. He gives two quick turns and suddenly is transformed. He is now a man, with a drab suit and vague features.*) Is this what you wanted?

WOMAN: You! You!

NAHUAL: It is I, you wild beast. Why are you this thing I cannot recognize? I saw a cool stream in your depths that has been dried up among the melting stones of your lust. Let it flow again. Forget the boiling that scalds you. The Devil? Why? Cast him away from you. Come, look at me. Look at me and refresh yourself. Burn no more, so that I may love you.

(*The Woman looks at him thirstily. She drinks him with her eyes, she is overwhelmed. The man returns to his nahual form. The Woman is motionless. Then, she begins to cry, not great sobs, but calmly*)

MAIDEN: You've saved her! You've saved her! Do you see? (*To the Devil*) Now she won't go with you.

DEVIL: I see it. She wouldn't have done me any good anyway. Let's go. (*Exits with his devils.*)

(*The sky has been turning paler. Now a star is visible.*)

MAIDEN (*looks at the Nahual, moved*): You are admirable, do you know that?

NAHUAL: Yes, I know.

MAIDEN: As I dissolve, I will think how you are the last living, admirable thing I have seen.

NAHUAL: That will be good. I don't know whether I'm going to dissolve, but I'm going to think of *you*.

CRITIC: That transformation of yours wasn't bad, really!

NAHUAL (*imitating him*): That transformation of yours wasn't bad.

CRITIC: Go on, just because you did one little thing, you want me to admire you. You're not bad, but I don't intend to fall apart praising you.

NAHUAL: I don't care whether you praise me or not. I'd rather you shut up. Your cold, slobbering voice irritates me. I know I did well. Didn't you see her? That's the opinion that matters to me.

CRITIC: Some opinion! A dummy you'd made would have had the same effect. I can be impartial.

NAHUAL: You can't be anything. Not even the Devil wanted you.

CRITIC: Blind man. So proud of your little transformation that you don't see the defects you could eliminate. I thought maybe you were worth something because you have a dash of ingenuity. But when you do something really impressive, I'll let you know.

NAHUAL: Something impressive? Would you like the two of us to do something impressive? (*He approaches the Critic menacingly.*)

CRITIC: What do you mean? Don't come near me. Don't look at me with a face like that. As if you'd like to eat me up. No. Let go, let go. (*The Critic breaks into a run and the Nahual follows him. They exit one after the other. Outside, the Critic screams.*) No, leave me alone, what kind of game is this! Stop following me! Don't!

MAIDEN: He won't hurt him?

FIRST ASSISTANT: I don't think so. It's just a game.

(*The Woman sighs and, at last, moves. She looks about. She runs her hand over her face. She barely murmurs.*)

WOMAN: So alone. God, I'm so alone.

MAIDEN: Do you feel better now?

WOMAN: I'm cold. It's almost night.

MAIDEN: Come, sit down by me. Don't think about anything. Rest.

WOMAN: Let me think. It's so long since I've thought. I'm so tired. I saw him, you know? I hadn't seen him for so long. I had him right in front of me, but I didn't see him. It was the thirst, it was horrible, and he said nothing to cool me off. I burned more. Perhaps he has suffered as much as I.

MAIDEN: You no longer want to see him?

WOMAN: What for? I didn't know how to keep him. I would like him to think a little about me. Do you think he will?

MAIDEN: I know he will. Cry some more. It's good for you.

WOMAN: I don't want to cry any more. Do you hear the music?

SECOND ASSISTANT: It's the night music. Now I'm going to loose the first breeze.

(*There are several stars in the sky. It is still pale. The light is indecisive, blue.*)

FIRST ASSISTANT: Prepare the moon. It has to come out in a minute.

(*The Nahual, satisfied, gnawing a femur, enters through the door. He carries a skull in his other hand.*)

(*First Assistant, frightened*) What's that you're carrying? What have you done?

NAHUAL: I ate him.

FIRST ASSISTANT: You ate him!

SECOND ASSISTANT: What! But you couldn't have done it.

NAHUAL: Yes, I could. But he doesn't agree with me very well.

(*He sits on the floor, gnawing his bone.*)

SECOND ASSISTANT: And now what? What will the Angel say to us when he comes?

FIRST ASSISTANT: I don't know.

SECOND ASSISTANT: It's the most frightening thing that's ever happened here. What shall we do?

FIRST ASSISTANT: What can we do now? I don't think they would have received him anyway.

SECOND ASSISTANT: Do you realize what you've done, Nahual?

NAHUAL: Yes. Whether he dissolves in the air or I eat him, what difference does it make?

MAIDEN: Don't scold him. He's never been a human. And he isn't bad.

SECOND ASSISTANT: No, nor good. So what do we do now?

FIRST ASSISTANT: Don't worry. I'm responsible. And I don't think it will be too serious.

(*The Nahual has finished gnawing the bone. With his fingers and his teeth he cuts it here, makes a hole there, and improvises a flute. He begins playing a sweet, strange tune.*)

SECOND ASSISTANT: And now he's playing the flute!

FIRST ASSISTANT: Leave him alone. There's nothing to be done. We'll see what the Angel says. The moon! You should have brought it out a while ago. Hurry, make it darker, much darker.

(*Startled, the Second Assistant takes charge of the levers. All at once the sky is dark. It is filled with stars. The flute sounds in the darkness.*)

No, let me take care of it. You must bring out the moon rapidly, but in an orderly way. A little bit first, you see? (*The light of the moon, entering rear, begins to illuminate the scene.*) The music of high night, let it loose. (*The music of high night and of the flute blend together.*) More moon now, more.

(*Suddenly the flute is still. There are moans.*)

MAIDEN: What's the matter? Someone is groaning.

WOMAN: It's the Nahual. What's the matter with him?

SECOND ASSISTANT: I'm glad. He must have indigestion.

WOMAN: Poor thing. Shine your light on him. After all, he did me a good turn.

(*The vivid moonlight illuminates the Nahual stretched out on the ground. He is very changed. He has no tail, and his animal features have disappeared.*)

FIRST ASSISTANT: But he's a man!

(*Everyone kneels around him. He moans and seizes the Maiden.*)

NAHUAL: I'm afraid.

MAIDEN: Don't cry. What's happened to you?

NAHUAL: I don't know. He wasn't good for me. I shouldn't have eaten him. It's worse than green apples.

WOMAN: He's suffering. He's a man! I'm going to cry for you, poor thing. Why did you make yourself a man?

(*The music swells. The moon becomes much more brilliant. In the door an angel is outlined against the stars.*)

ANGEL: You made night late.

FIRST ASSISTANT: That's true. Forgive me. There has been a lot going on.

ANGEL: Are these the nonhumans?

FIRST ASSISTANT: Yes. These aren't all. The Devil took one away. The Nahual ate another. Heaven knows how the Nahual got here.

ANGEL: The Nahual?

FIRST ASSISTANT: Look at him. I don't understand. He's turned into a man on us.

ANGEL (*approaches and looks at him*): Get up. Where are you?

NEW MAN: Let me hide myself. I'm afraid and ashamed. Don't you see? I'm almost naked.

ANGEL: Take this part of my robe. The clothes of the Devil are little covering for a man. (*He takes off his cape and gives it to him. The New Man covers himself.*)

NEW MAN: A man? I can't be a man. What will become of me?

ANGEL: You can't stay here, and you can't be judged. You have to return to earth. You will live with pain all the days of your life. You will produce thorns and thistles, and you will eat the grass of the field. You are a man because you have opened your eyes and you know at last the value of your acts. You are no more an amoral force, but a poor being who was taken from the earth and who will return to the earth in order to learn to bless your human condition.

NEW MAN: It's very sad to be a man.

ANGEL: Yes, but it is very noble, because you were created in the image of Someone. You must struggle to preserve your sacred condition. You must live, and inevitably you will know evil. Weep if it turns you from your way, but turn again to struggle with it, for if you surrender you will be lost.

NEW MAN: I don't know if I can do it, but perhaps I will be able to avoid evil.

ANGEL: No. If you only avoid it and maintain yourself in an intermediate zone, you will be still more lost, because you will have deprived yourself of everything, even your human condition. Everything negative is evil, falsehood, ugliness, injustice, evil itself. To struggle against all that must be your life.

NEW MAN: But won't I be able to make my changes any more?

ANGEL: Yes, you will, although in a different way. You can create them with words, with sounds, with action itself. You can mold them with your hands from the same clay of which you were molded. Go now. One like me is going to accompany you. But a devil will go with you too, always. You must decide for yourself between one or the other. You can doubt at times, but don't destroy them both, don't ever do that. (*Kisses him on the forehead.*) Go, to suffer, but also to be lord over the fishes of the sea, and the birds of the heavens, and over all the beasts that move upon the land.

(*The New Man looks at everyone. He caresses the hair of the Woman, kisses the Maiden. From the door he waves to the two assistants, while the first breeze moves his cape.*)

NEW MAN: God be with you . . . That is, God be with me. (*He exits into the night.*)

ANGEL: And you, Woman? Why are you crying?

WOMAN: I don't know. Perhaps because its nighttime and I'm very lonely. I haven't been worthy of going to Judgement, but let me cry a while in your arms. Then I'll be able to sleep in peace.

ANGEL: Cry in my arms if you want. But you are different now, and you must go to the Great Hall before the dawn of another day.

WOMAN: Are you going to judge me?

ANGEL: Not I. Another who is just and terrible is going to judge you, but he knows how to forgive. Aren't you cold, Maiden?

MAIDEN: No. I feel a calm tenderness. I am alone, but I think that it doesn't matter to me. You frighten me a little, too, and I don't want to come close to you. I think I am beyond help. (*The Angel is still. He caresses her hair.*)

ANGEL: Come, Woman. (*He starts toward the exits, with his arm around the Woman.*)

MAIDEN: Wait. (*They stop.*) Don't you want to give me a kiss, too? (*The Angel kisses her on the forehead. The Woman and she embrace.*)

WOMAN: God be with you.

MAIDEN: Forever.

(*The Angel and the Woman exit. There is a silence in which the music sounds softly.*)

FIRST ASSISTANT: Wouldn't you like to sleep a little? We're going to extinguish the moon now.

MAIDEN: So soon?

FIRST ASSISTANT: Time doesn't count here as it does in other places. I've already told you that.

MAIDEN: Will I still have enough time?

FIRST ASSISTANT: Enough?

MAIDEN: Yes, you know. Before ending like the clouds: white spume, a few puffs, then nothing.

FIRST ASSISTANT: I told you that our time is different. Everything must come, finally, but you still have several dawns left.

MAIDEN: Dawns. Will you let me help you a little?

FIRST ASSISTANT: Yes. We will make dawn together.

MAIDEN: Who are you? You aren't an angel.

FIRST ASSISTANT: No.

MAIDEN: Then?

FIRST ASSISTANT: You'll realize, little by little, while you're here.

(*The moon begins to darken.*)

MAIDEN: Now I'm cold.

SECOND ASSISTANT: We have loosed the second breeze. It's late.

(*The moon is almost gone. The night music is more intense.*)

MAIDEN: There's hardly any moon.

FIRST ASSISTANT: But there are still some stars. Do you see? There are a lot. And it will take them a long time to go out before tomorrow comes.

(*The cupola is dark. In the rear one can make out the sky, peopled with bright, nonhuman stars.*)

SLOWLY, THE CURTAIN FALLS.

The Clockmaker from Córdoba

A Play in Two Acts

Characters:

MARTÍN GAMA, CLOCKMAKER

CASILDA, HIS WIFE

DIEGO DOMÍNGUEZ, HIS BROTHER-IN-LAW

ISIDORA, DIEGO'S WIFE

NUÑO NÚÑEZ, A FRIEND OF MARTÍN'S

ALONSO PECH, SERVING BOY IN THE INN OF THE RAINS

THE JUSTICE

THE SCRIBE

DON LEANDRO PENELLA DE HITA, MAGISTRATE

ELVIRA CENTENO, A WIDOW

HER AUNT GALATEA

SEÑOR SALCEDO

MARFISA, A NEIGHBOR

LISARDO, A SHEPHERD

A PRETTY WOMAN

THE EXECUTIONER

HIS HELPER

AN OFFICIAL

TWO BLIND PEOPLE, A MAN AND WIFE

A CHILD, GUIDE TO THE BLIND COUPLE

CONSTABLES, AND CURIOUS BYSTANDERS

AND —SERAFINA

Córdoba and Orizaba, in the state of Veracruz, a number of years after the founding of Córdoba.

154

ACT ONE

1

THE BEDROOM OF DIEGO DOMÍNGUEZ

Diego is lying in bed, complaining. Very loud, the sound of four bells. Diego groans and moves. Isidora enters.

DIEGO: Why doesn't that idiot come?

ISIDORA: He's waiting for his clock to strike three.

DIEGO: And Casilda?

ISIDORA: She's helping him.

DIEGO: God knows why. Is that damned bell going to keep ringing?

ISIDORA: She says it will all be over soon.

DIEGO: For me! I shouldn't have paid any attention to you. I should have put Casilda in a convent.

ISIDORA: It was much more expensive: the dowry, charities . . .

DIEGO: More expensive! The dowry for the convent would have been paid just once. And how much is this hellish business costing us? As a husband, God is much cheaper than a clockmaker.

ISIDORA: Your sister didn't want to become a nun.

DIEGO: At this point, I'd make them both nuns—dowry and all.

(*The bell strikes stentorianly four times.*)

And that damned nuisance goes on! Wasn't he waiting for it to strike three?

ISIDORA: Yes.

DIEGO: I heard four.

ISIDORA: That always happens.

DIEGO: I don't see when they're going to get away to Orizaba.

ISIDORA: Did you tell them?

DIEGO: No.

ISIDORA: They won't want to.

DIEGO: Why not?

ISIDORA: He has his clients here.

DIEGO: What clients?

ISIDORA: I don't know. But Martín puts on airs. He's not going to want to be a porter.

DIEGO: I have to buy the buildings first. Then whether or not they want to won't be the question. He can have his clocks there in the porter's quarters, and ring his bells all he wants.

(*Casilda enters.*)

CASILDA: Diego.

DIEGO: Why doesn't your husband come?

CASILDA: A client came in . . .

DIEGO: Glorious! Let him sell something right away, I'll wait for him.

CASILDA: But . . . she's come for her money.

DIEGO: What money!

CASILDA: She bought a sundial, and we've had cloudy weather for two weeks.

DIEGO: And he's going to return her money?

CASILDA: She's the wife of the Justice.

DIEGO: Don't return anything. Let your husband take a lantern and walk around the dial. This isn't a time for returning anything.

CASILDA: Diego, we don't have the money and we thought you would . . .

DIEGO: Me, always me!

(*The great bell sounds three times.*)

CASILDA: Praise God! (*She runs to the door.*) Did you get it fixed, Martín?

MARTÍN (*offstage*): No, it should have struck five.

DIEGO: Give the woman an hourglass. No money.

CASILDA: We gave her one before, but the air is damp. The sand wouldn't run.

DIEGO: Well, give her a clock with a pendulum.

CASILDA: They're more expensive.

DIEGO: The most expensive thing of all is money! Leave me alone. (*Shouts.*) And I want to speak with your husband!

(*Casilda exits.*)

He is a prophet in business matters; he sells sun dials during cloudy weather, hourglasses when it's damp. Why are you waiting to put on my mustard plasters? (*Isidora sets to work.*) Be careful, you're burning me! My poor knees!

ISIDORA: On your elbows, too?

DIEGO: Of course on my elbows! If Casilda were a nun, she'd be praying to God now to cure my rheumatism. Instead, what good to us are her damned husband and her?

ISIDORA: You'll see, they're going to help you now.

DIEGO: I should hope so. (*The bell sounds, furiously, many times.*) But get that thing quiet and bring him here. And finish putting the mustard plasters on my neck. Don't you understand? And have him shut up with those bells, I don't want to hear them any more!

(*Isidora runs, stupified, from one side to the other with the mustard plaster in her hands. The bells are quiet. Casilda comes in.*)

What hour was it striking?

CASILDA: One.

(*Martín enters. He is a well-built man with the eyes of a visionary.*)

MARTÍN (*flustered*): Forgive me. I know, the bells, the clock. But it won't make any more noise.

DIEGO: Did you fix it at last?

MARTÍN: The bell cracked.

DIEGO: How much have you spent on that contraption?

MARTÍN: Well . . . a great clock is always . . . a little expensive. But you earn a lot when it's sold!

DIEGO: How much have you spent?

MARTÍN: When it's finished, the Archbishop will beg me to sell it to him for the Cathedral in Mexico City. But I'm going to tell him no, it's for Córdoba. I'm going to talk to every one of the thirty founding fathers. They can each one contribute a little and pay me for the clock. Then our parish will have what no other one has. Well, what no other in New Spain has, because in the world . . . I'm not sure. There's a clock in Venice with two apostles. Or two Moors, I'm not sure. And I don't think they walk, they simply strike the bell with a mallet, on the hour.

DIEGO: When do you plan to sell yours?

MARTÍN: Just wait till I finish it. There are four evangelists and two archangels. They all play the bells! And the best of all is, when it strikes twelve, twelve skeletons with scythes come out in a parade. Really there are only three, but it looks like twelve, and each one makes five different movements.

DIEGO: Skeletons! That's horrible!

MARTÍN: Precisely. To recall that this life is borrowed and every instant is precious.

DIEGO: A precious spectacle that will be: twelve skeletons cavorting in the tower of the church. When there *is* a church, because they only began work on it a year ago. In about ten years you may have a tower for your clock.

MARTÍN: Ten years! Well, I'm going to be a while, too . . . Not that long, of course. I may sell it before they finish.

DIEGO: Martín, your clockmaking is a disaster.

MARTÍN: It isn't going as badly as you think.

DIEGO: If you set up business somewhere else, in another town . . . Who wants clocks here?

MARTÍN: I've just got started.

DIEGO: Yes, I know. You've been beginning for a year. But I want to talk about something else. Here I am, laid low with this damned rheumatism . . . Ow! Ow! I forget it for a moment, but I say the word and here comes the pain . . . Isidora! The mustard plaster, quick!

ISIDORA: Another?

DIEGO: Another!

ISIDORA: And where am I going to stick it on you? You already have more plasters than skin.

DIEGO: Are you going to do what I say?

ISIDORA: All right, all right. Where?

DIEGO: On my wrists. (*She obeys.*) I was saying that here I lie, and in Orizaba they're selling—at a very good price—a patio and buildings. Don Úrsulo Téllez is going to the Court and doesn't want to leave his properties abandoned, so he's selling them. I'm going to buy his buildings, but here I am, in my prison of pain . . . Ow-w-w-w!

ISIDORA: I know, I know. (*She puts another plaster on him.*)

DIEGO: You see? I can't move from here. Martín, are you capable of not getting lost on the road? Are you capable of not losing two hundred and fifty ounces of gold?

MARTÍN: Two hundred and fifty ounces? Of what? Did you say win them or lose them?

DIEGO: I said for the purchase! Haven't you understood anything? I can't go. You must take this money to don Úrsulo. I'm going to lend you Serafina, my best mule. You must leave today. I'm going to give you one ounce for the journey. You won't have to spend even half that much, but there will probably be some taxes, or some gratuity. I'll expect the bills for everything. (*He groans.*) Listen how my bones creak. Crack! Crack! I wish my joints would mesh like gears, and see if that way . . .

MARTÍN: Joints that mesh. But of course, naturally. (*He starts to leave.*)

DIEGO: Where are you going?

MARTÍN: Oh, nowhere. It's just that . . . something occurred to me. (*He moves his arms and legs in various angular postures; he continues thinking and calculating. He exits rapidly. He looks in again.*) When everything is ready to go, let me know. (*He exits.*)

DIEGO: He's mad! He'll lose the money!

CASILDA: Why did you say something a little while ago about settling somewhere else?

DIEGO: I say whatever strikes my fancy. It's an idea of mine.

CASILDA: This is our parents' house. It's yours and it's mine.

DIEGO: What about it? Go on, prepare the saddlebags for that idiot. He ought to leave this very day.

(*Casilda is about to say something. She exits.*)

2
THE WORKSHOP

All the floor is covered with enormous wheels, springs, cords and pieces of some monumental clock. At right, Martin's masterpiece, half dismantled, from which a skeleton sadly peers. Bells, archangels, apostles. Martín is working on another skeleton.

MARTÍN: Here it could mesh, of course . . . And then each gesture . . . (*He works. A pretty woman enters.*)

WOMAN: Good morning.

MARTÍN (*abruptly*): Good morning. (*He sees her.*) Good morning. (*He smiles amiably as he continues to look at her.*)

WOMAN: I have this clock that doesn't work.

MARTÍN: Doesn't work?

WOMAN: No.

MARTÍN (*perplexed*): When did you buy it from us?

WOMAN: I didn't buy it here.

MARTÍN: Ah, that's good. I mean, do you want it repaired?

WOMAN: Yes, that's it.

MARTÍN: It isn't a bad clock. Although I have better ones. How is it possible that it isn't working? When you enter, all the clocks start ticking—like hearts beating. (*The woman titters.*) Casilda! Casilda! Bring a chair! Let's see, let me open it. It's a French clock.

WOMAN: My parents brought it to me from the Court.

MARTÍN: In Mexico City?

WOMAN: Madrid.

MARTÍN: I've never been to Madrid—yet. Perhaps in the coming year . . .

(*Casilda enters with a chair.*)

CASILDA: Here is the chair.

MARTÍN: What are you waiting for? It's for the señorita.

(*Casilda obeys. The woman sits down.*)

WOMAN: So you're going to go to Madrid?

MARTÍN: It will be necessary. When I finish this clock, everyone will be talking about it. Caravans will come here. And if they summon me from the Court . . .

(*Casilda looks at them, then exits.*)

WOMAN: With skeletons?

MARTÍN: Yes. On the hour. I'll show you! Such a shame, the bell doesn't ring because it's cracked.

(*He moves the hands toward the hour. The skeleton makes a few movements.*)

WOMAN (*laughs*): Oh, how amusing.

MARTÍN (*annoyed*): You don't get the full effect, because it's . . . only half completed. It's going to be solemn, impressive.

WOMAN: When will my clock be ready?

MARTÍN: Ah, your clock. (*He opens it.*) It's not much. Cleaning, changing the pin . . . adjusting . . . Will you come for it yourself?

WOMAN: I don't know.

MARTÍN: If you came for it yourself, you could have it very soon.

(*The woman titters. Casilda enters.*)

CASILDA: Martín . . .

MARTÍN: What do you want? I'm attending to this client.

CASILDA: Everything's ready.

MARTÍN: That right, the trip. (*To the woman*) I have some urgent business in Orizaba. That's the way it is in the profession, one is needed everywhere. I have to travel . . . In some cities a clock is never repaired until I arrive. Orizaba, for example. For two months now no one's known what time it is. That's why I'm going.

WOMAN (*titters*): How much is this going to cost?

MARTÍN: It's a simple job. It would be difficult, perhaps, for any other clockmaker, but . . . don't even talk about price. I'll tell you when you pick it up.

WOMAN: Tomorrow?

MARTÍN: Within a week. Because of my journey.

WOMAN: All right. Good-by.

MARTÍN: See you soon. A week.

(*She exits. Martín sees the look on Casilda's face.*)

Well, I have to be pleasant to the clients, don't I? Why are you looking at me like that? I was only joking. If she believed it, so much the better. If not . . .

CASILDA: I was just thinking.

MARTÍN: What?

CASILDA: How everyone who knows you sends girls, so you won't charge them anything.

MARTÍN: Who says I don't charge them anything? Who says so? Do you say that?

CASILDA: Martín, my brother wants us to go away.

MARTÍN: Where?

CASILDA: He's ill. The bells bother him.

MARTÍN: And . . . ?

CASILDA: Well, he says the house is small.

MARTÍN: So why doesn't *he* go? The house is as much ours as it is his.

CASILDA: I know, but . . . He's been supporting us, and he says . . . That is, Isidora told me . . . He wants us to go to Orizaba.

MARTÍN: To Orizaba? (*He thinks.*) It hadn't occurred to me, but . . . No, of course not, I . . . It's very small here, but . . . it has . . . We're *from* here, aren't we? And our clients . . . No. No, we aren't going.

CASILDA: He says he spends a lot on us. And that in those buildings he's going to buy . . . there's a porter's cottage . . .

MARTÍN: Do you and your brother think I'm going to become a porter? Who do you think you married?

CASILDA: I know, Martín.

MARTÍN: Do you know what the Master said about me?

CASILDA: I know.

MARTÍN: Do you know how many other girls I could have married?

CASILDA: I'm not saying . . .

MARTÍN: I'm going to speak to your brother. (*He starts to leave, determined. He stops.*) Well, I'll speak with him when I get back.

CASILDA: He says . . .

MARTÍN: *He* says! And what do *you* say? Nothing? You must be good for something—to spare me disputes with him, at least.

CASILDA: But you never say anything to him!

MARTÍN: Never! I should have married Francisca, that's what I should have done.

CASILDA: Why are you angry with me?

MARTÍN: I preferred you to all of them. Why? I don't know.

CASILDA: Because I didn't have another man's child—like Francisca.

MARTÍN: No one else's, *or* mine.

(*Casilda cries, and moves away.*)

All right, all right . . . I didn't say that to make you cry. Come here. I didn't love that Francisca!

CASILDA: Nor she you.

MARTÍN: And how do you know? What are you saying? Because of that business with Nuño? She took up with him out of spite, because I preferred you.

CASILDA: You didn't even know me when Nuño got her pregnant!

MARTÍN: What do *you* know? Don't talk nonsense. Let me work in peace! And dry those tears, you look like a fountain. The whole blessed day, tears and more tears. That's enough.

(*He turns to the skeleton and moves it aimlessly. Casilda blows her nose.*)

CASILDA: Everything's all ready—your saddlebags, the mule . . .

MARTÍN (*in a sad voice*): Good. I have to close things up here. Notify my clients that I'm away on a trip.

CASILDA: What clients? Yes, yes. I'll notify the clients.

(*They exit.*)

3*

A STEEP ROAD

Dusk. Shreds of fog. The murmur of insects. Martín enters, mounted on a mule. He stops.

MARTÍN: Don't heave so. This is the end of the climb. Going down

---

* After this play was published in Spanish, the author made two deletions in this scene, one of about seven lines, one of about four; they have also been made here. *Tr.*

will be easier than coming up. You see it? Those roofs and hills. They've already lighted the lights on the bridges. A little more and night will be overtaking us again. (*Truculently.*) The wanderer's night, Serafina, the traveler's night. Damp earth, your clay-heavy hooves, terrible cold, and many strange little noises beyond the circle painted by our fire. Night air, black as crushed charcoal. A traveler. This is traveling. I am a traveler. (*They move on. He sings.*)

> A colorful bird sang above me
> In the shade of the green lemon tree,
> His beak played among the branches,
> His tail stirred the flowers.
> Ah, yes, ah, no,
> Oh, I love you so.

(*He stops and dismounts.*) This is the end of the perils of the road. We were fortunate. No highway robbers, no wild beasts. Because there are tigers, you know. Well, wildcats—and two years ago don Lope was robbed and beaten on this very road. (*He sings.*) "A colorful bird sang . . ." Was it on this road? Yes, this road. And now, I'll dig into my saddlebags, and . . . . (*He searches.*) All gone? (*Sighs.*) A tiny piece of cheese, almost no bread . . . Well. (*Eats a few mouthfuls, then looks over the precipice.*) Deep, eh? (*He tosses some stones; they take a long while falling. A few more mouthfuls.*) And that's all. (*Of the food.*) Casilda ought to have realized that it's not a short journey. Or didn't she have any more? She should have demanded some from Isidora. She's silly. A rich silly woman is worse than a poor one. Casilda is silly. She has the house, she has . . . Well, maybe she isn't *very* rich, but . . . The dowry's all gone now. Bad business. Bad. And there are too many clockmakers in Orizaba. I won't go to Orizaba. The Master told me, "I have nothing else to teach you," and he said to the others, "You see Martín? Well, now he could teach me a few things." That's nice. Satisfying. (*He drinks.*) Casilda isn't so ugly. If she didn't have that mustache . . . (*Drinks.*) Why does Casilda always have to do what Diego wants? I don't believe we could have used up all our money. Diego, on the other hand . . . Two hundred and fifty ounces of gold! (*He jumps up, feels himself.*) Here it is. It's heavy. (*He removes a few leather pouches from his clothing and places them on the ground.*) If someone were following us . . . (*To Serafina*) You can't run worth a darn. I'd stand up to them! Or . . . I'm standing here, unaware, looking down . . . One push, and . . . (*He whistles sharply, then says soberly*) Look. Vultures. Some poor cow fell down there. (*Shakes his head, drinks.*) Buzzards. A bad sign. They say that the broth of vultures is good for rabies. (*Drinks, then throws a stone over the precipice.*) Oooh, if there were someone below! (*He leans over.*) No, how could there be? (*Laughs.*) If Nuño had been down there . . . (*Laughs.*) That damned lily-skinned . . . Things will never go well for him. He's an awful clockmaker. You'd be a better clockmaker than he is. And him running away because of . . . (*Drinks.*) Women are blind. What could Francisca have seen in him? The white skin, of course. Francisca . . . Nuño's going to come to a bad end, a very bad end. He'll be destitute, and close to death. Maybe he'll become a highway robber, an assassin . . . And they'll end up hanging him. (*Pleasing idea.*) I wouldn't like that, poor thing, hanging him . . . (*Laughs, imagining the scene.*) It would be the only way for people to know him for what he is. (*Drinks.*) You'll see, I'm going to finish that clock. Ah—when it strikes twelve . . . (*He moves like the skeletons.*) What a clock! (*He leaps and dances about.*) Martín Gama, you've had a lot to drink. (*Laughs.*) If my clock were in Mexico City, it might be striking as they put the rope around Nuño's neck. That would make him think. Poor thing. (*A bird sings.*) Well, let's go. (*He mounts. The mule begins to move. He fumbles in his clothes, terrified. He jumps down. He picks up the leather bags and ties them on.*) Martín, you're an imbecile, that's what you are. (*He drinks, and mounts the mule. He sings dejectedly.*) "A colorful bird sang above me, in the shade . . ." Giddap, you stupid animal! You stinking mule! Giddap! (*He exits.*)

4
ORIZABA. THE INN OF THE RAINS

The serving boy, Alonzo, dozing. A man in a corner playing a guitar. Two or three tables. At one, Nuño and two men are gambling.

NUÑO: Seven and a half!

FIRST MAN: Son of a bitch! (*He throws down his cards and looks at the other men.*) No offense to anyone present.

NUÑO: Queens follow me—since they're female.

SECOND MAN: I'm selling the bank.

NUÑO: I'll buy it.

(*Lisardo, a shepherd, enters.*)

LISARDO: Alonso! (*He beats on the counter.*) A glass of wine.

ALONSO: Do you have any money? (*Lisardo pays.*) Did you find your goat?

LISARDO (*shakes his head*): It must have been stolen. Or it could be down there in the ravine.

ALONSO: Sure. Easy. Since goats don't know how to climb and are always falling off cliffs. (*Laughs.*) What are you going to buy your sweetheart?

LISARDO: Idiot.

ALONSO: Or if that's not it (*he hits Lisardo in the belly*), you like roast goat, don't you?

LISARDO: Give me another glass.

ALONSO: The money? (*Lisardo pays.*) You're carrying quite a bit. Hey, don't you taste a little something in the wine? Goat, maybe? No? (*Laughs.*) Hey, who's your sweetheart? We saw you with her the other day, but a long way off. (*Laughs.*) Aren't you going to tell me who she is? (*Lisardo drinks.*) Well, so . . . Are you going to have to pay for the goat? What kind of person is your boss?

(*The guitarist finishes his song and exits lazily.*)

LISARDO: A good person. Give me another glass and I'll pay you for it later, all right?

ALONSO (*laughs*): It'll have to be water. We'll trust you for that.

NUÑO: The bank wins!

LISARDO: It's getting foggy.

(*Lisardo exits. Alonso goes back to his place. A muleteer looks in.*)

MULETEER: Listen, there are scorpions underneath my pallet.

ALONSO: What did you expect? Peacocks? Kill them and be done with it.

(*Muleteer exits. Martín enters.*)

MARTÍN (*claps twice*): Where is the owner?

ALONSO: What do you want him for?

MARTÍN: I want lodging in this hostlery.

ALONSO: The owner isn't here, and this isn't a hostelry. It's the Inn of the Rains.

MARTÍN: Who's going to receive my steed?

ALONSO: Nobody. You're going to take him to the patio out back. Do you want a cot or a pallet?

MARTÍN: I will want a bed, and a good room.

ALONSO: A bed! (*He looks him over from head to toe. He rises.*) You pay in advance.

MARTÍN: Do you have change? This is the smallest I have.

ALONSO: Blessed Host! Well, no . . . I guess you can pay later if you want. I'll take care of your steed. May I serve you wine?

MARTÍN: Serve it.

(*Alonso pours, and runs out.*)

NUÑO: The bank wins!

FIRST MAN: Well, this is as far as I go.

SECOND MAN: Me too. I have to get up early.

NUÑO: Man! No need to doubt your luck!

FIRST MAN: I doubt a man who's lucky all the time. (*Exits.*)

SECOND MAN: Good night. (*Exits.*)

NUÑO (*beats the table*): Alonso!

(*He rises, goes to the counter, and helps himself. He sees the piece of gold, picks it up, and whistles.*)

MARTÍN: It's . . . it's mine.

NUÑO: Of course, here you are. (*Looks at him.*) Martín Gama!

MARTÍN: At your service. (*Looks at him.*) I don't know . . .

NUÑO: You don't know *who*? Nuño Núñez! Nuño, man!

MARTÍN: Of course, Nuño. That's who I thought it was.

NUÑO: Well, greet me, then! (*Embraces him.*)

(*Alonso enters.*)

ALONSO: Sir! Sir! Someone stole your steed!

MARTÍN: How could that be!

ALONSO: I looked everywhere. The only thing outside is an old mule.

MARTÍN: Ah, yes, of course. She's mine. Uh . . . her name's Steed.

ALONSO: Steed? Well, that's a fine thing. You might have told me. (*Exits.*)

NUÑO (*laughs*): Well, how have you been?

MARTÍN: Fine. Just fine.

NUÑO: But this really is a surprise. What are you doing? What kind of job do you have? Where have you been?

MARTÍN: Here. In Córdoba.

NUÑO: Doing what?

MARTÍN: Oh, you know.

NUÑO: Making clocks? Are you still making clocks?

MARTÍN: Well, yes. That's my business.

NUÑO: Sure. That's what I thought. I always said you'd never change. Strange, isn't it?

MARTÍN: What?

NUÑO: That I was ever an apprentice. So! You must have got married.

MARTÍN: Yes, I got married.

NUÑO: You see! I always said you'd get married. I've been wandering around. Traveling. Madrid, of course. And I was in Italy. You've never been there, have you? But it's been a long time since I saw you. What are you doing in this inn? Things going bad for you?

MARTÍN: Well, I got this far . . . and I saw it . . . And what are *you* doing here?

NUÑO (*laughs*): So no one will find me. Women, you know. They'll never look for me here. So you got married. That's great, man. Who to?

MARTÍN: I married . . .

NUÑO: Don't tell me, let me see if I can guess. You liked . . . (*Laughs.*) Well, it wouldn't be her. What happened to her? To Francisca?

MARTÍN: I don't know.

NUÑO: Is she still in Córdoba.

MARTÍN: She left. You got her pregnant.

NUÑO: Yes, man. I guess so. (*Smiles.*) Well, well. But have another drink. I'm really glad to see you. You look a little older, eh? Who could you have married? Rosa! The one with the moles. Right?

MARTÍN: No . . .

NUÑO: Because you liked that one. Well, then, it must have been . . .

MARTÍN: I married Casilda Domínguez. Your health.

NUÑO: No! (*Laughs.*) That's a good joke. The one with the heavy mustache. I remember. I think you're . . . (*He wonders, and looks at Martín.*) Or are you?

MARTÍN: I'm telling you I married her. (*He serves himself.*)

NUÑO: Well, friend, she was . . . nice. Right? What a . . . Yes, a good woman. Very good. And do you have any children?

MARTÍN: No.

NUÑO: That's strange. Married and no children. And I have at least three. At least.

MARTÍN: Oh? Is that right?

NUÑO: Without counting Francisca, who wasn't sure yet. But they wanted to get married. And listen, there are a lot of things to do in this world before you get married. That's why I went off to Spain. Man, you ought to cross the ocean sometime. Have you heard all the stuff they tell about the Court? Lies, all of it. You can make a fortune there. Look at me. Of course you have to have . . . strength of character, and you can't dwell on . . . unimportant things. I made a fortune (*laughs*) and then lost it in Italy. But, listen, those Italian women! You've got to see, in Venice!

MARTÍN: Were you in Venice?

NUÑO: Venice, Florence, Rome . . .

MARTÍN: Did you see . . . ? (*He stops.*)

NUÑO: What?

MARTÍN: Oh, nothing. A clock.

NUÑO (*laughs*): A clock! You think I was looking at clocks? Finally, I lost everything. I went back to the Court and got on my feet again, because they gave me a good post. And gambling . . . I did pretty well. I came back with . . . enough. Not a fortune, but enough. Perhaps I'll get involved in mining now, or . . . (*Drinks. Laughs.*) Casilda Domínguez. You must be happy, right?

MARTÍN: Yes.

   (*Alonso enters.*)

NUÑO: Hey, we finished our drinks. Bring us another.

ALONSO: Who's going to pay?

NUÑO: I am, naturally!

MARTÍN: *I'm* going to pay. Isn't the money right in front of you? Why do you ask? Serve us.

ALONSO: I don't have change.

MARTÍN: Well, keep the change, and get us something to eat! (*He sits down, amidst the noise of table and chairs.*)

ALONSO: What did you say, sir?

MARTÍN: Are you deaf?

ALONSO: Yes, sir! No! No, sir! Whatever you say! Many thanks, sir! (*He puts the ounce of gold in his pocket.*) We have rabbit, it's very good. We have . . . we could kill a hen!

MARTÍN: Kill two, and be quick about it.

ALONSO: Yes, sir! (*Exits running.*)

NUÑO (*sits down*): Well! It seems that the clock business pays off.

MARTÍN: It's not a bad business.

NUÑO: And . . . just from making clocks?

MARTÍN: You know that Casilda is rich.

NUÑO: Rich?

MARTÍN: And I do other things. Smuggling tobacco, and . . . things like that. It pays, but . . . you have to have . . . strength of character, and not dwell on . . . unimportant things. I have men at my command, I travel . . . And there are other things that come up, and . . . you catch them on the fly. (*He drinks.*) Like just now on the road, I had a piece of luck. I met a businessman (*laughs*), the poor fool. He was having supper right on the edge of the ravine. He had laid his money pouches aside. These. (*He takes out the pouches and drops them noisily on the table.*) Feel them. It's gold. And the poor innocent was eating and drinking right on the edge of the ravine. (*He laughs.*) I drank a toast with him, and . . . (*He pushes the table, which turns over.*) Things are going great with me, there's always some way to get a little money.

(*Alonso enters running.*)

ALONSO: Did you call, sir? Oh, doesn't the gentleman like this table? Does he want a different one?

MARTÍN: No. Show me my room. Will you excuse me? I'm a little tired, I'll eat there. Take these. (*The pouches.*) Lead the way. See you in the morning, Nuño. Listen, don't forget to bring this gentleman his hen. And more wine, if he wants. He's my guest.

(*Alonso and Martín exit.*)

5
THE COURTROOM

Alonso, Nuño, the justice, the scribe, a constable. The scribe is recording the proceedings. Alonso, stunned, has just testified; he has his ounce of gold in his hand. Silence. The scribe finishes writing.

JUSTICE: Have you put everything down?

SCRIBE: Yes, sir.

JUSTICE: This ounce of gold is held on deposit as evidence. (*He takes it from Alonso's hand.*)

ALONSO: But . . . (*He stops.*)

(*Two constables enter.*)

FIRST CONSTABLE: Just like they said! Here is the gold!

SECOND CONSTABLE: We found the pouches underneath the mattress.

JUSTICE (*weighs them in his hand*): These are held on deposit, as evidence. We must verify the amount.

(*He walks upstage. He and the constables begin to count the gold.*)

ALONSO (*in a thin, small voice*): Well, if that's all, I'll be going. With your permission, good day.

(*No one pays any attention to him.*)

NUÑO (*with more assurance*): Yes, I think we can go now.

(*They start to leave; the constable detains them.*)

CONSTABLE: Where are you going?

NUÑO: We made our statements, didn't we?

CONSTABLE: You still have to confront the prisoner. Sit down.

(*They obey. The scribe approaches the justice.*)

JUSTICE: Go finish your record of the proceedings. I can count by myself.

SCRIBE: I can help you, if you wish.

JUSTICE: It isn't necessary. And you two, bring the prisoner.

(*The scribe and the constables obey, unwillingly. Silence.*)

SCRIBE (*interrupting his writing*): They say that don Leandro Penella de Hita is coming to Orizaba.

JUSTICE (*impressed*): Really? Why is he coming?

SCRIBE: He must be working on some deal.

JUSTICE: Of course.

SCRIBE (*laughs*): My uncle, the parish priest, told me a few things . . .

JUSTICE: Yes?

SCRIBE: The canon told him. It was really good: the Cachimba's birthday was two weeks ago.

JUSTICE: Cachim . . .? Ah, the funny one. What a woman! She's the . . . (*Quietly*) She's the Viceroy's protégée.

SCRIBE: Well, it was her birthday and all the important people, the magistrates, everyone, brought her incredible gifts—as a contest, to see who could bring the best. Well, don Leandro summoned some masons, who went to the end of the aquaduct and dismantled the fountain! They carried it back stone by stone and put it together again in the patio of the Cachimba's palace. What do you think of that? (*They laugh.*) It didn't cost a thing, and he made the best gift. They say the Viceroy laughed till he cried, and that afterward the Cachimba danced a special dance for don Leandro, something indecent where she showed her ankles.

JUSTICE: I heard there were some complaints about the fountain.

SCRIBE: Why, no . . . That was all they needed!

(*The noise of a cell door. Martín enters in chains. He sees Alonso and Nuño, who lower their eyes.*)

MARTÍN (*making an effort, but not quite achieving the tone he wants*): Was the hen . . . good? You, did you take good care of him? Yes? I'm glad.

(*Silence.*)

JUSTICE: Martín Gama, you are accused of robbery, and murder upon the person of an unknown. Nuño Núñez and Alonso Pech accuse you. Are you guilty or innocent?

MARTÍN: I am innocent, sir.

JUSTICE: I should warn you about something. If the evidence accumulates against you, and you refuse to declare yourself guilty, the interrogation will be conducted under torture. This Alonso Pech testifies that you arrived at his inn spending money with both hands. What do you say to that?

MARTÍN: I spent one ounce, sir. That is, I spent some and I gave the rest to this boy. I gave it to him because . . . he was guileless, and a nice boy.

JUSTICE: One hundred and thirty-eight ounces of gold were found in your possession. This Nuño Núñez . . .

MARTÍN: That's not possible: There are two hundred and fifty ounces!

JUSTICE: We have stated one hundred and thirty-eight, and the scribe and I are witnesses to it.

MARTÍN: Two hundred and fifty, sir! Exactly! My brother-in-law entrusted me with them for the purchase of the property of don

Úrsulo Téllez! Two hundred and fifty! They were in these pouches!

JUSTICE: I have said one hundred and thirty-eight! However . . . Constable! Come here!

(*The constable approaches.*)

Constable, do you have anything to state?

CONSTABLE: Well, I had the impression that I handed over . . . two hundred. I think we found two hundred. Isn't that what you thought?

SECOND CONSTABLE: That's what we thought.

JUSTICE: Did you count it?

CONSTABLE: No, no.

SECOND CONSTABLE: We didn't count it.

CONSTABLE: It *seemed* like that.

JUSTICE: Well, I am witness that there are one hundred and thirty-eight ounces. The said Nuño Núñez . . .

MARTÍN: That can't be, sir, that can't be! This man, the constable, or perhaps . . . (*He looks at everyone. He stops, horrified.*)

JUSTICE: Silence, accused, or the interrogation will be made with the assistance of the executioner. The said Nuño Núñez has accused you of a crime committed upon an unknown person who was thrown into the Infiernillo ravine and then robbed after death. Do you admit you're guilty?

MARTÍN: No. No, sir. I am innocent! Sir, we drank too much wine. This man, Nuño, he . . . he told me things. He told me . . . falsehoods. That he . . . Things, falsehoods. He awakened my worst instincts. And he made mock. He made mock of . . . of certain things. And I was drinking, and I had a fire here (*indicating his chest*), and sweat was running down my eyelids. It was a question of . . . lying, and I told lies. That money was given to me by my brother-in-law to buy the property that don Úrsulo Téllez is selling. But it was two hundred and fifty ounces of gold! You can send for don Úrsulo, or my . . . No, not my brother-in-law, because he's ill, and in bed. That's the reason he couldn't leave Córdoba.

JUSTICE: Note that the accused declares himself innocent and offers as witnesses his excellency don Úrsulo Téllez and a certain brother-in-law.

MARTÍN: Diego Domínguez, sir. Who lives in Córdoba.

JUSTICE: Noted?

SCRIBE: Yes.

NUÑO: Listen, Martín, I . . . Don't think I wanted to accuse you. But the boy had overheard and . . . he could have thought I was an accomplice.

ALONSO: I hadn't heard anything. You started telling me how that one had thrown some poor Christian to the bottom of the Infiernillo . . .

NUÑO: Me? I was just telling you about it to make conversation. The idea of accusing . . .

ALONSO: Was yours.

NUÑO: It was yours! I don't . . . I don't even have time for such things . . . I have affairs to . . .

JUSTICE: Silence! This confrontation is declared terminated. Do you insist on that figure? Do you insist that you were carrying two hundred and fifty ounces of gold?

MARTÍN: Yes, sir. Surely, sir. Two hundred and fifty ounces of gold, counted and recounted.

JUSTICE: If the statement of an accused noticeably contradicts the facts as observed by the executors of justice, the interrogation shall proceed under torture. Our direct observation of the truth reports the quantity of one hundred and thirty-eight ounces of gold. Do you wish to have your conflicting opinion put down in writing?

MARTÍN: I . . . I don't know what . . .Ye . . .. N-n . . . I don't know.

JUSTICE: You two. It is hereby prohibited that you absent yourselves from the city. In the event that the said Martín Gama be proved innocent, you will suffer the punishment accorded to the crime of false accusation.

NUÑO: But, sir! I haven't accused anyone. It was this imbecile boy who . . . I didn't make the accusation.

ALONSO (*at the same time*): I came as a witness! This man brought me! I haven't accused anybody! How can I . . .!

JUSTICE: Silence! Lead the accused away. You two may go. One step outside the city will be punished by three years imprisonment. Silence!

(*All exit except the justice and the scribe*).

SCRIBE: There is one point I have been unable to word exactly. The gold . . . It's one hundred and eighteen ounces, isn't it?

6

THE COURTROOM

Diego, Casilda, Nuño, Alonso, Señor Salcedo, the justice, the scribe, constables.

SALCEDO: I suppose I may withdraw.

JUSTICE: We pray you to wait one moment more. We're going to bring the accused.

SALCEDO: This whole affair seems to me terribly offensive for don Úrsulo.

DIEGO: Oh, I understand that very well, sir. It's a question of whether we can recover the money so that we may terminate our negotiations. It's . . . very shameful, all this.

SALCEDO: I don't see why you call it "our negotiations."

DIEGO: It's . . . a term, it's . . .

SALCEDO: Being manager, as I am, for don Úrsulo, I can clarify the situation. There are no such negotiations. There is simply a benefit that His Excellency is disposed to make you. Any real negotiations of don Úrsulo have to do with mines, tobacco, spices, and not small properties. As you may imagine, we are going to Mexico City, summoned personally by the Viceroy.

DIEGO: I understand all that, I'm . . . (*Gestures.*) I understand. If my bones were a little less creaky . . .

SALCEDO: Don Úrsulo—His Excellency—it would be better if we began now to address him as he deserves, His Excellency— called to testify in a murder trial!

DIEGO: It's terrible, terrible.

SALCEDO (*to Nuño*): You, you're the one who's making the accusation. Exactly who was murdered?

NUÑO: Well . . . No, it's that . . . I'm not sure he murdered anyone. *He* said, and . . . This boy and I . . .

ALONSO: Don't get me into it.

NUÑO: We didn't want to look like accomplices. It's a duty, isn't it? If anyone says he committed murder, we should declare it.

SALCEDO: Very true. His Excellency has always preached zeal. When he assumes his position, he is going to establish prizes for those who make accusations. Informing is a civic action, and our only defense against heresy and social dissolution.

(*The justice and the scribe applaud—a few approving claps —and smile.*)

If we do not defend New Spain against all of these new and foreign ideas, the colonial system runs the danger of collapse.

JUSTICE: Yes, sir.

SALCEDO: By the way, in this murder, would there be anything involving social dissolution?

JUSTICE: No, sir. I don't think so.

SALCEDO: Too bad. But at any rate, to involve the name of don Úrsulo . . .

DIEGO: He didn't murder anyone, sir, he didn't murder anyone. What happened is that my brother-in-law is worthless, and an idiot. Here is his wife, ask her yourself. Isn't that right, Casilda? Stop whimpering. She's an idiot, sir. But the buildings . . . If don . . . if His Excellency would be kind enough to . . . If he might wish to consummate the sale, I mean, the charity . . . The money's here, on deposit. Isn't that correct, sir?

SALCEDO: One would think so.

(*Noise of bars. They bring Martín, in chains.*)

MARTÍN: Diego!

DIEGO: Yes, Diego. I should have come in the first place. Even though I'm coughing out my bones one by one, I should have come. Do you know what a trip I've had?

JUSTICE: Silence! Accused: Señor Salcedo, here present, represent-

ing His Excellency don Úrsulo Téllez, and this Diego Domínguez, confirm your story that the money was entrusted to you
for the purchase of certain properties. It remains to be clarified
who is guilty of the crime of false accusation, if it be the said
Nuño Núñez and Alonso Pech, or you.

MARTÍN: Well, sir, it is obvious that I was joking. This man, Nuño
Núñez, he knew that I hadn't . . .

NUÑO: How could I know? He's the witness! (*indicates Alonso.*)

ALONSO: I didn't hear anything.

JUSTICE: Silence! If this divergence of opinions continues, and if
there are no witnesses, torture will be applied to the two accused to clarify the point.

NUÑO: But . . . me, accused?

JUSTICE: Silence! For the total removal of the charges, it will be
necessary to conduct investigations in the Infiernillo ravine, cer-
tifying in this manner that such a cadaver does not exist. The
exploration will have to be made at the expense of the accused.

MARTÍN: At my expense! But I don't have the means!

JUSTICE: It can be done and charged against the gold we have
here on deposit.

DIEGO: No, sir! That money is mine!

JUSTICE: In that case, the accused will provide. Once the clarifica-
tion of the charges has been completed, we can proceed to the
return of this money to its legitimate owner. But from the said
quantity, which amounts to one hundred and two ounces of
gold, we will discount . . .

DIEGO: How much?

JUSTICE: We will discount a percentage for safekeeping.

DIEGO: How much? How much did you say?

MARTÍN: In the record they wrote one hundred and thirty-eight!

DIEGO: One hundred and thirty-eight!

JUSTICE: One hundred and two!

DIEGO: Two hundred and fifty! And where's the rest?

MARTÍN: They wrote one hundred and thirty-eight! I saw it!

DIEGO: And the rest? But . . . what money are you talking about?
About mine?

JUSTICE: Since there seem to be certain doubts in respect to the quantity, here is the record. Read it yourself.

(*Señor Salcedo yawns.*)

DIEGO: That isn't my money they're talking about.

SCRIBE: Here is the paragraph: "A recount of the money found in charge of the accused was made, and it was one hundred and two ounces of gold." Here it is. And we the authorities swear to it.

DIEGO: And the rest? What did you do with the rest? (*To Martín*) Thief! You spent it! The property! I want to speak to don Úrsulo! I don't know what's going on! And the rest? Did you keep it, or spend it, or what? Speak! My savings for six years! I feel sick. I shouldn't have come.

MARTÍN: I didn't touch it. It was them, or . . . I don't know anything. First they said a hundred and thirty-eight, and now they come out with a hundred and two! But if I say anything, it will be to the torture for me. How could I have spent it! I spent one ounce, only one, and *he* knows what I spent because I gave it to him.

ALONSO: I don't know anything about anything!

JUSTICE: Silence! This will be clarified later. Note these new charges: abuse of trust and embezzlement. Who's going to pay for the investigation of the area? Without an investigation, he will remain jailed under suspicion of murder for an indefinite period.

DIEGO: Nobody's going to pay! Let him rot! Let them hang him! And torture him! Nobody's going to pay anything!

(*Señor Salcedo yawns.*)

CASILDA: How much is there to pay, sir? (*She unties a handkerchief.*)

DIEGO: Where did you get that? Are you robbing me, too?

CASILDA: I sold the necklace that Mother left me. And . . . Martín, I sold the skeletons, and the apostles. Because I knew we were going to need money.

MARTÍN: The skeletons! And the apostles! (*He sits down.*)

CASILDA: How much is there to pay, sir?

JUSTICE: Make the usual count—two men to search, two to guard, salaries and meals.

CASILDA: Don't cry, Martín.

JUSTICE: Remind the accused that he must remain standing.

7
INTERIOR OF A CELL

Dusk, turning from reddish to violet tones. Martín, in chains. Casilda is with him. Silence.

CASILDA: Do the chains bother you?

MARTÍN: Hardly at all.

CASILDA: I should have brought you something to eat. You're turning yellow. But I never thought this would take so long. At the inn they're charging me four *reales*. I still can't orient myself in the city; it's much larger than Córdoba. It has its parish church all finished, with towers. There's a river to go across. The bridges have lanterns . . . If there's no fog, you can see hills all around. I've spent seven *pesos*. (*Silence.*) Martín, why did you say those things?

MARTÍN: Oh . . . well . . . one says things.

CASILDA: How could it be that you'd kill anyone?

MARTÍN: There's *one* I'd like to kill.

CASILDA: Don't say that. If our friends could only come from Córdoba, and your clients . . .

MARTÍN: What clients?

CASILDA: They all know you're not capable of . . .

MARTÍN: But I'll deny it, and deny it, until they torture us both. Until they burn us and stretch us on the rack. Oh, how I'm going to enjoy that. You'll see. Don't cry. (*Silence.*) Who did you sell the skeletons to?

CASILDA: To the blacksmith. He paid more for the apostles.

MARTÍN: They moved so well. Five movements every one. The apostles . . . Well, they weren't bad, but they only played the bell. I was thinking, I know now why they sounded bad. The pulleys. You see? They needed . . . It doesn't matter now.

CASILDA: I had a few savings . . . Perhaps something will be left over.

MARTÍN: We have to pay Diego. (*Silence.*)

CASILDA: They're taking so long to explore the ravine. When they come back, they'll withdraw the charges. Then I think Diego isn't going to accuse you. As for the rest . . . the rest is easier. (*Silence.*) I was saving because there's a woman who knows a lot, about herbs and everything, and she took off Lucina's mustache. Well, hers wasn't as heavy, mine would cost more . . . I would like to be less ugly.

MARTÍN: Don't be silly.

(*He embraces her, as well as he is able. He kisses her. Noise of bars. The justice and the scribe appear, dressed in black, very solemn; the constables are with them, also a man dressed in black carrying a drum. They carry lights. They open the cell door and enter.*)

JUSTICE: Will the accused rise?

(*Martín rises. A drum roll.*)

SCRIBE (*reads*): "Having terminated the investigation of the Infiernillo ravine, those charged with the same—Gerónimo Bribiesca and Agustín Aguilar, constables by the grace of God—report that on the first day they found the skeletons of two burros; on the second, the wheel of a diligence, a broken, rusted sword, and the remains of a saddle. On the third day they came across a flock of vultures pecking at the headless cadaver of a man. Having frightened away the birds, they ascertained that the body had begun to decompose, and the constable Gerónimo Bribiesca felt ill and began to vomit. Later they explored the environs, without finding the head of the man. Having declared such, it is hereby set down in this document, with the end of initiating a trial for the treacherous and premeditated murder which the accused, Martín Gama, clockmaker, committed upon the person of an unknown."

(*Drumroll.*)

JUSTICE: Depending upon the circumstances in which the crime may have been perpetrated, and upon the clemency of the judges, it will be determined whether the accused be simply condemned to death by garrote, or whether first his two hands be cut off.

(*Drumroll. Casilda faints. Martín kneels, slowly.*)

CURTAIN

ACT TWO

1

THE SAME STEEP ROAD

The road is now dotted with awning-covered stalls; under some, fried foods are being sold; under others there are large earthen jars of cool drinks, sunk in damp sand and decorated with flowers. People are coming and going, or are settled as for a day in the country. Two blind people enter, a man and a woman, with guitars; a young boy leads them.

BLIND MAN: For this respectable gathering, in God's name, we are going to sing the exemplary ballad of the Clockmaker from Córdoba. My son, put down the stools and open the parasol. (*He kicks him. The boy obeys.*)

BLIND COUPLE (*singing*):

> I'm going to tell you the story
> Of a clockmaker crafty and sly,
> Who under the spell of the grape
> Caused a good man to die.
>
> It was twelve o'clock of midday,
> And the sun burned high overhead,
> A ball of glowing hell-fire
> Whose coals by the devil were fed.
>
> Hide yourself, traveler, take care!
> Prepare to meet your Maker.
> The sun now glints off the knife
> Of the cursed Córdoba clockmaker.
>
> At the edge of the deep ravine—
> "Infiernillo" it was called—

He met the traveling merchant
Who under his blade was to fall.

He said to him, "You are my brother,"
He greeted him there as a friend,
But in less than the flick of an eyelash
The merchant had met his sad end.

Let citizens close up their houses,
Let priests and penitents pray,
For the cursed clockmaker approaches,
Now silently wending his way.

Because he was a smuggler,
A thief, and a rustler of stock,
The constables captured the villain,
The Córdoba maker of clocks.

"Good-by, dear wife, good-by,
Farewell, who knows how I'll fare,
My life they'll be taking from me—
After all, what do I care?"

With these words I bid you good-by,
For now my story is over,
The devil has come to reclaim
The clockmaker from Córdoba.

(*A constable shakes them.*)

CONSTABLE: Let's see your license.

BLIND MAN: What license?

CONSTABLE: You need a license from the justice to sing here.

BLIND MAN (*loudly*): I have no license other than that God has given me. Ask the birds for a license to sing.

A GIRL: Well said.

CONSTABLE: You're not going to tell me who I ask for a license. I'll ask the birds—or your mother!

BLIND WOMAN (*sweetly*): Constable, be kind to us. We have a recommendation from the parish priest.

CONSTABLE: Let's see it.

BLIND WOMAN: The boy's carrying it. Sonny. Sonny, where are you? (*She feels around.*) Where's our boy?

CONSTABLE: If he's a real dirty one, he's drinking a cool drink.

BLIND WOMAN: Come here, sonny. (*The constable starts her in the right direction.*) Is this you? (*She finds him. She raps him with*

her cane.) Show the gentleman the priest's recommendation.
(*A family—mother, father, and three children—are sitting in the grass with their picnic basket.*)

BOY: Papa, shall I give some bread to the poor blind people?

FATHER: Don't give them anything.

A LADY (*to another*): Are you going tomorrow to see them burn the printer at the stake?

SECOND LADY: I haven't been able to get a balcony, but we'll see.

THIRD LADY: I have one, be my guest.

SECOND LADY: Oh, how good of you. I thank you with all my heart.

FIRST LADY: This government is very energetic. It's taking care of the heretics.

SECOND LADY: This one wasn't a heretic. He printed some things about the French Revolution—about the rights of man, and I don't know what.

FIRST LADY: The rights of man! But that *is* heresy.
(*Two constables climb over the edge of the ravine.*)

ONE OF THESE CONSTABLES: All's ready now to bring it up.

A MAN: Yes. They're bringing it now!

CHILDREN: Hurrah! Hurrah! They're bringing the dead man!
(*Excitement. People cluster together.*)

VOICES (*offstage*): There's the widow, there's the widow.
(*Elvira Centeno enters, followed by a group of people.*)

ELVIRA: Where is he? Where is he?

CONSTABLE: Watch where you're going. Be careful, you'll fall!

ELVIRA: Yes, I want to fall and accompany him. Let me go!

MURMURS: It's the widow of the headless man . . . Poor woman, she's desperate . . . I can't hear what she says . . . How she's crying . . . !

CONSTABLE (*to the other*): Is she coming to identify him?

SECOND CONSTABLE: And how's she going to identify him if he doesn't have any head?

CONSTABLE: Hasn't the head been found?

SECOND CONSTABLE: No. They're still looking for it.

ELVIRA (*drops to the ground*): One night your husband doesn't come home. And you think bad things. He's drinking, he's with another woman, he's . . . That's the devil of evil thoughts. And nothing happens, the pictures don't fall, the clocks don't stop, no signs appear on the walls. You cry, from rage, you toss in the bed because he doesn't come home. At last you fall asleep, exhausted, with a salty face and a bitter mouth. And in your dreams, there's no revelation, no forewarning. And another day passes and he doesn't arrive and there's the uneasiness, the doubt. And another day, and another, and another. Did he abandon me? Did something happen to him? What? When the news comes, you don't want to believe it. *He's* the one who's dead, the one the blind couple sings about. *He's* the victim. The victim. And I'm alone now, and I'm a widow now. (*She cries.*) A widow! Forsaken. (*She sobs and twists.*)

(*The crowd is moved. Murmurs, tears.*)

A LITTLE BOY: Mama, what does "victim" mean?

A CONSTABLE (*enters running*): A litter's coming! I think don Leandro's coming! (*He descends into the ravine.*)

MURMURS: The magistrate . . . Don Leandro's coming . . . Who'd they say's coming?

AN ELDERLY GENTLEMAN: Don Leandro Penella de Hita! A great man!

(*An official runs in.*)

OFFICIAL: Clear everything away. Disperse the crowd. His Excellency the Magistrate is coming. Disperse the crowd!

(*The constables push the crowds off stage rudely.*)

CONSTABLES: Let's go! Get along!

CROWD (*leaving*): But the Camino Real belongs to everyone, doesn't it . . .? Why are they sending us away . . .? I know Don Leandro personally . . . Things were just getting interesting . . . How can I leave my merchandise . . .? Papa, why are we going?

(*All exit. The constables look at the widow, who is still on the ground.*)

OFFICIAL: Who's this?

A CONSTABLE: It's the widow. Shall we send her away?

OFFICIAL: No, leave her here.

(*Two men enter carrying a litter. Don Leandro Penella de*

Hita, Magistrate, rides on it. It is deposited on the ground; don Leandro gets out.)

DON LEANDRO (*rubbing his body*): What bad beasts of burden men are.

OFFICIAL: Did they do something wrong?

DON LEANDRO: They dropped me twice.

OFFICIAL: I'll have them lashed.

DON LEANDRO: No, no. By no means. Go in peace, my sons.

(*The two men exit, carrying the litter.*)

OFFICIAL: His Excellency is kindness itself.

DON LEANDRO: That's true. But more than that, I've lost faith in lashings. You castigate an ass and he establishes a clear relationship between the fault committed and the pain in his back. But men! They don't establish any relationship, they argue whether the punishment was just, they judge their judges, and they end by saying that lashings are the illegal product of a misguided system. The next time I'll travel on muleback.

OFFICIAL: What times! As our Viceroy said, there are foreign influences filtering in. There are French agents.

DON LEANDRO: That's true, my son. Was there a pilgrimage?

OFFICIAL: A crowd. Curiosity seekers.

DON LEANDRO: Give me a cool drink.

OFFICIAL (*goes to serve him*): There are flies in it.

DON LEANDRO: Take them out. Who is this?

OFFICIAL: It's the widow.

DON LEANDRO (*touches her with his cane*): Are you the widow, woman?

ELVIRA: He's gone from me, killed, sir.

DON LEANDRO: I'm very sorry, dear. What is your name?

ELVIRA: Elvira Centeno, at God's service. (*Sobs.*)

DON LEANDRO: Get up. (*Helps her.*) You have a strong body, and that's good, because that way you will be better able to withstand pain. Come, sit in the shade. You weren't left with a fatherless child, were you?

ELVIRA: No, sir.

DON LEANDRO: I imagined not, because you have such a small

waist, such . . . (*He lets go of her waist.*) When did you recognize the body?

OFFICIAL: She hasn't seen it yet. Who knows if she can identify it? It's headless.

DON LEANDRO: Man, a wife doesn't need the head to know if a dead man's her husband. She can be sure she's a widow without seeing him. Has there been a vigil kept?

OFFICIAL: Two constables, since the cadaver appeared.

DON LEANDRO: And who's been watching the constables?

OFFICIAL: I have.

DON LEANDRO: I hope the jewels are still on the body, his . . .

OFFICIAL: He had no jewels. He was very poorly dressed. Old pants, a threadbare jacket.

DON LEANDRO: Córdoba, Córdoba, whoever had the idea of founding you?

OFFICIAL: Thirty gentlemen.

DON LEANDRO: I know that. I'm one of them. But we must have made some mistake when we founded it. There was the Mulata some years back, remember?

OFFICIAL: Vaguely.

DON LEANDRO: Infernal. Delicious. She had a body . . . And the great advantage of being able to duplicate it—she could be in more than one place at the same time. You'd see her in the plaza and in the gardens, simultaneously. Or in the arcades and in the market. Or in Córdoba and in Mexico City, simultaneously. I don't know how they proved it, since the ones who saw her weren't ubiquitous themselves. They locked her up in Mexico City and it was a difficult case. She escaped from prison in a ship painted on the wall, before the very eyes of the Chief Inquisitor. He was an idiot forever after. A shame, he had such a brilliant mind. (*Spits out a few seeds.*) Very good. Watermelon juice. Do you want some, dear? No? (*Sobs from Elvira.*) When are they bringing up the cadaver? (*More sobs from Elvira. Don Leandro pats her all over her body, consoling her.*)

OFFICIAL (*shouting to those below*): When are you bringing up the cadaver?

CONSTABLE (*below*): It fell down to the bottom again!

DON LEANDRO: Didn't I tell you? Very bad beasts! We'll have to go see where they found it, and it would be good to proceed with the identification. Do you feel up to seeing it, my daughter? (*Elvira sobs, nods.*) Go on, help her go down. And have them bring me the clockmaker.

(*They help Elvira to the edge of the ravine. A constable appears over the edge to assist her. They exit. The official exits on one side. Don Leandro now eats some of the fried things that were for sale. Martín enters, between constables.*)

So you're the famous clockmaker.

MARTÍN: I'm innocent, sir!

DON LEANDRO: You're the only one who thinks so. Let's see your hands. Let's see your arms. (*Feels them.*) The man was decapitated in two strokes, they tell me. You're strong enough to have done it.

MARTÍN (*with a certain apathy*): I didn't do it, sir. By God and the Virgin, I've sworn it a hundred times.

DON LEANDRO: Well, don't swear it any more. Each time you have less conviction in your voice. If I haven't forgotten, the facts were these. You accused yourself in front of witnesses of having assassinated a man in this place. They looked and found the cadaver. You accused yourself of having stolen, and a quantity of money appeared in your possession.

MARTÍN: Sir, that gold . . .

DON LEANDRO: I know. Your brother-in-law, et cetera. It still isn't known whether your family is involved or whether you spent one quantity of money and stole another. This seems the most logical theory, but the amount your brother-in-law mentions doesn't coincide with that you were carrying. Now, son, we have a small problem—where to find the head of the dead man. Where did you hide it?

MARTÍN: I didn't hide it, sir.

DON LEANDRO: The tribunal thinks otherwise. If you don't find it, they will torture you so you'll remember where it is.

MARTÍN: Sir! Torture if I tell, or if I don't tell. Torture if I know, or if I don't know. Let them torture me now, or kill me. I only want the whole thing to be over.

DON LEANDRO: Well, then, you ought to look for it and find it. As long as it's still missing it isn't possible to close a case of murder. Who can guarantee us he didn't have the head of a bull, or a dog?

(*The constables cross themselves. Elvira's scream is heard, far away, in the depths of the ravine.*)

OFFICIAL (*yelling*): What was that?

CONSTABLE (*distant, deep*): The widow has made the identification.

DON LEANDRO: Good, son, start looking. Take him wherever he says.

CONSTABLE: He doesn't want to say where.

DON LEANDRO: Well, let him walk, and follow him step by step. I'll be here, in the shade.

(*He sits down on the blind couple's stool. Martín sobs once, abruptly.*)

MARTÍN: Where am I going to look? Where? And what's worse, I might well find it.

(*He exits with the constables. Don Leandro sighs. The blind couple's boy guide is trying to steal a piece of food.*)

DON LEANDRO: Don't hide, little fellow. The constables won't let the owners pass. Go on, eat. And give me another piece. It's pretty good.

(*The child approaches slowly, timidly, with the piece of food in his hand. Don Leandro takes it. The two of them calmly eat.*)

2*

THE TORTURE CHAMBER

There are various apparatus. The executioner and his assistant are wearing hoods. The executioner is enormous; his assistant, small. The justice and the scribe. Martín enters. He trips, steps back, advances.

* When this play was published in Spanish it contained another scene between this and the preceding one; the author later decided to delete it. *Tr.*

JUSTICE: Why did you take so long?

CONSTABLE: He can scarcely walk, look at him. Come on, act like a man. (*He hits him.*)

JUSTICE: Martín Gama, you have refused to say where you hid your victim's head. Once more we insist that you confess what you did with it.

MARTÍN: I didn't . . . I already told you, sir . . . (*His voice chokes in his throat; he makes drowning noises, and trembles.*)

JUSTICE: All right, he refuses to speak. Put him on the rack.

SCRIBE: Always the same thing, the rack. Why don't we begin this time with the funnel and the water?

JUSTICE: With the funnel in their mouth they can't confess.

SCRIBE: I don't think he's going to confess anyway.

EXECUTIONER: We could hang him by his thumbs, couldn't we?

JUSTICE: Well . . . perhaps.

EXECUTIONER: I also have the pincers hot.

CONSTABLE: Yes, the pincers! It's a long time since we used them!

JUSTICE: Well . . . Put him on the rack and then we'll try a little of each.

(*Martín faints.*)

EXECUTIONER (*disgusted*): He's already begun to faint. He won't be able to stand anything.

CONSTABLE: Help me get him up.

EXECUTIONER: Shall I throw water in his face or put a hot coal on his belly?

(*Noise of bars. They are placing Martín on the rack when don Leandro enters. Everyone stands.*)

JUSTICE: Sir, what an honor to have you here!

SCRIBE: Sit down, please.

DON LEANDRO: Have you already begun?

JUSTICE: No, sir. You haven't missed a thing.

EXECUTIONER: Sir, I . . . forgive the boldness . . . I've always wanted to go to the Inquisition in Mexico City. Nothing ever happens here! If you'll permit me, I can show you now, I know many special treatments. Here, you! Bring me the splinters! And the needles, put them in the fire!

DON LEANDRO: Don't exert yourself, my boy. If there's anything we have too much of lately in Mexico City, it's executioners. They have so little work that they devote themselves to sowing flowers in the gardens. (*He approaches Martín.*) Throw a little water in his face. (*They obey.*) Are you awake, boy? What have you told them?

JUSTICE: Nothing, sir. He continues to deny everything.

DON LEANDRO: You see, boy. It's not advisable for you to deny it. You killed that man, didn't you?

MARTÍN: No, sir.

DON LEANDRO (*sighs*): What foolishness. Where did you hide the head?

MARTÍN: I didn't hide it. I don't know where it is.

DON LEANDRO: Well, suspend the torture.

JUSTICE: But it hasn't begun yet.

EXECUTIONER: We're just getting ready to . . .

DON LEANDRO: Suspend the torture. It's very clear. This man cuts off the head, throws it who knows where, loses it . . . He's not going to remember because you torture him.

JUSTICE: Why isn't he going to remember?

DON LEANDRO: You. Have you cut off heads?

EXECUTIONER: Yes, sir, and I've garroted people.

DON LEANDRO: And you've never lost a head?

EXECUTIONER: Well, only once. I left it in a theater and the actors carried it away, thinking it was John the Baptist's.

DON LEANDRO: You see? And he's a professional.

JUSTICE: I was thinking, sir . . . A little torture is always a good example.

DON LEANDRO: Not in this case. If he were the master of some guild, or if there were people backing him up . . . But he's alone, and everyone detests him. Take him away.

(*General bad humor. Martín is untied and taken off the rack.*)

JUSTICE: If you would permit me, sir, it's my opinion . . .

DON LEANDRO: I don't permit it. (*Exits.*)

(*The constables and Martín exit, followed by the justice. The scribe gathers his papers. The assistant climbs up on the rack and ties himself on it. The executioner helps him.*)

SCRIBE: And this?

EXECUTIONER: We're going to practice a little.

ASSISTANT: Almost nothing ever happens here.

(*As the scribe exits, rapidly, the executioner is already turning the rack and the assistant is yelling.*)

3

RECEPTION ROOM

Galatea and Elvira are waiting.

GALATEA: I was thinking . . . Elvira, we didn't leave the bird outside, did we?

ELVIRA: No, aunt.

GALATEA: The cats might come and eat it up. Or the possum. The other night the possum got into the chicken yard and killed two hens. I heard the poor things. What a commotion! When I went out (*she begins to sob loudly*) they were fluttering around. Headless, gushing streams of blood . . .

ELVIRA: Be quiet, aunt. (*She shudders.*)

GALATEA: It was so horrible. I remember and remember and remember.

ELVIRA: Don't cry any more, aunt.

GALATEA (*drying her tears*): Well, I've hardly cried at all. You've been crying more than I have. Yes, you tore your clothes and ripped them to shreds and you rolled around all over the yard. Don't go and do that here.

(*Don Leandro enters. The women rise, greet him.*)

DON LEANDRO: I'm glad to see you, woman. Who's this old lady?

ELVIRA: This is my aunt Galatea. She was like a mother to my deceased husband.

DON LEANDRO: You shouldn't have brought her with you. She's too old to wander through the streets.

GALATEA: And she's too young to wander around here.

ELVIRA: A constable came to get me, sir, and told me to come here.

DON LEANDRO: Yes, I sent for you. I've found out all about you and your means of livelihood.

ELVIRA: My means of livelihood?

DON LEANDRO: A piece of land, two cows.

ELVIRA: My deceased husband was our only means of support. (*Tears.*)

DON LEANDRO: So I found out. You've seen how we are preparing to punish the crime. Besides that, I've been wondering what other way I might help you. I am a magistrate and you are a young widow. It's my duty to look after you, aid you, see that you're not . . . abandoned. (*He has been moving closer to her.*)

ELVIRA: It's true, sir. Since . . . all that . . . happened, we've been living off our neighbors' charity.

GALATEA: You've been. Not I. I work. Feel, sir, feel my arms. (*She makes him feel.*) They're strong, aren't they?

DON LEANDRO: It's true, very strong. Let's see yours. (*Voraciously, he feels Elvira's arms—and other parts.*) You're weak, woman. Delicious muscles, but too feminine. (*She pulls away, blushing.*) I am a magistrate, and I have called for you in order to help you. (*Very close.*) Ask anything you want.

ELVIRA: When my husband set out, he was going to buy some land. The money he was carrying hasn't been returned to me.

DON LEANDRO: How much was it?

ELVIRA: I don't know. He never spoke to me about his business affairs. But it was a lot, and in gold. If they would only return it to me right away, sir, it's all I ask. And, of course, any assistance that could relieve my state of widowhood.

DON LEANDRO: Is that all?

ELVIRA: And that justice be done to the murderer.

DON LEANDRO: And you, woman? What do you want? Speak. You've been forsaken, too.

GALATEA: My skin is wrinkled and my muscles are dried up. I'm not delicious or feminine. I'm an old woman, so no one will come to my aid, or supply my needs.

DON LEANDRO: That's why I'm asking you, to know what I can do.

GALATEA: With all respect, I don't think you can do anything, Your Mercy.

DON LEANDRO: Ask me, and we'll see.

GALATEA: It isn't easy. Because I want people to remember him as a living person, a boy who made my years happy. Not like that . . . that horror and pestilence they brought in. Elvira, are you sure it was him?

ELVIRA: Naturally, aunt.

GALATEA: I'm not. But it's possible. You see, my Ginés has become that *thing* for everyone. I would like to tell them . . . so many things. That he had blue eyes and that his whole face crinkled when he smiled. And here, on his hands, he had a soft down. His father was Spanish . . . and, well, you know, my sister never saw *him* again. Both of us looked after Ginés, and my sister died when he was ten years old. No one remembers now, but he used to sing so well. He had a light, fine voice that always reminded me of my sister's. First he wanted to be a soldier, but he changed his mind later. He knew a lot about the earth, and here, near his neck, he had a mole. He always danced at the fiestas, you should have seen his feet go. He played the guitar a little, too, but not much, because he couldn't ever buy one. He was happy, happy . . . Well, not lately. Lately he was serious, and tired. Age, I guess. He was more than forty, and that changes your character. I would like everyone to remember him the way I see him. But I walk around, and I listen, and it's as if Ginés had always been . . . *that.* (*She begins to cry, increasingly louder.*) But he wasn't, he wasn't. He liked peppers in walnut sauce better than anything. When he carried the water pails, he limped a little, so he carried all the weight on this side. He was especially devoted to Saint Onofre. He knew how to weave cane! He wanted a child, a girl, so he could give her my name! He was getting bald! And he always said hello with a gesture . . . like this, a gesture . . . Now I can't say how it was, a gesture of his, of his . . .

ELVIRA: There, there, aunt.

(*Galatea calms down.*)

GALATEA: Let's go, daughter. I don't know if I put the bird inside. Tell the gentleman good-by.

DON LEANDRO: We will do what we can for you both. I'll keep you informed. About the gold, I don't think I can hand it over to you now. (*He opens the door.*) Call the justice, have him come here. (*To the women.*) It's on deposit here until the trial's over. And we can't close the trial until we find the head.

ELVIRA: They're taking so long, sir.

DON LEANDRO: The weight of the machinery of justice is terrible and because of that weight it advances very slowly. Nevertheless, there is some oil that never fails to speed it up a little.

(*The justice enters.*)

I've just had a good idea. We must offer a reward to the one who brings us the head. Fifty . . . or perhaps a hundred, yes, a hundred *pesos*. Announce it in a proclamation. You'll see, now things will move more quickly.

ELVIRA: Thank you, sir.

DON LEANDRO: And the next time, come alone. Your aunt shouldn't be involved in this any more.

GALATEA: If you had only known him, Your Mercy. If you'd heard him sing. Good-by, sir.

DON LEANDRO: Good-by, old woman.

(*The two women exit.*)

JUSTICE: A hundred *pesos* to find the head? I don't know how many they'll decapitate to get money like that. They'll bring us dozens of heads.

DON LEANDRO: Perhaps you're right, but send out that proclamation. Better a dozen than none.

4
THE COURT

The scribe, the justice, constables. Lisardo enters.

LISARDO: With your pardon, sir.

CONSTABLE: Where are you going?

LISARDO: I wanted to see the justice.

CONSTABLE: What do you want him for?

LISARDO: It's about that proclamation that came out.

CONSTABLE: What does the proclamation say?

JUSTICE: Let him pass.

(*Lisardo advances.*)

LISARDO: With your pardon, sir.

JUSTICE: Take off that cap. You're standing before the law.

LISARDO: With your pardon, sir. I want to find out . . .

JUSTICE: Speak and get it over.

LISARDO: It's about the proclamation. Is it true they're giving one hundred *pesos* for the dead man's head?

JUSTICE: Yes, man. It's true.

LISARDO: And who's giving it?

JUSTICE: I myself, when you find it and bring it here.

LISARDO: Well, I'm a goatherd. I take care of my herd. I go up and down and around. And a while back I lost a female goat. I kept looking for her, and then . . . in a cave . . . well, that's where it was.

JUSTICE: Your goat?

LISARDO: No, the head.

JUSTICE: Well, why are you waiting to take us to the cave? Constables! Call His Excellency. Bring the prisoner here!

(*Much running around by the constables. Noise of bars.*)

LISARDO: Well, there's not much reason for me to take you there now, because the head is here. I left it outside, you see? Out there in a corner. It's in such a state that . . . really, it's better out there than in here. Do you want to go out and see it, sir?

(*The scribe is still writing.*)

JUSTICE: Surely. What is your name?

LISARDO: Lisardo Guadaña, sir. Sometimes known as Goaty Lisardo.

(*Martín enters, between the constables.*)

JUSTICE (*fiercely*): Martín Gama, Providence will not permit you to continue enjoying a delightful imprisonment. Come with us. Lead us, shepherd.

LISARDO: It's right out here.

(All exit. Don Leandro, with the constable, enters.)
DON LEANDRO: What's happening? Where is everybody?
CONSTABLE: I don't know, sir.
DON LEANDRO: Find out.
(The constable exits. Don Leandro reads the proceedings that have been recorded. The constable returns.)
CONSTABLE: Come here, sir. They're looking at the head! The prisoner doesn't say anything, but he's turned white as a mushroom. Everybody's holding his nose.
DON LEANDRO: I believe you, it won't be necessary for me to go.
(All return. The justice is triumphant.)
JUSTICE: Add to the record that the assassin remained impassive.
(Martín mumbles something.)
SCRIBE: What did you say?
JUSTICE: Speak up!
(Martín mumbles. A constable hits him.)
CONSTABLE: You've been ordered to speak up.
MARTÍN *(looks at them)*: The skeletons.
JUSTICE: Are you making fun of us? Haul him to his cell!
(Don Leandro stops him.)
DON LEANDRO: A strong impression may produce a certain degree of incoherence, but it's worthwhile because of the truth that follows. What skeletons are you speaking of, son? Come on, tell us. You mentioned skeletons.
JUSTICE: He must have committed other crimes. That's it, note it down.
DON LEANDRO: Let me listen. The skeletons?
MARTÍN *(quietly)*: Yes. Now I won't make . . . I intended to make . . . It was a dream, sir. A great clock with skeletons . . . to warn . . . They'd move, like this. *(He makes some vague mechanical gestures.)* They'd be golden in the sun, at the tip of the parish church . . . But no, it wasn't that, that would be . . . happy, wouldn't it? A skeleton in movement, like a clock without a case, but walking, alive. That, life, that's what it would be, as I feel it here, mine, my skeleton *(feeling himself)* with its parts functioning . . . The image, the warning, would be *that* *(pointing*

offstage)—that's death. That color, that putrefaction crowned by hair, and that little moving mass, pullulating in the eye sockets. And I see, and these, my eyes, will be like that! I hear, I smell, I touch myself, I feel revulsion. I would like . . . I would like . . . (*He stops.*)

DON LEANDRO: What would you like?

MARTÍN: I don't know. To do something. Pray. I want . . . I don't understand it, sir. (*With astonishment.*) I don't believe it. I can see it, but I don't believe it. I see myself here, and it's someone else who's here. Am I crying? Who's crying? This pain, this sadness, I think they're for someone else. The things that are real, this air . . . (*He breathes deeply, several times, with his eyes half closed.*) This pain here, where the chains hurt me . . . These steps, that lead me . . . (*He walks aimlessly.*) It's like something very sad that I am about to find out. Here, I see him, is Martín, the clockmaker, and he's walking toward his cell. I think he's crying. He doesn't understand anything, and it's better that way, because if he understands it will be *me*. The pain will be bared, the desperation, the butting of his head against the wall . . . There he goes. *I* only feel . . . Such sweetness . . . This fetid air, going in and out . . . This physical pain, so sweet . . . This dampness covering my face . . .

(*He stops. He walks toward the cell. He exits.*)

LISARDO: Who's going to pay me my hundred *pesos*?

5
RECEPTION ROOM

Marfisa and Elvira enter.

MARFISA: Holy Mother!

ELVIRA: What's the matter with you?

MARFISA: What class! Just look. I'm so glad I could come with you and see this. It's more to my taste than the church. And you've already been here?

ELVIRA: Yes. Once.

MARFISA: I tell my son, don't be a bum. Get into things, Pascual,

get into things. And the boy's pretty sharp, he runs errands for
the justice and the priest, he knows how to flatter people, and
they give him good tips. He's going to make it. Look, look at
this!

ELVIRA: What is it?

MARFISA: A solid gold inkwell.

ELVIRA: Could it be gold?

MARFISA: Do you think they'd have an inkwell that wasn't gold?
I tell Pascual, the world belongs to the clever, son, not to the
stupid. Look at the ones in the government, there's the example
you ought to follow. And the boy's clever, he's clever. Look at
this rug! (*She drops on all fours.*) Dragons! And butterflies!
(*Don Leandro enters.*)

DON LEANDRO: I'm glad to see you, woman, very glad. Did you
finally get here without your aunt?

MARFISA: Oh, yes, sir. The poor old thing went on so about my
taking care of Elvira.

DON LEANDRO: Who is this woman?

ELVIRA: A neighbor, sir.

MARFISA (*stands up*): Marfisa Lagunas, at God's service, and
yours.

ELVIRA: I convinced my aunt that she ought to stay home. Then
she talked to Marfisa . . .

MARFISA: How could I refuse, sir? I know what a neighbor should
be.

DON LEANDRO: I, too, and I don't think we are in agreement. Well,
my dear, this is how it is. The trial's finally going to be ended
and the guilty one's going to die. Aren't you happy?

ELVIRA: Yes, sir. I thought the day would never come.

DON LEANDRO: Well, it came. Everything comes to an end, everything passes. Your husband's in heaven now, or in . . . Yes, surely
in heaven. Life goes on. People forget. You'll forget.

ELVIRA: I, sir? Never!

DON LEANDRO: You'll forget, slowly, by the grace of the God who
sends us consolation. And I've thought of a way to help you.
There's only one. See that you get married.

ELVIRA: Get married!

DON LEANDRO: Yes, my child. Married.

ELVIRA: But, sir, to whom? I mean, I can't even imagine it. My pain is so great still . . . And a widow ought to observe her mourning.

MARFISA: Why should the poor little thing want to get married? You should have heard her, Your Mercy, only a few days ago. Such screaming, and such dragging herself over the ground. She seemed like a mad dog. I remember she even foamed at the mouth once.

DON LEANDRO: She can't go on like that. She'll be getting calmer, little by little, she'll smile again. I only want to make time pass a little more swiftly for her.

ELVIRA: But my mourning, sir . . .

DON LEANDRO: You should begin to moderate your mourning. We'll send out a proclamation explaining your circumstances, and my will. That will reduce the gossiping. I will give you a dowry and offer a small gift to the suitor. Of course, *you* will say "yes" or "no" to those who present themselves.

MARFISA: But this man is a Solomon! What more do you want, woman? For that I'd have my husband's head cut off. Well, just in a manner of speaking.

ELVIRA: I don't know what to say, sir. It's so unexpected . . . What will people think?

DON LEANDRO: Did you hear *her*?

ELVIRA: What will my aunt say?

DON LEANDRO: That the dead man's place in your bed is still warm, that by doing this you're burying him deeper in the ground, that . . . You can imagine what she'll say.

MARFISA: It's true. The poor thing can't put things together very well any more. She's so old-fashioned!

DON LEANDRO: What do you say, woman?

ELVIRA: Well, I . . . I still suffer for my deceased husband, sir. It's true, the Church orders me to console myself. But there's no man in the house, and we women . . . we don't know how to think well, in an orderly way. Your Mercy is a man of intelligence, and . . . I don't want to seem arrogant, and I don't want Your Mercy to think that I pretend to know what's best for me. I . . . I respect the disposition of Your Mercy. That has to be the best thing for me.

DON LEANDRO: Very well said. We'll send out the proclamation. We can't let a woman like you worry about . . . working . . . and . . .

MARFISA: I'm thinking about some of the biggest and strongest single men around. You'll see, I'm going to tell several . . .

DON LEANDRO: It seems we could forget the proclamation now that you're here too. But we'll send it out this afternoon. Go on, woman, run, spread the news.

MARFISA: Sir, I was thrilled to come! Happy to meet Your Mercy! I kiss Your Mercy's hand! Good-by, Your Mercy!

(*Exits, bowing.*)

ELVIRA: Sir, so much interest in poor little me. I don't know how to thank . . .

DON LEANDRO: I could give you a few ideas. (*He approaches her.*)

ELVIRA: Sir, well . . . I'm going to . . . I'm going to catch up with Marfisa! (*Flees; almost at the exit she stops.*) I don't know how to thank you, sir, but I shall do as Your Mercy orders . . . Whatever pleases Your Mercy . . .

DON LEANDRO: Very well said, my dear. I hope you will demonstrate your gratitude . . . a little before your new wedding.

(*Elvira exits.*)

6

THE CELL

Martín alone. A bird sings. Silence.

MARTÍN (*quietly*):

A colorful bird sang above me,
In the shade of the green lemon tree . . .

(*He stops. Noise of cell door. Casilda enters. Crying, she falls at Martín's feet.*)

Is it very sunny outside? A bird was singing. I think it was a lark.

CASILDA: How can it be, O God, how can it be!

MARTÍN (*shouts*): Don't be like that! Do you want to see me screaming too? (*He begins to cry. They embrace. He becomes calm, rises, walks.*) They put more chains on me today. You know what? I've been thinking a lot about Córdoba. Isolated fragments, images. For example, the poles in the fence. Remember? I cut them, and polished and seasoned them. And after a while they put out branches and leaves. I remember, too, I fell asleep once on a hill, just at dusk, in front of the door in the high wall. As I went to sleep I thought, when I wake up that door will be open. And it was. I woke up and they'd opened it, and through it you could see the tile roofs and the plaza and the unfinished church. The lights were beginning to come on. And I remember, too, the orange trees in the patio at night, full of white flowers and fireflies. That fragrance . . . And the coffee trees of the Franciscans . . . The fruit of the coffee tree is sweet. They don't mean anything, they're just things that come to my head, I don't know why.

CASILDA: Isidora came to get me. Diego doesn't want me to be here when . . . (*She stops.*) But I'm not going to go. Afterwards, they're going to put me in a convent.

MARTÍN: There's one thing I've been thinking about a lot. I want you to remember it. I've thought it out very carefully so I can say it when I go to confess. It's all my own fault.

CASILDA: Your fault! Martín! *Your* fault! (*Starts to cry again.*)

MARTÍN: I haven't been bad, but it's because I wasn't able to. I never knew how. I watched everyone and I wanted to be like that, capable of the kind of things people talk about when they say, "*He's* really sharp," or "*He* knew how to live." I married you because . . . because I loved you. Because one day you fell as you were going into church and everyone laughed. Because your brother shouted coarse things at you in the street, and because one day when you saw me you dropped your shopping basket and nobody helped you pick up your vegetables. For all that. For your . . . (*He caresses her face.*) And I was never capable of saying it. I wanted it to look as if I married you for your money. Because I wanted to think so, too. I would have liked to be like Nuño, like all the others. But I didn't know how. I never knew. And now, they're going to . . . This thing they're going to do to me, the person I wanted to be *deserves* it. That's it. This is the end I was looking for. Nevertheless, you can be glad that I don't deserve it as much as the others.

CASILDA: No, Martín! You've been good! You've made me so happy! You didn't want to be bad, and even if you wanted to, you never really were. We all have feelings that push us to imitate the crafty ones, the dirty ones. That feeling comes from the devil, and people like that encourage us in it. Sometimes I wanted to be like the Viceroy's mistress, the funny one, you know. But thanks to God I'm ugly and stupid. Francisca wanted to, too, and . . . she's turned into a whore, poor thing. There are ugly, silly people who imitate the crafty ones, the pretty ones, all those . . . hungry people! Because that's what they are, hungry! They swallow up banquets, palaces, horses, people, gems . . . And that doesn't take away their hunger. Of course, we watch them, and they make us want things too. Who doesn't? And if we haven't eaten, well, we belch so they'll think we're full.

MARTÍN: And they're going to hang me for belching.

CASILDA: No, no, no, don't say that! I'm still praying, I'm still praying. You're not guilty of anything. You and I have made do with our own. They've taken things away from us, and I don't know what. What we can earn and touch with our own hands is enough for us. What's life for if not to enjoy it! Life's been too short for you and me! *You* bad? Everyone knows how good you are!

MARTÍN: *Do* they know? If I had lived, if I had gone on dreaming about my clock, selling things that they returned later, putting up with your brother . . . If I had died that way, no one would have said, "Martín was a good man." They would only have said, "Martín was a horse's ass." And my clock . . . (*He shrugs his shoulders.*)

CASILDA: It would have been beautiful! Martín, if we had had a child . . . If I could learn to make clocks . . . It would have been . . . I should never have sold the skeletons!

MARTÍN: The skeletons . . . By now they must be scrap iron scattered along the road. Yes. That would have been something good. That would, yes. When it struck twelve, all of them, one after another, like a parade. I would change their movements, that I would. So they seemed happy, so they'd invite . . . So they'd say . . . things! That we're alive! That would be a clock! And instead of apostles and archangels, I think I'd put . . . I don't know . . . people! You, me, children . . . people!

(*The little bell of the viaticum sounds. They look at each other.*)

CASILDA: That's . . .

MARTÍN: I think they're coming to confess me.

(*They embrace, sobbing out loud. Noises of cell door. A priest and altar boys enter, with the viaticum. Casilda flees, still crying.*)

7
RECEPTION ROOM

Dusk. The lights are already lighted. Music offstage. Marfisa looks out the balcony.

MARFISA (*very excited*): Your suitor brought those musicians. Are you nervous?

ELVIRA: Yes.

MARFISA: Black wasn't becoming to you. White is better. You should have worn all white. Or a bright color.

ELVIRA: This is hardly half mourning. I was ashamed to come out this way.

MARFISA: Who's going to be your sponsoring lady?

ELVIRA: I don't know.

MARFISA: I imagine some important lady. Too bad. I would have liked to. Be lively!

(*Don Leandro enters.*)

DON LEANDRO: My dear, we've taken quite a while interviewing the suitors, to better guarantee your future. The choice will be yours.

ELVIRA: The suitors? How many are there, sir?

DON LEANDRO: There are two.

ELVIRA: Two?

DON LEANDRO: Were you expecting only one?

MARFISA: She's so modest, sir. But I knew, I knew.

(*An official enters.*)

OFFICIAL: Sir, your baggage is ready.

DON LEANDRO: There isn't any hurry. I'm still planning to go to Córdoba and (*looks at Elvira*) do one or two things before I go.

MARFISA: Are you leaving, sir?

OFFICIAL: Don't question His Excellency!

DON LEANDRO: Let her be. Yes, I'm leaving. I have several business affairs pending in China, and the ship is waiting for me in Acapulco. First (*approaches Elvira*) you and I will have a little chat.

ELVIRA: You and I, sir?

DON LEANDRO: I have a friend in China who will be glad to hear your story. His name is Pu Sung-ling, or however you say it. These Chinese names. He's written some very curious stories.

OFFICIAL: Shall I order a carriage for Córdoba, sir?

DON LEANDRO: Order it. I want to go there because I had a remarkable dream.

MARFISA: It must have been a prophecy!

DON LEANDRO: It's possible, although it seemed absurd. A divorce was being completed in Córdoba. A lady from the Court in Madrid was repudiated by her husband. And the husband was an Indian, or a mestizo.

OFFICIAL: And *he* repudiated her? That really is an absurd dream.

DON LEANDRO: Yes. It all happened near some white arches. The judge who executed the sentence was a man who looked something like that Martín, the clockmaker. On the other hand, there was a Viceroy testifying in very humble fashion. An intense sun was shining over everything, and many cloths, painted the colors of watermelons, were floating in the air.

OFFICIAL: Like watermelons?

DON LEANDRO: Yes. Green, and red, and white.

OFFICIAL: That's a very strange dream.

DON LEANDRO: Yes, very strange. I don't know. The Mulata, the clockmaker, and now this dream. I tell you, I think we made a mistake when we founded Córdoba.

(*The justice looks in.*)

JUSTICE: The document is completed, sir. Shall I have the suitors come in?

DON LEANDRO: Let them come in.

(*The justice exits. The door remains open.*)

DON LEANDRO: Come in, man. Don't just stand there, come in.

(*Nuño enters.*)

NUÑO: Sir, may I greet my betrothed?

DON LEANDRO: Greet her, man. Go over there, Elvira. But don't call her your betrothed yet, she still has to decide. Where's the second?

(*Lisardo enters.*)

And here comes the other one. He's much more humble, he offers you considerably less . . . But I don't mean to influence your decision.

MARFISA (*quietly, to Elvira*): They're so handsome! And strong! Of course, this one's a gentleman, you can see that. No choice between the two.

DON LEANDRO: Be quiet, let her think. These two men have contributed a great deal to your cause. That one, exposing the crime, this one, allowing us to close the trial and punish the criminal. All right, you, what do you have to offer?

NUÑO: Sir, I've been to the Court in Madrid, and I discharged a few humble responsibilities there.

DON LEANDRO: I know. You were a spy and a constable.

NUÑO: I hardly dare hope I may expect, because of your kindness, some charge in which I could demonstrate my capabilities. May I expect that, sir?

DON LEANDRO: Yes, you may expect it.

NUÑO: Elvira, your dowry isn't important to me. I think I have a future. I have a good name, and experience. I can write verses. I offer you all this. I may call you Elvira, mayn't I? May I speak affectionately to you? I've done it so often in my dreams. I even composed a sonnet for you:

> As if in competition with your hair,
> That burnished gold, the sun shines—in vain . . .

DON LEANDRO: My son, *she's* brunette, and that sonnet isn't yours. But it doesn't matter. He knows what to offer, don't you think? And you, shepherd, what do you offer?

LISARDO: Well, I bought myself a few goats, and I'm going to buy more. And I . . . Elvira, I . . . I don't know how to say things, but she understands!

DON LEANDRO: Well, Elvira, say something.

ELVIRA: Sir, Your Mercy has brought us to this point, and . . . I'm a poor undecided woman . . .

DON LEANDRO: If you want my opinion, Nuño's going to go far. He's a good boy, he understands how things are.

ELVIRA: Sir, I told you I'm a poor woman, and although I am undecided . . . this gentleman seems of very fine estate . . . and I'm not. I would say . . . (*She is moving closer to Lisardo.*) Well, I'd say every lamb seeks its ram, sir.

DON LEANDRO: You're talking about sheep and he, about goats. It's true, there's some relationship.

MARFISA: How could she! Oh, but there's no comparison! Use your head, woman.

DON LEANDRO: "The heart has reasons that reason cannot understand." Who said that? Well, for the moment, I did. Well, Lisardo, take Elvira's hand.

NUÑO: Madam, I do have some property, but I grew up in a humble family. That you see me now with certain advantages doesn't mean anything.

LISARDO (*fiercely*): She's said *me*, isn't that clear?

DON LEANDRO: Have you said so, Elvira?

(*She nods.*)

NUÑO: Yes, yes, it certainly *is* clear. (*Moves away.*) If Your Excellency will permit me, I will go send the musicians away.

MARFISA: He even brought musicians! Oh, Elvira.

DON LEANDRO: Well, I see I was mistaken. I would have sworn that you would choose him, because from the very beginning he was the one who was precipitating things.

NUÑO: May I leave, sir?

DON LEANDRO: No, you may not. First you must go to the dungeon, and then to the pillory, where you will be given fifty blows for the crime of false accusation.

NUÑO: I, sir? Me?

DON LEANDRO: Yes, you. For being an imbecile. For accusing the clockmaker. Call the constables.

OFFICIAL: They're waiting, sir.

(*The door opens, the constables enter.*)

DON LEANDRO: And you, you never knew what your dowry was to be. It's the gallows.

(*Elvira screams, steps back. Lisardo embraces her.*)

MARFISA (*yells*): Is it possible! I understand it all! It was her! She killed her husband!

DON LEANDRO: In a way. Actually, it was *he*.

MARFISA: Because she knew who the dead man was! Of course. If even the poor aunt couldn't recognize him, how could she?

DON LEANDRO: What I needed to know was who had helped you. A lover, no doubt. It had to be either the one who exposed the crime or the one who found the head. That was why it was good that you choose.

(*Lisardo and Elvira are still embracing. She begins to scream and cry.*)

ELVIRA: It isn't possible, sir, it isn't true! (*She throws herself at his feet.*) Sir! My gratitude, my affection. Don't they mean anything? Let me speak to you alone, Your Mercy! I will prove my innocence!

DON LEANDRO: Do you think so?

MARFISA: *I* know how she's going to prove it. (*She spits on her.*) I don't want to watch that. How revolting. I'm going. Let me pass!

DON LEANDRO: Let her pass.

(*Marfisa exits.*)

Go, *vox populi*, run off to tell the news and ring the bells. And you, my children. How did you think you'd get away with it? You hid the head of the dead man to confuse the issue. And then you found it to precipitate the death of that other idiot, the clockmaker. And you, you wanted to get the dead man's gold back? Not even the constables were interested in the dead man's clothes. And your poor husband never scraped enough money together to buy a guitar! I can give you the reason. It was a shame that a forty-year-old man with a soprano voice, bitter and tired . . . and you, young, with your firm body (*pulls her to her feet*) with your desire to have things . . . But here life is taken only by God and Ourselves. And always for important causes, as an example to others, so it will be known who commands and who invents justice.

(*Lisardo tries to run away. He battles spectacularly. He is felled by a blow to the head. Elvira throws herself upon his body.*)

ELVIRA: Lisardo, Lisardo! Not you! No, Lisardo!

DON LEANDRO: Yes, Lisardo. He isn't dead, daughter, not yet. Take them away. And don't cry so, woman. After a while I'll come to your cell to console you.

(*The executioner and his assistant look in, happy, jabbing each other with their elbows.*)

NUÑO (*leaving*): Sir, after the pillory could I have a job?

DON LEANDRO: It's possible. Men like you are always useful.

(*The constables lead Lisardo and Elvira away. Everyone exits except Don Leandro and the official.*)

Go out and have the clockmaker and his wife brought in here. She'll be crying. She's probably thrown herself on the ground outside the jail.

(The official exits.)

Such is the way with the affairs of justice. Everyone loses, and in the end those who win have less than they did at the beginning. Greed for pleasures and material gain corrupts the public. This impatience, this thirst, this desire to possess things, that's man's heaviest burden. The people throw it on the backs of those of us who govern, and it's very difficult. And in exchange, only bitterness and worries. The remote temptation that comes, at times, to be, simply, a good man. The temptation to watch cabbages and lettuce grow, to know what day the tulips will bloom. It isn't possible to have everything. It isn't possible to listen to everyone say how good, how just, how noble we are, and be it at the same time. It isn't possible. There's the humble fire in the kitchen hearth and there's the lightning bolt. There's the plain and there's the mountain. There's the pleasure of being humble and that of being Magistrate. I chose, and the world and its opinions helped me choose. And if something of this adventure remains in the memory of man, it will doubtless be I. Because . . . who's going to remember whether a poor clockmaker lived or died?

(The justice looks in.)

JUSTICE: Sir, that woman, that Marfisa, has created a riot. People are coming with torches shouting for the clockmaker to be freed.

DON LEANDRO: Asking for his freedom? Aren't they asking instead for the death of the guilty ones?

JUSTICE: No, sir.

DON LEANDRO: That's how they are. Sometimes they get the idea of asking for the life and liberty of the innocent, and that isn't good, because you never know where it will end. Open the balcony and announce that they will be satisfied.

(Martín enters, in chains, between two constables. The justice opens the balcony, and then yells.)

JUSTICE: They've wounded me! They threw a rock in my face.

DON LEANDRO: Take him to the balcony. What are you waiting for!

(They place Martín on the balcony, and the shouting stops.)

MARTÍN: I don't understand, sir. Is it time?

(Casilda runs in.)

CASILDA: Martín! Martín! Everyone knows! They're asking for your freedom!

(*She falls at his feet.*)

DON LEANDRO: Get the light on him. Surround him with candles and lamps. And take off the chains. And you! Get out of here! You're getting me all bloody.

JUSTICE: Yes, sir. As you say, sir. (*He exits, moaning.*)

(*Clamor of the crowd. Music. Martín raises his hands, free.*)

MARTÍN: Is it true? Is it true?

CASILDA: Your freedom, Martín!

MARTÍN: Justice!

DON LEANDRO (*smiling*): Yes, justice.

CURTAIN

Theseus

A Tragicomedy

To José and Mary Vázquez Amaral

And to what end have you called to
mind sacrifices which time had buried
in forgetfulness?

Sor Juana Inés de la Cruz

(From a *loa* presented on the occasion
of the birthday of His Excellency the
Count of Galve preceding the comedy
Love Is More Labyrinthine)

Characters:

THESEUS
AEGEUS
SHIP'S CAPTAIN*
ARIADNE
PHAEDRA
FIRST LADY OF THE COURT
SECOND LADY OF THE COURT
PASIPHAË
THE MINOTAUR
ATHENIAN SOLDIERS (TWO OR MORE)*
TWO SAILORS*
CRETAN SOLDIERS*
THESEUS' THIRTEEN COMPANIONS (It is not necessary to see them all.
    Only two of the girls and two of the boys speak.)

In Athens and in Crete.

> A hero does not feel death; an affront,
> yes, for it is infamy that one born to
> such high estate should die so basely.
>
> Sor Juana Inés de la Cruz
>
> (*Love Is More Labyrinthine*)

THE DOCKS OF ATHENS

A blue sky, in which several constellations may be seen painted in gray on white rectangles or outlined against the sky. In dark colors there are figures which recall the celestial charts of the Renaissance. The Gemini are there, Pisces, Aries, Scorpio, and—very prominently—Taurus.

* In these roles an actor may play more than one part.

There are two or three packing cases, labeled in Greek. A gang-plank rises from center stage to some high point off stage at the left: shipboard. And from this point run ropes to a stone mooring ring. In a slightly more elaborate production, the ship can be at stage rear, three dimensional, with sails that can be raised at the end of the play.

Nightfall, although there is still a great deal of light.

AEGEUS: I am just a sentimental old man. I look at you and I am astounded. My continuation, that is what you are. The blood that courses in torrents through your body is the same that flows so sluggishly through my arms. And the skull hidden behind the burnished symmetry of your face is the echo and fruit of this other, the one that scarcely suffers the weight of my teeth and that looses its hold on my eyes—which are too small now, to judge by the crystalline liquid that pours from the shadowed caves where they are housed, to continue contemplating the emptiness and penumbra of a world in which the only important thing is to perceive you.

THESEUS: It's a splendid evening. The breeze smells of fried fish and rusty metal. I'm hungry. I'm going to eat as soon as we leave.

AEGEUS: I know. You say that to prevent my getting sentimental. But this is a farewell. Who are you? It surprises me to see you here by me. You are my son. I cry without realizing it. To find you only to lose you.

THESEUS: I will be back, don't doubt it.

AEGEUS: I want to think about how you came. How long ago?

THESEUS: Three weeks.

AEGEUS: Three lifetimes. Three centuries. Three universes. One would think, almost, that I had seen you grow up by my side. Wouldn't you think so? Three weeks of knowing you. I forget easily what has just happened, but I remember things in the remote past. For example, that trip. The oracle forbade me to lie with any woman until I reached my kingdom. But I met Aethra, and she was as sweet and white and tiny as a bunny. I saw her running through a meadow. I think she was wearing . . .

a chiffon gown, or something like that. She was like a spring cloud, white, untouchable, ready to bend to any caprice of the wind. And I was the wind.

THESEUS: Wrap up well. The wind is rising. And sit down. Your asthma might come back.

AEGEUS: I was the wind. I fled, because the oracle had spoken. You already know that. I could never understand that prohibition by the oracle. You were born!

THESEUS: Yes. I have already told you I don't mind being a bastard. That way, I am the son of my own acts.

AEGEUS: Aethra, sweetness, Aethra. How is your mother now? She must be beautiful still.

THESEUS: Well . . . She is a tiny, proud-looking old woman, of bad character. She wears black. She suffers palpitations during the day, and breaks out in a sweat at night. I told you that.

AEGEUS: Of course, of course. I forget . . . some things.

(*A young girl, repeatedly screaming, is dragged toward the ship by two soldiers.*)

Someone is screaming.

THESEUS: A girl who is afraid. Let her go! (*She clings to Theseus.*) Don't cry.

GIRL: My parents have just gone away. And from a distance, as she left, Mama cried, "Take care of yourself." Take care of myself! I want someone to take care of me!

THESEUS: There, there. It's all over. Get on board the ship. There is music and wine and food, there are hangings and baskets full of flowers. It will be an enjoyable voyage.

GIRL: And when we get there . . . The Labyrinth! The Minotaur! (*She weeps.*)

AEGEUS: I don't want to cry, but I hear her, and . . . Forgive me, son. Child, Theseus will go with you. The heir to Athens. The king's only son. And I am the king.

GIRL: You are the king. Yes, you must be. You look like a dried-up old crocodile. Why are you crying? Look at me. A ruler should contemplate the results of his pacts. Every seven years you have your drawing, and you pick us out. Fourteen young people who owe nothing, who have done nothing. And you send us to Crete, to the Labyrinth, and you shut us up there with a monster. We don't even know what he'll do to us. They say he is half man and half bull! What is it he's going to do to us? I want to die here, close to my parents, in the place where I was born. I want my mother, I want my . . .

THESEUS (*slaps her*): There. Did you hear? There. Ask the King's pardon. On your knees.

GIRL: Pardon.

THESEUS: If you and I, and the other twelve, did not go to Crete, there would be war. King Minos demands this sacrifice, every seven years. This has saved the life of your city, it has made it strong. Your name will be inscribed in gold, on marble. You ought to give thanks on your knees to the gods.

GIRL: Forgive me. You are right. I know now.

THESEUS: Get on the ship. (*She obeys.*) Is this your basket?

GIRL: Yes. Fish, wine, and a cake. My . . . mother brought them.

THESEUS: Well, take it with you, but you won't need it. There is plenty of everything on the ship.

(*She takes it, and boards the ship. Exits.*)

AEGEUS: I have never watched them leave. You shouldn't have entered the lottery. You shouldn't have killed your cousins and uncles.

THESEUS: No? That bunch of corrupt, ambitious men who were hanging around waiting for you to die? They would have assassinated me.

AEGEUS: I know, but . . . there's been a lot of talk among the people. They have been cleaning the palace a whole week . . . and today there was still dried blood on the entrance steps, and on the dining room columns.

THESEUS: I told you that you should punish the servants. They clean very badly.

AEGEUS: Medea, in spite of everything, was a great help in those matters.

THESEUS: She would have killed you, as she killed her own children and Creon and the princess. She is a witch, and not very appetizing, except for that red hair. Her body is all withered and her glance is shifty. Beware of political refugees who have been run out by an entire people.

AEGEUS: I know. But she is so wise. (*Whispers to him*) She had given me back my virility.

THESEUS: And she had convinced you that you should poison me.

AEGEUS: Don't remind me of that. Another cause for remorse. Luckily you drew your sword at the banquet.

THESEUS: It wasn't luck. I cut the roast with my sword deliberately, so you would see it.

AEGEUS: This sword. I will strap it on again. It is terrible that they do not permit you to carry arms on the voyage. The only token I left so that I might recognize the son to be born if he should some day come to me. It is strange to touch it.

THESEUS: But anyone could have come. You left it under a stone in the field.

AEGEUS: Only my son, if he were strong enough, could lift the stone.

THESEUS: Or be clever enough to use a lever, or astute enough to have four laborers lift the stone for him. Besides, it could have been a girl.

AEGEUS: But you were born. And you raised the stone with your arms.

THESEUS: With my right arm. What a face Medea put on when you overturned my cup and called me son. She fled like a rat, like an evil red rat, toward her fiery cart.

AEGEUS: You don't believe it, but in intimate moments . . . she knows how to be sweet. Yes, she lies. She pretends. I didn't truly love her. But you understand (*whispers*) she gave me back . . .

THESEUS: I know, Father. You told me that before.
(*Singing on board ship.*)
Good. The night wind is coming up now. The sailors are singing as they raise the sails. The drum already marks the rhythm for the oarsmen. It is time to say farewell.

AEGEUS: Wait. There is so much I want to say to you. (*He takes out some scrolls.*) Son, as king I must tell you that the nation appreciates your sacrifice, voluntarily entering the lottery . . .

THESEUS: Leave it alone. If I hadn't entered, they would be judging me for assassinating your fifty relatives. Now, on the other hand, the people acclaim me. I know that the lottery was rigged. What a coincidence, my being picked! It doesn't matter. I will be back.

AEGEUS: You will be back. I know you will be back. If you don't come back, I shall die.

THESEUS: Why must you die? You have a kingdom, for your lifetime. And a three-week-old son. You will reign. You will fortify Athens.

AEGEUS: No. No. I mean it seriously. I have ordered the captain of the ship . . . Is that he over there? I don't see well.

THESEUS: It is he.

AEGEUS: Captain. Don't forget. Repeat my instructions.

CAPTAIN (*from memory*): I will wait in Crete the designated time and two days more. If Prince Theseus has not emerged from the Labyrinth, I will raise the black sails as a sign of mourning, and thus the disaster will be known in Athens from the moment in which my ship is only a funereal dot hovering on the horizon. And if the prince conquers, and returns, I will raise the red sails. And Piraeus will see floating toward her docks a flame of enthusiasm, a rose more fiery than that of a windswept dawn.

AEGEUS: That's it. That's it.

THESEUS: Did you dictate the instructions?

AEGEUS (*humbly*): The palace poet helped me. A metaphor here and there lends solemnity . . . and it's a mnemonic device, too.

CAPTAIN: We're going to cast off, sir.

(*Boards ship. Exits.*)

AEGEUS: Son, when it is time for the ship to return, I will be on the highest walls. If the lookouts discover a black spot on the horizon, I will leap into the sea. I am not going to survive you.

THESEUS: But why? I don't understand.

AEGEUS: I lived the life of a king. I was not a bad ruler, neither was I excellent. However, I had little time for the trivial things that so delight men—to look at the sky, to talk with friends, to tend some plants. And I discovered one night, many years ago, that instead of taking my new concubine, I wanted only to read a while, and sleep. I was growing old. And after that it was as if there were a constant caustic breeze corroding me, which was subtly and tenaciously divesting me of my own being—my clear sight, my strength, the color of my hair, the tautness of my skin, my memory, my will, my desires, what I was. And I no longer knew what I was doing, alone in a world that was becoming devoid of friendly faces. Then, when you arrived, I understood suddenly what I had been lacking. I understood that all I had lost was there in your powerful arms and in the polar brilliance of your look. This was I again. The secret of the phoenix, my eternity, is in your body. My face will spring forth on your sons, my gestures will be reproduced some day by someone who never saw them, and the timbre of my voice will give commands, will speak sentences to a world that I cannot even imagine. So, if you do not return, what point would life have? I shall leap from the cliffs and let Athens suffer the fate that the gods dispose. At any rate, what good is a solitary and nostalgic old man? And if you come back . . . I will be waiting with the most immense procession ever seen by mortals. There will be an altar, to anoint you, at the foot of the throne. I will rest the weight of my remaining years on your shoulders while you learn to be a king. Embrace me.

THESEUS: Good-by, father. Until later.

AEGEUS: Good-by, son. Good-by. Son. My son.

(Song of the seamen. Theseus boards ship. Wind flutters his garments. He waves, exits. Two sailors have cast off the ropes. They pull up the plank.)

(Shouting) Son, be careful!

(Darkness.)

2

THE ENTRANCE TO THE LABYRINTH

> I don't know what attraction unhappi-
> ness holds for arrogant souls; the being
> it, alone, serves as recommendation.
>
> Sor Juana Inéz de la Cruz
> (*Love Is More Labyrinthine*)

*A ruined, overgrown façade that should suggest what is con-
tained inside. Cretan motifs. Theseus, Ariadne, and a Girl are
upstage, backs turned to each other.*

ARIADNE: I'm jealous. (*Theseus laughs.*) You're going to enter
with all those girls, all the ones who came on the voyage.

THESEUS: You could ask your father to leave them outside.

ARIADNE: Don't be foolish. But I know what those voyages are
like. I've heard things.

THESEUS: Naturally. They have to be that way. For twenty-three
days we sang, we drank, we danced, and we made love.

ARIADNE: You had all seven, didn't you? Don't deny it.

THESEUS: I don't deny it.

(*Ariadne walks away. She sits down on a broken column.*)
Are you going to cry?

ARIADNE: No.

THESEUS: Listen, foolish princess, somber child, baby. In general,
the voyage to Crete is not a round trip. It ends here, in the
Labyrinth, and there is no return ticket. On shipboard people
could go crazy, or mutiny. It's better to bring musicians than
jailors. You have to be happy, and sing, and be promiscuous. I
had all seven girls. We all did. We had the happiest, most complicated parties you can imagine, as they do in plague-stricken
cities, as they do in towns on the edge of a war. And when
the lookout cried "Land ahoy!" the music stopped and we all
went up to see the sooty line that was beginning to show
through the dirty light of dawn. Then we ran to the prow,
and the girls began to cry, and some fell to their knees scream-

ing prayers, still drunk and half nude. And we seven young men became seven figureheads, our eyes fastened on that floating line constantly changing shape and color, our breasts tense and hard as the wood of the prow, seven lugubrious, distorted figureheads with the taste of copper in our mouths, livid circles under our eyes, and skin the color of hyacinths. Then the wind brought us a burst of trumpets, and soon the sun shone on the marble wharves. We had to wash, and shave. And there was the procession, awaiting us, and in the procession . . . (*Caresses her.*) Do you know who was in the procession? The daughter of King Minos, her face drawn up in the grimace of official business, trying to be very adult and very efficient in her role of mournful princess awaiting the victims for her brother, the Minotaur.

ARIADNE: Don't call him my brother.

THESEUS: But he is. You have to call things by their names.

ARIADNE: My nightmare, my shame, not my brother.

THESEUS: Come, now. There are minotaurs even in the best families.

ARIADNE: Don't joke. (*Embraces him.*) There is almost no time.

THESEUS: Are you going to begin portioning out the soup?

ARIADNE: Yes. They think I'm in the kitchen now. Phaedra has been very good, she's helping us. She's lying, pretending to be talking with me so no one will notice my absence.

THESEUS: Your sister is . . . a very clever girl.

(*They kiss.*)

(*While he nibbles at her*) It's nice that princesses must publicly display charity for those of us who are condemned. Very nice.

ARIADNE: I have thought of a plan.

THESEUS: Yes?

ARIADNE: I don't know whether you can overcome the Minotaur. I couldn't even think of a way to bring you a weapon. This whole area is guarded. They even watch us. No one can come close to the Labyrinth if he is carrying a weapon. But if you win . . . I have thought of a way for you to get out.

(*Fanfares, distant.*)

THESEUS: They have finished the purification of the second couple.

ARIADNE: I am going to the kitchen. They might see me here. Listen closely. Take this.

THESEUS: A ball of yarn?

ARIADNE: Yes. Fasten the end at the entrance to the Labyrinth. Unwind it carefully, don't drop it. The thread will always guide you to the entrance. By the gods, it's so simple. I thought and thought. And yesterday, while I was knitting, my black cat took the ball of yarn and ran away, rolling it, downstairs. I followed her, guiding myself by the thread . . . and suddenly, I understood: your salvation. Take it. Take care of yourself.

(*Exits running.*)

THESEUS: Everyone seems to want me to take care of myself. A thread. It's not a bad idea. Only a woman . . .

ARIADNE (*returns running*): Here they come. Give me a kiss. They're bringing the second couple.

(*They kiss. She flees. The girl upstage comes up to Theseus.*)

GIRL: Are you going to be able to save us?

THESEUS: It's better if you don't think, or ask questions.

GIRL: That was Ariadne, the princess.

THESEUS: Yes, it was.

(*Music nearby. The second couple enters, alone or with a procession that performs a small ceremony and leaves them there, going off afterward. They may also enter between guards.*)

BOY: They're taking a long time purifying us. At this rate all fourteen of us won't be together here until morning.

THESEUS: Nothing but the best for the Minotaur. The flower of Athens—us—well perfumed and purified.

BOY: I reek of incense from head to foot.

SECOND GIRL: I'm afraid.

THESEUS: If you cry, I'll slap you.

SECOND GIRL: I know, you already have.

THESEUS: We are living examples. We are Athens.

SECOND GIRL: I know that already. Let me alone.

(*Goes to rear of stage. At a sign from Theseus, the first girl accompanies her.*)

BOY: It smells like food.

THESEUS: The princesses are bringing some soup before we go in.

BOY: It'll be ice cold before the last ones arrive.

THESEUS: There are pots and pots in the kitchen. Ariadne told me the whole procession will eat here.

BOY: And...? Already?

THESEUS: From the first night. She slipped out of the palace and came to look for me at the temple.

BOY: Ah! She was the one who was whistling.

THESEUS: Yes. She.

BOY: She was the owl you went out to frighten away.

THESEUS: She was the owl, but I didn't exactly go out to frighten her.

BOY: And...? Where?

THESEUS (*laughs*): Standing up, behind a column. She was a virgin.

BOY: And the guards?

THESEUS: She bribed them. Be quiet. Here comes her sister.

(*Phaedra enters. Two ladies behind her carry a cauldron of steaming soup.*)

PHAEDRA (*declaims*): I have here the soup of friendship. Minos, the king, sends it as proof that his acts are dictated by inherent justice and not by personal rancor or . . . or . . .

FIRST LADY (*prompting*): Or by ambition for strength and power.

PHAEDRA: Or by ambition for strength and power over the sister kingdom of Athens. (*Exhales a sigh.*) I forgot. It's the first time I have tended the propitiatory victims. Seven years ago I was a child. (*Maliciously*) Ariadne is twelve years older than I. She's a little older than the Minotaur. Where are the plates?

FIRST LADY (*reproachfully*): Your Highness should have brought them.

PHAEDRA: I forgot them. Run get them.

(*The ladies exit running. Phaedra winks at Theseus, watches them leave.*)

(*Hurriedly*) Theseus, there is a sword in the third cauldron. Don't try the soup, it must taste like thunderbolts—the sword boiled in it all morning. Oh, I hope that you kill that odious Minotaur. I think Ariadne has thought of a way for you to get out.

THESEUS: Thank you, princess.

PHAEDRA: Call me Phaedra. You also are a prince. How handsome you are. I tell you that only in case you should die in there. I know it isn't nice to say such things to men. You're enchanting. Let me touch your arm. Don't tell him to go away, let him stay. I like him too, but not as much. Is it bad that I like boys? Kiss me. You first.

BOY: Me?

PHAEDRA: Yes, you. (*He kisses her.*) Now you. (*They kiss. Pause. Sigh.*) Your kiss is much better. Be serious. Here come the harpies.

(*Two ladies enter with the plates. Phaedra serves.*)

You're really supposed to say a prayer while you serve, but I didn't learn it. And if you two go buzzing to the priest to tell him, I'll have you flogged till your skin falls away.

FIRST LADY: Your Highness cannot speak to us that way. We are ladies of the nobility, not slaves.

PHAEDRA: You'll see whether I can or not when two strangers grab you and beat you on some dark corner. (*To Theseus*) I learned this method from my father. Since he is a just and democratic ruler, governed by laws, his punishments take place by surprise on the darkest corners of the city. There are never executions. Prisoners commit suicide in their cells. He has also invented some very vague and convenient crimes that he applies to whomever it most suits him. His greatest aspiration is that when he dies he be made judge in Hell.

THESEUS: May he achieve it speedily.

PHAEDRA: You can tell them to reserve him a place.

FIRST LADY (*can stand no more*): If Your Highness continues speaking to the prisoner in that tone, I shall leave. I am a patriot.

PHAEDRA: Go, then. Just be careful crossing streets. Chariots often run away, and accidents may occur at any time.

(*The ladies continue serving. Phaedra laughs. The ladies finish and exit solemnly.*)

They're going to bring us the second cauldron now. Remember, the third. Why didn't you pay any attention to me when you arrived? All your glances were for Ariadne.

THESEUS: I saw you.

PHAEDRA: What color was I wearing?

THESEUS: Red.

PHAEDRA: Idiot, idiot. Blue. Do you like my dress? I'm wearing it for the first time. (*To the Boy*) Don't eat that, imbecile!

BOY: No?

PHAEDRA: No. The soup of friendship has a narcotic in it. They prefer to take no risks. After all, the Minotaur is one and you are seven. Or fourteen, if we count the girls. I would fight.

BOY (*terrified*): I already ate half a plate.

PHAEDRA: Well, go throw up. Not here, though. And tell your companions to pretend to eat.

(*He flees.*)

I don't really know for sure, but it's probable. I know Papa. And I wanted to be alone here with you. Do you like Ariadne a lot?

THESEUS: Well, she looks like you.

PHAEDRA (*sarcastic*): Yes? Really? Thanks. I think that's she coming. Pretend you're eating.

(*Ariadne and the two ladies enter with another cauldron.*)

I already said the prayer. You can save yours.

ARIADNE: Has everyone eaten?

THESEUS: We've eaten.

PHAEDRA: Let's bring the *third* cauldron now.

(*Exits with ladies.*)

ARIADNE (*embraces Theseus*): I can't stand any more. I'm afraid. If everything goes well, if everything goes well . . . what will happen?

THESEUS: The treaty establishes that there will be no further sacrifices. Peace will be signed. Our commerce will continue, under more advantageous conditions. Athens is no longer the poor city she was twenty-one years ago. Give us time.

ARIADNE: You're not going to attack my country.

THESEUS: Why should I? If I'm going to marry you.

ARIADNE: Going to . . . (*Pulls back.*) My father won't like it.

THESEUS: He'll like it. I am Theseus. My fame is not very great, yet. But I am a friend of Heracles, and after I emerge from the Labyrinth my name will resound in every crashing of the waves and in every gust of the wind. Theseus! It will suit him to have me as a son-in-law.

ARIADNE: You frighten me. You're a vain child, and I'm going to take care of you. I am going to be your minister, your treasurer, and your chatelaine, your . . . wife. Something pained me here, when I saw you disembark. You were pale, and you were staring blankly into space . . .

THESEUS: I had had a lot to drink the night before.

ARIADNE: No. You can't deceive me. You were asking for help. Then you saw me, face to face, and gave me a long, disconsolate look.

THESEUS: I was looking at your body.

ARIADNE: You looked at my belly as a child might look at his home. You looked into my eyes as if asking me to take you by the hand. (*Fanfares.*)

THESEUS: Here comes another couple.

ARIADNE: Take care. Fight. Win. (*Phaedra and the ladies return.*)

PHAEDRA: Well, here's the *third* soup cauldron. And now it's more important that we receive the next couple. Let's go. (*Phaedra and ladies exit. There is a bellow, repeated in several echoes.*)

THESEUS: Your brother is getting impatient.

ARIADNE: When you enter the Labyrinth, I will have the end of the ball of yarn in my hands. I will clutch it to my belly. I will feel it like an artery that pulses and draws my life toward you. I will feel it like the cord that unites the mother with her newborn child. I will support it and through it I will be sending you my prayers, my strength, my ancestors, my name. When you emerge, you will be my husband and my child.

(*Kisses him. Exits. Pensively he watches her leave. Then he plunges his arm into the third cauldron, searching. He withdraws it, clutching a short sword from which soup pours, as from his arm. He raises it triumphantly, showing it to his companions, who slowly come up and form a circle around him. Fanfares, distant. Darkness.*)

3

THE LABYRINTH

> . . . So that human blood may nourish
> the Minotaur, monster of contradictory
> forms . . .
>
> Sor Juana Inés de la Cruz
> (*Love Is More Labyrinthine*)

It will be formed by earth-colored screens stained by dampness, with friezes. They will be mounted on wagons, or they may have wheels and be moved from behind by the actors themselves. Thus the Labyrinth will be changing constantly as indicated. The actors will interweave the walls, they will perform a dance, constantly opening new passages, new depths. Downstage right there is a stone grating that can be covered by changing the position of the walls. All of this is inside a dark chamber. Lamps hang overhead but emit almost no light. No one. Pause. Intense light behind the grating. Pause. Behind the bars we see Pasiphaë.

PASIPHAË: Son. Darling. My son. (*She sings a sort of cradle song.*)

> Let us go play
> In the fields of alfalfa
> Where a white bull
> Breathes a silver haze.

(*Calls.*) Son. Come. It is I. It is Pasiphaë, your mother. Don't you want to see her? (*Sings.*)

> He was a baby bull
> With skin so dark,

Eyes big as saucers,
Horns like crescent moons.

Little son! It's always so damp in here. No one comes to clean up and it smells of spoiled meat and mushrooms. Son!

MINOTAUR (*surges out of the shadows*): What do you want?

PASIPHAË: They're coming. Do you feel well?

MINOTAUR: I feel bad. Something's wrong with my legs and my breathing.

PASIPHAË: You have a cold. You don't take care of yourself. I brought you a muffler. This place is so damp. Didn't you light the fire as I told you to do?

MINOTAUR: The wood was wet.

PASIPHAË: How could it be? I picked the driest.

MINOTAUR: I didn't notice where I was pissing. I got it all wet.

PASIPHAË (*reproachfully*): Son.

MINOTAUR: And I don't like the fire. Can you see me well?

PASIPHAË: Yes.

MINOTAUR: Do you notice anything on my head?

PASIPHAË: Where?

MINOTAUR: Here, near this horn.

PASIPHAË: It's so dark. What is it?

MINOTAUR: A gray spot. And here, near my neck. I have more and more white hairs. I saw them today in the pool when I started to drink. What does that mean? Why are you crying and not answering me?

PASIPHAË: They are gray hairs, son.

MINOTAUR: Gray hairs? Why? I'm not an old man. (*Coughs.*)

PASIPHAË: Your body time passes as if you were a bull. If they hadn't sacrificed your father . . . he would be very elderly now.

MINOTAUR: You're a mad, deceitful old woman. I wish my mother were a cow and not you. And that my father were a man.

PASIPHAË: You're always in a bad humor. I loved your father because he wasn't a man. Because he had skin as white as the winter sky and soft as the dawn mist. Because his eyes were large and pure. Also because the gods arranged it that way, of course.

MINOTAUR: I shit on the gods.

PASIPHAË: Don't be vulgar.

MINOTAUR: So my father was white.

PASIPHAË: A white bull that Zeus caused to emerge from the sea.

MINOTAUR: And he had four horns.

PASIPHAË: Two, as you do.

MINOTAUR: Four. His and those you put on him.

PASIPHAË: Son!

MINOTAUR: If he was white, how is it I have black hair? Eh? You must have gone to roll with any common bullfight bull.

PASIPHAË: Son! You always insult me! Your hair is black because you favor me, and I am dark. Of course, I have white hair now. Don't insult me, I have never loved anyone but your father. They wed me to Minos when I was still almost a child, and I couldn't love him because . . . I don't know, I just couldn't.

MINOTAUR: That was centuries ago, wasn't it? As long as I can remember you, you have been a crazy, weeping old woman. What did you bring me?

PASIPHAË: Your muffler.

MINOTAUR: Give it to me. What else?

PASIPHAË: A handful of salt.

MINOTAUR: Give it to me.

(*She passes her hand through the stone grate. He licks the salt.*) Gray hair, right? I'm getting old. An old bull's head on the body of a young man. And these passageways that never seem the same, but really are. I've never found out how many pools there are, nor how many recesses, nor the number of statues: one of each thing, or thousands, or ten, or twenty. I never know if I've turned around and come back to the same point, or if it's another pool, another statue, another recess. And in the center of the whole universe, this grate. I always come back here, to find you whining and recalling my father. What is it all like out there?

PASIPHAË: I've told you before.

MINOTAUR: But I think you lie. Tell me again.

PASIPHAË: Well . . . there are passages and passages, and corridors that turn back on themselves.

MINOTAUR: And what is it that resounds and that the guards call the sea?

PASIPHAË: It's . . . a very long tunnel with many echoes.

MINOTAUR: I don't believe you. Somewhere there's a peephole—or many of them in many places—and I look out and I listen to the guards talk, and they mention many things. And up high you can see something blue, and they call it the sky. What is it?

PASIPHAË: It's a very high corridor, filled with lamps, and its ceiling is painted blue.

MINOTAUR: The books you bring me say something else.

PASIPHAË: Books are the inventions of poets, to kill time. They don't mean anything. Just believe in your senses. Look. Do you know what intestines are?

MINOTAUR: Of course. What my victims have in them, the things that get tangled in my horns.

PASIPHAË: That's what the world is like. A tangle of guts where we constantly lose our way while the gods direct us slowly.

MINOTAUR: I don't believe you. You're a cunning, crazy, deceitful old woman. And your songs make me sick. Before, when you sang, I put my head on your lap and drank milk from your breasts.

PASIPHAË: Before, you were a child.

MINOTAUR: A child or a calf?

PASIPHAË: Both.

MINOTAUR (*roars and kicks his feet, like a bullish child*): You're fooling me, you're fooling, you're fooling! You're fooling me! (*He begins to cry.*) You used to come in and scratch my flea-bites, and now you never do it. Mama, come here. Tell me who I am. Tell me what's happening to me. Tell me what day and night are. Tell me what this is I move about in, what happens while I'm speaking, what these images are that pursue me while I sleep. Why, when I open my eyes, the cows and women have gone away. Why, if you sang me lullabies yesterday and I was a calf, I now have these whitish spots between my horns. I don't understand anything. I read and suddenly I believe I'm a man, and I almost believe what I think, and I learn words and I almost think I understand them. Then, from deep inside me, comes a muddy, confused wave, a reddish wave filled with violent images, with the sensation of great space and of alfalfa extending through waving, wall-less corridors, with a great blue ceiling and a great hanging lamp. And I run and I bellow. And then everything is the same, and I have run into a wall, and I'm here, on the same day, in the pale light, and my whole body hurts and I have asthma. (*Pauses.*) Why don't you ever come in?

PASIPHAË: The king doesn't permit it.

MINOTAUR: Who is the king?

PASIPHAË: Minos. My husband.

MINOTAUR: Adultress! Whore!

PASIPHAË: Don't insult me. Zeus, our lord, ordered that a great bull be made of his own divine substance, the only thing worthy of being sacrificed to him. And my husband wanted to deceive Zeus and to keep your father, to keep the divine bull as a seed bull for his herds. Deceive the gods! Minos was insane! His punishment was my blessing—I loved your father. It wasn't adultery. It was the will of the gods.

MINOTAUR: The gods are mad. The gods are a herd of mad, infuriated bulls. They're a bunch of idiotic men. I shit on the gods. Tell me more about my father.

PASIPHAË: I suppose that what Zeus ordered must have been predestined, because I had a presentiment of the bull in my nuptial bed. I always dreamed confused dreams in which he used to appear. I daydreamed of his image while I lay between the conjugal sheets, tired of the impeccable correctness of Minos. I loved your father the moment I saw him, as he was coming out of the sea. He too was shining, as brilliant as the sea itself, and he was streaming salt and spume. I loved him when he ran swift and potent and free, pursuing the cows. I wanted to be a cow too. I *was*! I swear to you I *was* to him! I loved him with screams of anguish and when they raised the efficient sacrificial knife above him, I wanted to die, to be sacrificed beside him. I loved him as I sang to you, and as I suffered the inexpressible pain that your birth produced in me. And now, when I see traces of him in your head, a furious gust of memories and of love shakes my ancient entrails, and I love him.

(*Distant fanfares. Music.*)

MINOTAUR: What is that?

PASIPHAË: The captives are arriving. For you. Seven maidens, seven young men.

MINOTAUR: And that noise?

PASIPHAË: The music that accompanies the victims as they are committed to your home.

MINOTAUR: They brought them to me yesterday, didn't they?

PASIPHAË: No, son. It was seven years ago.

MINOTAUR: It's all the same. I like them. Especially the women. I like cows, too.

PASIPHAË: Soon they will bring some to you. I must go.

MINOTAUR: First, scratch my head. (*She does.*) Ah, ah. (*Moos.*) Ah, what delight. How good you are. How much I love you. You are a precious little cow. I love you a lot. A lot. A lot.

PASIPHAË: Good-by, dear son. Put on your muffler. Drink your medicine.

(*She leaves. The light behind the grate goes out. Fanfares.*)

MINOTAUR (*sniffs the air*): They're coming. I smell them. I like the smell. I like it.

(*He rushes down a corridor. Disappears. The walls of the labyrinth move, and form a new composition. We see Theseus, with several of his companions. He has the sword in his hand and is unrolling the ball of yarn. They advance silently.*)

THESEUS: Don't get separated. We must form a group.

(*Their advance has become the dance of the captives, and the walls of the labyrinth hide them and reveal them, separate them and reunite them. There are cries and growing panic. Two captives find themselves face to face, attack, and then recognize each other. Now fear seems to overcome Theseus. He is alone, he looks in all directions. He lies in wait. He attacks a surging figure. Screams. He has wounded her; it was the frightened young girl.*)

YOUNG GIRL: Were you . . . were you . . . the Minotaur? (*Dies.*)

THESEUS: I'm sorry. You won't be afraid any more. Forgive me for hitting you that time.

(*He straightens up, pauses, and advances. The body is hidden by the walls. Suddenly, the Minotaur surges out. Bellowing. Theseus plays him with his cape. The bull attacks. The struggle recalls a bullfight, but* NOT TOO OBVIOUSLY, *or the result will be comic. The Minotaur coughs, becomes tired. He attacks. Theseus wounds him fatally. He falls, bellowing. Theseus runs his sword in him repeatedly. Gouts of blood, death rattle. Theseus has triumphed. He stands panting.*)

Here! Come here, everyone! Here! The Minotaur is dead! Come here! I killed the Minotaur.

(*There are echoes of his cries. His companions arrive slowly. The music ceases.*)

I have Ariadne's thread tied to my wrist. Come on. Follow me.

BOY: This was the Minotaur?

GIRL: I'm afraid. He won't move any more, will he?

ANOTHER BOY: An old bull, that's what he was.

GIRL: A weak man, that's what he was.

BOY: A man with the head of a bull.

(*They exit. Only the corpse of the Minotaur remains. Silence. Darkness.*)

4

THE DOCKS OF CRETE

> . . . The nearer it is, the more I attempt to avoid the danger that I touch and do not believe.
>
> Juan de Guevara
> (*Love Is More Labyrinthine*)

Identical almost to those of Athens. Constellations, except that Taurus is missing. Downstage, flowers and festive adornments are also hanging. Crates. A mooring ring. The deck of the ship goes from center to right. Theseus. Ariadne. A young man is boarding ship.

THESEUS: Are they all on board?

BOY: All on board.

ARIADNE: I counted eleven.

BOY: There is one girl missing who was killed by the Minotaur. And one boy who got lost.

THESEUS: His cries were heard through the openings for several days.

ARIADNE: Didn't anyone try to get him out?

THESEUS: It's a well-constructed place. And since yesterday, nothing has been heard.

ARIADNE: We're going to seal up the entrance to the Labyrinth.

THESEUS: At least, your father offered to do it in his speech.

ARIADNE: He has promised. (*Pause.*) On our wedding day, Papa was very somber. I think it hurts him to see me leave.

THESEUS: Perhaps he resents other things. For example, your own people acclaimed me, more than any of your Cretan heroes.

ARIADNE: No people loves minotaurs.

THESEUS: A skillful ruler—and your father is skillful—knows how to make his people feel a terrified love for their local monsters. Nevertheless, it's a relief to see them die. But that is the custom of fear. The killer anoints himself with the force and attributes of the monster. Your people have acclaimed me, you have heard how. Who can stop me now?

ARIADNE: If they learned their lesson—the people. If you love the people—you yourself. If you keep on loving me—I will.

THESEUS: What is your father waiting for? It's late. We ought to leave today. The affairs of Athens await only one stimulus. I see . . . a great hegemony. I see many small kingdoms grouped around our own. I see power growing in my hands.

ARIADNE: I see wars. I see the growth of a pathetic class, that of the slaves. I see dangers. Minotaurs. Ruins. No, Theseus, we will unite Crete and Athens. We will live in peace. We will have children. We will love each other. We will make trips, remembering.

THESEUS: Why do you always dress in dark colors? You look very pale.

(*He walks away from her. Phaedra enters.*)

PHAEDRA: There is a state of great confusion in the palace. Something horrible has happened. Mother has gone mad.

ARIADNE: Phaedra!

PHAEDRA: She took down her hair and covered her face with it. She hopes to isolate herself from the world behind it, forever. Had you noticed how white and thick her hair is? And she moos, and bellows, and calls her son with the craziest and most foolish names. Let's go to Athens right away. I don't want to stay here any longer. I've spent enough years sharing the nastiness of our palace. Papa is crying, and they've had to tie her up because she was running around banging into wall after wall, screaming for them to lock her up in the Labyrinth. I think that Papa, in spite of everything, is still in love with her. He won't come to tell us good-by.

THESEUS: All right, then. We will go.

PHAEDRA: Have they put my luggage on yet?

THESEUS: They have, Phaedra. Twenty-six boxes, full.

ARIADNE: You shouldn't have come. To leave Papa alone . . . When does he want you to come back?

PHAEDRA (*looks away*): I don't know. In three or four months . . .

ARIADNE: Something tells me . . . that you shouldn't come.

PHAEDRA: And am I going to stay in that horrible palace, with Mama crazy and Papa crying?

ARIADNE (*with rancor*): Mama never loved us. She only loved . . . Poor Papa.

PHAEDRA: Well, as for me, I loved my wet nurse. And after Papa threw her out, nobody else.

ARIADNE: I want to tell him good-by.

THESEUS: There isn't time. A good wind is coming up.*

ARIADNE: The sea frightens me. I've been on shipboard only once, and I was dreadfully seasick.

THESEUS: There are islands on the way. If you feel bad, we can stop at Naxos and allow you to rest. Let's go.

---

* After this play was published in Spanish, the author rewrote this scene from here to the end; his revised version has been used in this translation. *Tr.*

ARIADNE: Theseus. Look in my eyes. Tell me that you love me as much . . . as much as the first night, as much as before the Labyrinth.

THESEUS: I love you exactly as much as then. (*Kisses her lightly.*) Get on!

(*Helps her get on board.*)

PHAEDRA: I read in a travel book that Naxos is a horrible island. That pirates maroon people there. And there are wild animals. And . . .

THESEUS (*puts his hand over her mouth*): There are no wild animals on Naxos.

PHAEDRA: But the pirates maroon . . .

(*Theseus touches his finger to her lips. Then he kisses her on the mouth. Then he looks at her, smiling.*)

Don't smile like that, that's the way my father smiled. If you ever became like him . . .

THESEUS: Then what?

PHAEDRA: I don't know . . . But I like young men.

THESEUS: Captain!

(*The captain appears from the ship.*)

Raise the black sails.

CAPTAIN: The red ones, sir. Those of celebration.

THESEUS: The black ones.

CAPTAIN: Your father will be waiting to see us appear on the horizon. The red ones.

THESEUS: I said . . . the black ones. (*Unsheathes his sword.*) Did you hear?

CAPTAIN: Yes, sir. The . . . black ones. (*Exits.*)

(*The sailors are singing. Ariadne, with an expression of nostalgia, appears at the top of the gangplank. She gazes at her fatherland, bidding it farewell. Theseus and Phaedra move apart.*)

ARIADNE: It feels to me now as if the ship were throbbing like a great heart.

THESEUS: It is the drum for the oarsmen.

ARIADNE: Do you know what the sea seems like with the foamy weaving of its waves and the open web of all its invisible ways? A labyrinth. When we have crossed it, we will be different people. In a way, a story ends here.

THESEUS (*giving his hand to Phaedra and climbing the gangplank with her*): And another begins.

CURTAIN